JESUS LOVES OBAMACARE

AND OTHER LIBERAL CAUSES

BY

BARBARA YOUNG WITH STUART YOUNG

Bluegrass Press
Louisville, KY 40204

www.JesusLovesObamacare.com

Copyrights and Credits

Jesus Loves Obamacare and Other Liberal Causes
by Barbara Young with Stuart Young

Kindle edition: Jesus Loves Obamacare and Other Liberal Causes, © January 2017 by Barbara Young with Stuart Young

    ISBN 10: 0-9986227-0-2
    ISBN 13: 978-0-9986227-0-5

Epub Edition: Jesus Loves Obamacare and Other Liberal Causes, © January 2017 by Barbara Young with Stuart Young

    ISBN 10: 0-9986227-1-0
    ISBN 13: 978-0-9986227-1-2

Print Edition: Jesus Loves Obamacare and Other Liberal Causes, © January 2017 by Barbara Young with Stuart Young

    ISBN 10: 0-9986227-2-9
    ISBN13: 978-0-9986227-2-9

Publisher: Bluegrass Press, Louisville KY

Credits

Contents

Acknowledgments

Many thanks to all who helped me this far through life's journey, especially to my parents. Dad, you're no longer with us, but I know you worked hard to provide for us; you gave us an economic floor for our family, and you were always there when I really needed you. And to you Mom, you continue to inspire me in countless ways. You're still going strong at 98, and you're a phenomenal force of nature. You reared me to learn and study Scripture, taught me to follow the light that was personally revealed to me, and by example showed me how to brave the world and stand alone for my convictions. Decades ago, you preached a series of sermons on "The Four Corners," where you demonstrated Mosaic law on caring for the poor, the widow, the fatherless, and the stranger. Those lessons first made me aware of the Old Testament standards that I further explain in this book. You may not always agree with my progressive interpretations, but your sermons helped me to see that Jesus was speaking in the context of His Jewish legal tradition when in Matthew 25 He commanded us to do the things that the law of Moses required, taking care of "the least of these." I stand on your shoulders, and I am eternally grateful for my strong biblical heritage.

I thank all my teachers and mentors along the way who helped me learn to read, write, and think critically and holistically, to challenge assumptions, to advocate for my truth, and to speak up for those who have no voice. At the University of Louisville, I encountered many outstanding professors who went to great lengths outside of class to help me hone my writing and thinking skills, first in the English department and later in the Brandeis School of Law.

Thanks also to my son Stuart, who needled me, challenged me, and then worked with me to make this book possible. You put your own life on hold and put in long hours late into the early morning to get this book completed.

I acknowledge my beautiful daughter Faye, who has always encouraged and supported me and understood when I had to miss family dinners because I was working on this book.

Thanks to my grandson, Scott, who took time, despite his heavy engineering school schedule, to work a math problem that I needed for this book, and who enthusiastically promised to read the finished product and share it with his friends.

Here's a shout-out to my younger grandson, Austin, for being cheerful and able to discuss the issues in this book, intelligently holding his own with any adult in the room. And to my son-in-law Harold who always helps me see the humor in every situation and whose example helps us all to remain calm. I have a wonderful loving family that is fun, energetic, and interesting, and I am grateful.

To our friends Amos Jones, Tom Korbee, Dee Allen, Lauren Morton, Vonnelle Tingle, Gary Barch, and Debra Wells, who took their time to review our book and give us encouraging feedback, you guys are the best!

And I am blessed to have so many more good friends in my Highlands neighborhood and from my long-ago community college days. You all cheered me on and patiently listened to my monologs as I excitedly shared my Bible discoveries and book's purpose, regardless of your own individual allegiances.

Thanks goes to my copy-editor Paul Hawley, who meticulously brought my mechanics into the twenty-first century, noticed content errors, and reminded me to play nice; and to my cover designer Jeff Gerke, who was patient with my nitpicking and who improved the book's visual statement.

Most of all, I give thanks to God, the ground of my being, for all the wonderful blessings I have received, for the privilege of being born in America and for being alive, healthy, and able to share my vision of the Holy Scripture with the world.

Foreword

If you're reading this preface, you may have purchased this book, or you may just be having a peek on Amazon or iTunes. In either case, thank you for your time. I hope this book will engage and inform, but I'd like to encourage anyone reading this page, whether you buy the book or not, to immediately start using the phrase:

Jesus Loves Obamacare!

While all authors hope that their books are successful, most aren't hits. My mom and I have no illusions about this book being a *New York Times* best seller, although I think it has tremendous value. We've put countless hours into the research. And because we wanted to get this book out as soon as possible, we spent our time writing and developing the book as best we could. We are both accomplished academics, but we aren't novelists or publishers. Had we devoted our time to chasing down various publishing houses and getting their input and feedback, we feared it would have delayed our project for months. We also passed on lucrative paying projects to devote our time to this book, because protecting Obamacare is the moral thing to do, and we felt compelled to do it. Given the stakes where millions are facing the loss of their health insurance, which risks lives and livelihoods, my mom and I decided that it was better to get the book published so people can use it *before* the Affordable Care Act is repealed.

This book is an excellent summation of my mother's life journey, her religious upbringing, and her work as a lawyer and civil rights advocate, but we had to do something *now*, rather than sitting around complaining, "Ain't it awful." This book is about lifting our voices and trying to make a difference. So whether people buy our book or not or give me credit for the phrase is irrelevant. Please just use the phrase "Jesus Loves Obamacare." And feel free to use the scriptures in this book to bolster your point. While I am hopeful that this book will be successful, you can make a difference by using this phrase in your everyday conversations and on social media. This phrase changes the narrative around the ACA and its potential repeal. Just as Republicans use phrases like the "death tax" to get poorer people to endorse yet more tax cuts for the super rich, Democrats need to start using powerful messaging to change hearts and minds.

"Jesus Loves Obamacare"—the phrase by itself transforms the debate. Suddenly, if asked whether "Jesus loves Obamacare" Republicans will be instantly on the defensive, and they will have to prove that Jesus wouldn't approve of universal health care. Opposing collective efforts to provide universal health care flies in the face of the theology of every established Christian denomination, except for some American white evangelical churches. Let them be on the defensive to prove that it is somehow "Christlike" to take away health care from people with preexisting conditions. There are no Bible verses to support this assertion. No doubt, they will try to play the "small government" card, but this book will be a resource to debunk that myth. If you choose not to buy this book, you can merely refer to it in passing in your arguments: "Well, I know that book *Jesus Loves Obamacare* had some really good points; you should go check it out." But even the phrase will prompt some Republican evangelicals to consider whether repealing the Affordable Care Act, which is in fact Obamacare, is moral and consistent with Christ's wishes.

That's how we find common ground with our fellow Christians across the aisle. We can't expect them to magically change their minds. We have to meet them on their turf and show how our common faith should compel us to protect one of the most Christian pieces of legislation passed in the past 30 or 40 years (yes, that statement is controversial, but it is true). This book will show how the Affordable Care Act/Obamacare saves lives and follows Jesus' commands and the commands of Moses and the Old Testament prophets.

Nancy Pelosi and Chuck Schumer have tried using the phrase "Make America Sick Again." That's not bad, but I think "Jesus Loves Obamacare" is far more powerful. Democrats are squeamish about appealing to religious authority, but they have to get over it if they want to save lives. If you want to win in red states, you have to connect with people on matters that are relevant to them. For millions of Americans, that's the Bible. Some people of Jewish faith may hesitate to endorse this book given the title. That's understandable, but note that the title is not saying, "Jesus is the Messiah." Whether you view Jesus as the Son of God, an inspired prophet, or merely a wise teacher, if you're a progressive person of faith, you can see how Jesus would certainly endorse the notion of universal health care, given His commands to take care of the sick, the poor, the immigrant, and the prisoner. The Bible is a great resource for ancient wisdom, even if you don't interpret it literally. It is political malpractice for national Democrats not to use it in making their case, and they'll never reclaim election victories in "red states" unless they get comfortable using the Bible to promote their policies. So for now, whether you endorse the book or are personally religious, it's key to get it into the lexicon of Middle America if we want to save the benefits of the Affordable Care Act. Let's improve it, not replace it. So whether it's on Instagram, Twitter or Facebook, please help us get this trending:

#Jesus Loves Obamacare!

– Stuart Young

Introduction

My Journey to Writing This Book

Before getting into the heart of the book, I felt compelled to share my own journey and life story that led me to write this book. You're free to jump into the next chapter if you're eager to get to the meat of the book. This introduction shares a bit about my unusual background that shaped my views and my search for a holistic, rational interpretation of the Bible.

I grew up in Louisville, Kentucky in the 1950s. My mother was a Pentecostal minister, who founded her own church, which later grew into an international organization. And as a result my family was devoutly religious. I grew up believing the Bible was the literal, infallible Word of God. I believed it and was steeped in it. I still look to the Bible for inspiration and guidance for my life, for deeper meanings to reality, though I've gained a few tools for interpreting it and historical facts I did not know as a child. And no matter how far out my own thinking may venture, my consciousness is grounded in the Bible. I have Bible running out my ears, and it pervades and shapes my views. I'm not pretending always to have followed it or even to be in integrity with all my espoused beliefs. I'm just acknowledging the Bible as a lodestar for my life.

I've always been amazed at how supposedly Bible-believing Christians pick and choose which verses to get up in arms over, while ignoring multitudes of scriptures that underscore important moral and ethical principles, scriptures that are crystal clear and leave little room for ambiguity. But I remind myself that it was the religious crowd who most viciously hated Jesus, for He called out

1

the Pharisees, mean-spirited hypocrites, who loved the show of piety, but who lacked compassion and mercy, religious leaders who "strained at gnats and swallowed camels," who nitpicked others for minor flaws while ignoring their own big wrongs.

This is what I see happening with today's Christian Right, ever since its inception as the Moral Majority decades ago. Many want to impose their personal morality on "sinners" to regulate their bodies and bedroom behavior, while they ignore essential admonitions of their founder, Jesus Christ. They want to kill in the name of God and country, to invade other countries to rid the world of evil dictators, but they have little room in their political or social philosophies for taking care of "the least of these" here at home—the sick, the hungry, the prisoner, the stranger (immigrant), the naked, the thirsty. Whenever I feel the sting of their cold, cruel words, my inner spirit convulses.

Yet I can never escape a deep connection to evangelical Christians, and I honor their devotion to God. I like their worship services, especially exuberant ones. It doesn't get any better than down-home gospel music. Singing "Amazing Grace" or "Precious Lord Take My Hand" still brings tears to my eyes. I used to attend a formal Presbyterian church with highbrow music and intellectual preaching. Yet when a special guest with a guitar would sing an old gospel hymn, worshippers would wipe tears from their eyes and loudly applaud. I never have understood why more "highfalutin" churches lack the sense of Spirit and Presence found in the more conservative evangelical churches. To be smart, do I have to turn cold? To feel the warmth, do I have to shoot my brain? I have often wondered, "Will I ever get my head and my heart in the same church at the same time?"

I am writing this book, perhaps to grapple with all this, to give a voice to many ex-evangelicals like myself, and to awaken people who consider themselves socially progressive to the power and untapped potential of Scripture to support their policies. A great many of us in America share a common heritage of the Bible. Whether we believe it literally or no longer believe it at all, the Bible is a wellspring of metaphors and morals that are rooted deep into our collective consciousness. It's part of our Judeo-Christian heritage, and three major faith groups in this country (Christians, Muslims, and Jews) share a reverence for the Old Testament, while Christians revere the New as well, and many Jews, Muslims, Buddhists, Sikhs, Hindus, and agnostics affirm the moral precepts of Jesus.

I have not written this book as an outsider, ragging on someone else's religion. I am proud of my biblical heritage, my roots, and all the good that was poured into me. I love the inspiring music in church and the strong sense of community and family. The scriptures I memorized as a child shape every area of my life and taught me hard work, perseverance, excellence, honesty, fair play, and the importance of being my word. It also taught me to transcend current circumstances, to be triumphant in the face of loss and adversity, and to look for the good in all things.

But I am a witness to much hypocrisy and cruelty done in the name of the Lord—not by con artists intentionally trying to bilk people, but by blind Christians who actually believe they are sincere and righteous but are ignorant and oblivious to the contradictions between their behavior and their beliefs, between their politics and their Scripture. Just getting people to acknowledge their inconsistency would be a big step forward. It takes some level of self-awareness to say, "I know I'm not following the Bible on this point, but this is what I choose to believe and do." At least, you'd be cutting out the pretense.

My Encounters with Religious Intolerance

I grew up in the mainstream of Christianity and yet apart from it in a Pentecostal holiness culture. My mom founded her own mission, which later grew into a large church in Southern Indiana, tens of churches in the US, hundreds in Mexico, and many around the world. As a preacher's kids, my sister and I were closely scrutinized, and we grew up "sanctified." We went to church four to five times a week. We studied the Bible daily and prayed for long periods—one to two hours. And when we prayed, it was intense. We made sounds like the Jews at the Wailing Wall, the ritual cries of Native Americans, or the high-pitched wailings you hear on TV when the Palestinians are grieving the death of their loved ones. Those were our expressions, which was our intercession to God's ears. It was all part of speaking in tongues and praying under the control of the Holy Spirit. We called it the Holy Ghost, for Holy Spirit was a fancy word.

Growing up, we sanctified girls didn't cut our hair or wear makeup or pants, the latter being "men's apparel." We didn't go to the movies, listen to worldly music (neither pop nor rock 'n roll), dance, or watch TV, which beamed loose morals and worldly pleasures into the home. It even had two horns on top, which proved its devilish origins. To enforce the necessity of separation from the world, we were given scriptures to support each of these stands. The Bible teaches people to dress modestly, to set their heart on eternal things, and to restrain the lusts of the flesh. Today, I see that the holiness perspective has a lot of good in it—but for different reasons. Watching TV is a huge waste of time, destroys the imagination, shrinks the attention span, and hooks young people on the values of lookism, sexism, and consumerism.[1] Parading young girls around scantily clad teaches them that their value depends on their looks and their sex appeal.

I also grew up believing that Jesus Christ was literally coming back soon to take over the world. When I was twelve, I worried about that, for the Lord would come back to earth before I could grow up, get married, and have sex—in that order, of course. The hushed tones of references to sex made it seem all the more alluring. As an adolescent, I did not see Jesus' return as a good thing, for He would usher in the great tribulation, and the world would be destroyed. Plus, in the afterlife, we wouldn't marry, have sex, or eat because we'd have a supernatural or spiritual body. Didn't sound like much fun.

My mom and dad decided they would sacrifice and send us girls to a private Christian school across town. It was evangelical and ultraconservative. My dad was a district manager of an insurance company, so they could afford the tuition. It was a nice school with caring teachers, who gave us a solid education, and I had some excellent experiences there. But that school was murder on my self-esteem. I felt judged and put down throughout junior and senior high. I felt like a weirdo, a freak.

Many Christians at that school were sincerely devoted yet dogmatic people, who acted as if they had the one and only true interpretation of the Bible. Alas, many groups are like that. Religious people seldom stop to question the arrogance of assuming that their finite minds can box in an infinite God or even how their finite minds can comprehend the "inspired Word of God." Rather, many are absolutely certain that they alone have the one true path to the infinite Almighty, and a lot of energy is put into proving that they are right while others are wrong. St. Paul's words, "now we see through a glass darkly," have little impact on their certainty that their theology is correct. Unfortunately, church history reflects such arrogance, given its multiple bans on sects, declarations of heresy, expulsions, and persecutions.

The church that sponsored our school allowed girls to wear makeup, pants, and even knee-length shorts, and their teens could go to the movies and listen to pop songs on the radio, but they didn't have musical instruments in their services, and they were adamant that women should never pray, speak, teach, or preach aloud in church—unless they said a prayer or read the Scripture in unison with the entire congregation.

They did allow women to sing in small ensembles and even perform solos or duets. I never figured out why a woman could get up in front of the congregation and sing the same words that she could not utter in regular speech. I guess if your words are set to chords or pitches of G, C, and E, your message transcends your gender. Of course, these same women could go across the seas and speak to "heathen" men in Africa, China, or India, for fewer men were inspired to make such a sacrifice, but when the women came home to America, they were to be silent in the church.

In this environment, telling my classmates or teachers that my mother was a self-proclaimed preacher was just one step above saying that she was a witch. No one made derogatory comments directly to my face, but I could see the sneers and feel the subtle digs, as my peers, perhaps just naturally curious, asked me about our holiness restrictions or why my mom was a preacher. Then I'd get sermons on the "correct" way of interpreting the Bible: women were not supposed to preach.

We also got jabbed because our church was Pentecostal. Today, being "charismatic" is widely accepted, but back then, our demonstrative form of worship was labeled either as self-induced hysteria or demon possession. Forget all the scriptures that affirmed exuberant worship. When it came to yielding to any joyful expression of Spirit (weeping, groaning, speaking in tongues, clapping, dancing), our fundamentalist friends easily left their literalism behind and relegated scriptures about ecstatic experiences and the "gifts of the Spirit" to the early church. "These scriptures do not apply today," they insisted, banishing their literalism. I still don't understand why church shouldn't be as much fun as Zumba or a Beyoncé concert. I understand the diversity of spiritual experiences: quiet meditation, Mozart's *Mass in C Minor*, or a soulful rendition of "His Eye is on the Sparrow"—not to mention a foot-stomping, hand-clapping round of "I'll Fly Away." But why should church be only one thing or one style? But at this point in my youth, I had internalized much of their stigma against women preachers. I figured that if they were right, then something must be wrong with my mother, and, by extension, with me. It never occurred to me that the Protestant mainstream might need to catch up with us.

The first big shock to my consciousness came when I was thirteen, and my Christian schoolteachers gave us students a tract on the evil about to descend on America, as John F. Kennedy made his bid for the White House in 1960. "A Catholic for President?" it read. Terrified, we just *knew* that our country was doomed, our freedoms would vanish, and the pope would soon rule America. Then there were all the jokes: "Hey, did you hear that Jackie Kennedy fell and broke her leg at the White House last week?... Yes, she tripped over the pope's luggage"—meaning that the pope was moving in with them. Today, we lionize JFK, but this view dominated even mainline Protestant culture in the late 1950s and early '60s.[2]

At a young age, I was petrified of Catholics. They were evil. Their priests and nuns fornicated, then murdered their babies, and buried them under their convents and monasteries. This slander, perpetrated since the early nineteenth century, no doubt, fueled the Protestant burnings of many Catholic churches and communities in the 1850s. Even in my hometown of Louisville, Kentucky, in 1855 Protestants rioted against Catholics and burned homes and a church. This was part of the resentment against a massive flood of Irish and German immigrants[3] Sound familiar? Yes, the history of Christian intolerance is abysmal and embarrassing. It reminds us that Jesus doesn't need enemies, for His friends have done Him in.

At the Christian school I attended, we were taught to believe that Catholics were morally corrupt because they allowed their members to gamble (i.e., play bingo) and drink beer. Catholic priests in other countries had ordered their members to persecute and kill Protestants as heretics. They had sponsored the Inquisition, which murdered thousands of sincere true Christians, such as the Huguenots. These were strongly held beliefs of good Christians, who were blind to all of the hate, gossip, and fearmongering they were promoting. But it was all done in the name of Jesus and country. And there was historical truth in some of this. The Inquisition and persecution of "heretics" are a great stain on the Roman Catholic Church. Giordano Bruno, one of the earliest scientists to assert that the earth revolved around the sun (thus questioning the official interpretation of Scripture), was burned at the stake. But the stories told to Protestant children were worse and implied that the Inquisition was descending on America. Soon we'd be called before authorities and jailed for asserting our right to read the Bible.

Of course, we were not told how Protestants persecuted Catholics, even in our own hometown. The dangers of bigotry never merited a Bible lesson. The history of England shows great persecution by each group against the other, depending on which king occupied the throne. And England first became Protestant not because of enlightenment, but because King Henry VIII had the hots for Anne Boleyn, and the pope would not let Henry dump his Spanish Catholic wife. Of course, Catherine of Aragon had failed to give him a male heir, and he hoped a younger woman would fulfill his dream. So Protestants must acknowledge that even our movements toward enlightenment had some impure beginnings.

It gets worse. As a teen, I listened to WFIA, a Christian broadcasting station in Louisville, Kentucky. Its call letters stood for "With Faith In America." Now, the Rev. Martin Luther King Jr., mind you, was a communist, so the white Christian DJs and radio preachers alleged. And if he wasn't an outright communist, then at a minimum, he was a communist sympathizer and ally. He "palled around" with communists, to use Sarah Palin's terminology. "He was going through the South, stirring up the good colored people, who were content to keep the races separate just as God had intended them to be. For the Bible justified segregation [so the "Christians" preached], and black people had been cursed to be an inferior and servile race." This belief had something to do with a curse from one of Noah's kids. As the 1960s protestors sometimes quipped, these good Christians "loved God and hated Negroes"—though that is not the N word they used. Today, many "good Christians" are still loving God and expanding their hatred to Mexicans and Muslims.

I also remember when, a few years later, conservative Christians thought it an abomination to name a holiday after Dr. King, who in their view had not done anything noteworthy for our country, had questionable ties, and had personal moral failings (he cheated on his wife).[4] Today, with the prominence of Herman Cain, Ben Carson, and Clarence Thomas, the Christian Right, along with most of us, has achieved amnesia over its racist past. Now, it staunchly insists that our society is and should be colorblind. (Well, the latter statement is questionable, given the advent of Trump's openly racist supporters, emboldened by his promise to return America to its great past—when white males reigned supreme.)

Nevertheless, the Rev. Martin Luther King Jr. and the Civil Rights movement did change the perceptions of the majority—even though many of us are insensitive to the vestiges of segregation and racism that remain. We wish to sweep aside the sins of our forefathers by suddenly proclaiming "all gone." It's as if you've been trying to run a race with one leg broken and set in a cast for centuries, unable to heal fully, move in a full range of motion, or grow any muscle. Then, we remove the cast from your leg and say, "Well it's fair now; no one's leg is bound, so why don't you get up off your lazy butt and run?" But your leg has already withered from centuries of non-use.

I vividly remember the hatred, the mean-spirited hypocrisy, and the unwavering defense of the status quo that dominated conservative Christianity in the first two decades of my life. Supporters of civil rights were labeled unpatriotic or "communists." It's always easier to attack someone else than to examine yourself.

Fortunately for me, my mom took a different point of view on race, as she had had experiences that sensitized her to racial and ethnic prejudice. In 1948, my mother was studying the Bible intensely but did not yet have an organized church. She participated in various inter-denominational Christian groups such as Youth for Christ. One of her friends told her of the plight of a young Mexican woman (from Mexico City—not an American of Mexican descent), who was moving to Kentucky to pursue a master's of divinity at Asbury College, but she had no place to stay when school was out between semesters, during summers, and on holidays. She could not afford traditional lodging or plane fair to and from Mexico—to say nothing of the fact that few white people would give her a place to stay, knowing her race. My mother, not knowing her but based solely on hearing of the need and feeling divine inspiration to bridge the gap, welcomed this foreigner into our home. My mother

saw that this brown-skinned lady had a limited wardrobe and supplies, so she set about making sure she had sufficient clothing, toi-
letries, and school supplies for her sojourn in America. So for two
years, this woman lived with us when she was not in school.

One day, probably somewhere between 1948 and 1949, my
mom took her new friend on a shopping errand. When they board-
ed the bus, the driver scowled and became indignant. "You have to
go sit back there," he said, pointing to the back of the bus, which
was designated for "Negroes." My mother saw that his attitude was
so hateful and angry that she was appalled. Suddenly the racism that
she had never before encountered was palpable, and it was being
perpetrated against a woman she cared for. My mother sat at the
back of the bus that day, but from then on, she refused to tolerate
racial discrimination.

My mother has told me that before she ever started her own
church, she spread the gospel by going into different neighborhoods
in Louisville, handing out Christian tracts, knocking on doors, and
gathering groups of children to listen to Bible stories. Her efforts
included going into black neighborhoods teaching all who would
listen. She used a flannel board and cutouts of Bible characters with
felt backing (imagine paper dolls that would stick to a board), so
that she could make the stories more vivid. She said that she never
felt unsafe, nor was she ever disrespected. She noticed that the black
parents were more eager to have their children attend Bible story
time than their white counterparts. They displayed a strong reverence for the Bible as they encouraged their children to listen and to
learn. Even adults who did not go to church thanked her for taking
her time to come tell their children that God loved them. In the
1940s, knocking on doors and organizing neighborhood study
groups was how people evangelized. And Mom was doing all that
she knew to do. She also did extensive visitation up and down East
Market Street, then known as skid row, bringing clothing and food
to people living in squalor above and behind beer joints.

When I was in elementary school, my mother started a store-
front mission on East Market Street, next to another beer joint,

among the people she had personally ministered to. Today, we'd call it the inner city. So perhaps it was not surprising that she welcomed African Americans into her church; they were nearby. Either way, she seemed to think nothing of it. It was no big deal having blacks and whites pray and worship together in her church, and yet that was monumental for the 1950s. We quickly learned that African Americans were an immense contribution. It was customary at the time for church guests to sing and testify (share a short sermon). We all loved the gospel music that they shared. I thought it was the coolest thing I had ever heard, and black preachers have a cadence that you don't find anywhere else. We enjoyed the spirit and the passion of their testimonies; we thought nothing of the revolutionary aspect of having guest black preachers share their sermons with a predominantly white audience.

Also, during the 1950s and '60s, a close family friend, one of my mother's first parishioners, a white woman named Lenora, said that she felt a special burden to minister specifically to African Americans, and my mom raised no objections to this but eagerly supported her work. Lenora not only preached at predominantly black churches in town and did neighborhood visitation, but she also made missionary trips to Africa, which my mother funded through her church. So she began bringing in black people to my mom's church. When people hear about my mother, they have always been curious to see her in action. She certainly is a force of nature. But I can't help wondering if many of them were also curious to see a woman preacher.

My mom did not grasp the political movements going on in America, but she understood that racism was wrong. If God's Word commanded us not to distinguish between Jew and Gentile, how could she segregate her church or deny black people entrance? She took some flak for welcoming black people into her church and into her home. Neighbors called the police when they saw black people coming to our home, which was located in a prosperous middle class white neighborhood. But Mom was just doing her part in her corner of the world. My mom says that one time, she looked out the door and saw a white man standing outside of our home with a rifle. That was the only time that she and her black guests entered and left through the back door, fearful of being shot. Nevertheless, she was undeterred.

Later, around 1965 a black minister wrote to my mother and wanted to affiliate with her church. She warmly invited him to visit her church and stay at our home, considering the hotels would not give lodging to African Americans (yes, the Civil Rights Act of 1964 had passed, but many states weren't enforcing it yet). But what she didn't know at the time was this black pastor had a white wife. This shocked everyone's sensibilities and assumptions about propriety. At that time, one of my mother's parishioners, who often drove my sister and me to church, lectured me on how interracial marriage was wrong, how blacks were supposed to be a servile class, separate from whites, and how they had been cursed through one of the sons of Noah. Such folklore has persisted and isn't even biblical. True, the Bible says that one of Noah's sons did get a curse for "uncovering his father's nakedness" (whatever that means), but in a logic-defying leap, these white evangelicals just *knew* it had to refer to the black race, since they reasoned that having dark skin and kinky hair must be a curse, and certainly they treated black people as if they were cursed with a contagion.

Troubled, I took this tale to my mother, and she handled it in typical fashion. The very next Sunday, she preached a sermon from the twelfth chapter of the book of Numbers. It went like this:

Moses married an Ethiopian woman—a black woman from Africa. Yet God never condemned Moses for his choice of a dark-skinned mate. Clearly, God had no problem with his interracial marriage. Yet when Moses' sister complained about his marriage, prejudice being alive and well even way back then, God smote her with leprosy. So we should not criticize someone for marrying a person of a different race. If God doesn't have a problem with it, neither should we, and remember, as we have studied in Galatians 3:28, in Christ there is neither male nor female, slave nor free, Jew nor Greek. That was the racial divisions in Jesus' day.

Remember, this was in Louisville, Kentucky, not exactly a hot-bed of liberalism—and well before the 1967 Supreme Court ruling in *Loving v. Virginia* that struck down state miscegenation laws. We knew nothing about the law or legal precedent when Mom preached that sermon. But here was my mom giving us divine authority to love black people and accept interracial marriage. My mother didn't change people's hearts and minds by calling them stupid or telling them that they were wrong. She knew her Bible and knew exactly what verses to share. And although many still held prejudices against blacks in their hearts, it was hard to argue with the fact that if God was okay with Moses' marrying an African woman, then they should be too. A few families did leave her church after numerous black people started attending, but the majority of her white parishioners stayed and remained receptive to her interpretation. Yet she demonstrated exactly why national Democrats need to use "Bible-speak" as authoritative justification for progressive policies. For many of her parishioners, a sermon with Bible verses was far more effective in prodding their thinking than a well-reasoned conversation about segregation.

Actually, Pentecostals have a history of interracial worship and deserve credit for being ahead of other denominations at the time. The phenomenon of speaking in tongues (glossolalia) began with black people on Azusa Street in Los Angeles[5] and then spread around the world. Prominent white revivalists, both men and women, integrated their churches and revival meetings from the 1920s to the 1950s. These include evangelists like Aimee Semple McPherson, Kathryne Kuhlman, Oral Roberts, and A.A. Allen—names that were familiar and respected in my parents' household.[6] Yet to this day, among mainline Protestants and non-charismatic evangelicals, Sunday morning remains the most segregated time in America.

These experiences with African Americans changed my life. I not only loved their music but also sensed a kinship because I, too, felt denigrated for being different—although I am not equating the religious slights I suffered to the harsh and dangerous realities of Jim

Crow. I loved the atmosphere of warmth, spirit, and acceptance in the black church. I loved the music and the shouting—a celebration of life. "Hey, I could have woke up dead this morning, but thank God I woke up, clothed in my right mind!... You may think it's crazy that I sing and shout, but you don't know like I know what He's done for me." I also loved their emphasis on justice as a biblical mandate.

In 1968, I started visiting black churches in Louisville as part of a project for a graduate class in sociolinguistics (my research was to analyze interactions between the gospel singers and the audience during the service, identifying rhetorical patterns). I visited Cable Baptist Church near the inner city and fell in love with the piano playing of the music director there. He was far better than the black guest pianists who visited our church, as he used jazz chords that were new to me. I persuaded him to give me private piano lessons. He insisted that he was no teacher. But I countered, "If you just meet with me, I will teach myself." And I compensated him fairly for taking his time to work with me. In about six months I got pretty good and soon began playing piano for a ladies' black gospel singing group. We traveled all around Louisville and surrounding towns to participate in Sunday afternoon gospel singing concerts. I was proud that as a white gal, I could play well enough for an all-black audience and had mastered the tempo and syncopation to keep up (something I'd have a hard time doing today). The ladies were kind and loving to me; I never felt "blamed" or judged for what other white people had done to them. If only the reverse were true today.

In the black church, I saw a continuity of values of Christian moral principles and social philosophy—unlike the hypocrisy I kept bumping up against in the white evangelical community. God's love required people to return good for evil and to lift up the downtrodden. That so many black preachers could keep nonviolence alive in the black community, given all the severe persecution it endured, is a testimony of divine grace. Had they taught revenge and "an eye for an eye," America would have experienced many great bloodbaths. As the Rev. Martin Luther King Jr. preached, "If we practice Old Testament retribution, we'll all be going around toothless and blind."

I loved the black churches' moral perspective on justice, racism, and the American ideals that we white people gave lip service to but ignored in practice. But the black churches used their Christian consciousness to embrace and advocate for what we now term *social justice*. In fact, Dr. King changed America by using our biblical heritage to get us to rethink our assumptions and open our hearts to justice. And that is one purpose of this book. We need to use the skills, tools, rhetoric, and legacy that he gave us. He proved that Scripture combined with the right moral vision has power to bring changes that no one ever thought possible. Today's Democrats have lost this type of vision, and they need to reclaim it—not by sipping coffee in Manhattan or idolizing Bill Maher but by engaging evangelicals in their churches in the flyover states.

I also loved the theology espoused by black preachers. They were just as devoted to serving Jesus as their white counterparts, but they had a natural compassion for the downtrodden and saw the push for justice as Bible-driven. The Israelites had been enslaved in Egypt, had worked hard, and had suffered long, but God sent them a prophet to break the yoke of oppression and set His people free. The New Testament affirmed that in Christ there are no racial divides. God is not black or white, not male or female, but a spirit, and God is love.

In addition to visiting black churches, I also got involved in local civil rights efforts, and I attended marches and rallies to protest segregation and racism, and I was pleasantly surprised to see other white Christians, even ministers, there participating with me, although these evangelical progressives were the exception and not the rule. But my activities must have raised suspicions with the authorities. One day, my older sister was meeting friends in a restaurant, and a man approached her. He asked, "Do you know this woman?" He then produced a picture of me and explained that I was a suspected communist. When she later told me about it, she was visibly distressed—worrying for my safety and troubled that it might be true. "No, I am not a communist," I assured her. But I had to admit that being under surveillance by the government was scary. How unfair to be labeled a "traitor" to America for pursuing a public policy that aligned with my faith and the Constitution of the United States. But I wasn't going to let this stop me, in part, because I had a deep moral conviction that I got from my mother. Segregation was wrong, and we had to do something to change it. I doubt I would have had that same fervor if she had not imparted a strong sense of the Bible into my consciousness.

And only two years after the 1967 Supreme Court ruling in *Loving v. Virginia,* which struck down state laws that prohibited interracial marriage, I began dating a black man, whom I later married. My father was livid and blamed my mother for her "damnable sermon on Moses." My mother was fearful for our safety. But she grew to love my husband, and she did much to support our family. It also made the civil rights struggle of the outside world more real for her. Actually, my dad, too, grew to like my husband. He would say, "It's just a damn shame that he's black." Obviously, not every white evangelical pastor will have the experiences that my mother had. My own experience confirms that the Bible is a powerful tool for changing hearts and minds. But I will never forget the intolerant and hateful views that permeated white religious culture throughout the 1950s and '60s.

Transcending Fundamentalism: Like Mother, Like Daughter

For a long time, my mom resisted the call of the ministry because she was brainwashed to believe that women were not supposed to be leaders in the church. She didn't want to be labeled as one of those bad women—bossy wives who dared to preach. She was intimidated by some dude who wrote a book called *Bobbed Hair, Bossy Wives, and Women Preachers*[7]—a book my father browbeat her with. So she struggled between her inner calling to preach

God's Word and her duty to conform to tradition. I watched my mom slowly transform her own thinking beyond the traditional fundamentalism of her day. Seeing her step out on her own empowered me to think for myself, though I was unaware of her bravery at the time. Yet her example has been a great source of inspiration to me. My mother has a rare passion for God and a conviction about right and wrong. But she had to overcome the prejudices of her day to be true to herself and her Lord.

Eventually mainstream Christianity "caught up" with her, and in a sense, I am attempting to do the same. Although I don't subscribe to all of my mother's fundamentalist views, I vividly remember her teaching a series of sermons on "The Four Corners of the Field, which corresponded with four classes of people Christians should help. She asserted that these four groups actually represented four points of spiritual growth that were laid out in the form of a cross. I don't know that this book represents spiritual growth as she saw it, but for me, it was certainly a milestone in my own development.

Not only were the 1950s and '60s a time of racial strife, but many were also worried about communism taking over our country and Russia's unleashing the atomic bomb, which would destroy us all. Given the number of loose nukes floating around today, maybe that fear was a good thing. A sort of fatalism hung over our world. We were not encouraged to get involved in changing the world, because it was all going to end disastrously anyway, and everything in this life is vanity and vexation of spirit. So the only recourse was to live pure, love God, and be ready to be transfigured with Jesus in the air.

When I lived in rural Indiana, I had neighbors who still believe the same way today. All the worry about pollution and living green is silly because Jesus is coming soon, and the entire earth will be blown up. Then God will supernaturally restore the universe, with a new heaven and a new earth (and a lake of fire for the bad people—and those who missed out on hearing about Jesus). Put eschatology (the end of times) together with Ecclesiastes (everything is vanity and vexation of spirit), and you can easily lose any motivation to work for justice, improve our government, or even end disease and hunger. Didn't Jesus say, "The poor we always have with us"? So that justifies not worrying about poverty, for you can never eradicate it. You should just focus on being pious and praising the Lord—while you fear the communists, liberals, and atheists coming to take away your guns and your religious freedom.

Today, I sense that same spirit of hatred, hypocrisy, and animosity in Christian talk about other social issues: marriage and family, abortion, health care reform, or immigration—or when Christians have asserted that Obama was a secret Muslim, or that his presidency was illegitimate because he wasn't born in America. It's one thing to criticize him because you think he had bad policies or made mistakes. Saying that someone is misguided or out of touch with essential American values is a far cry from demonizing him as a threat and playing on the fear and hatred generated by terrorists who attacked us on 9/11. Yet this same distorted, fearmongering logic has pervaded political ads for decades, and both parties play this game. That is why John Lewis said in 2008 that McCain and Palin were sowing the seeds of hatred and division, reminding him of the atmosphere George Wallace fostered in the 1960s in Alabama. He wasn't saying that they were segregationists but that they were using the same tactic: evoking fear and hatred of blacks by demonizing their opponent.

We've seen the seeds of fear and hatred come to fruition with several absurd proclamations of Trump during the 2016 presidential election. Now we want to drive out eleven million undocumented immigrants, build a multibillion-dollar wall, and impose a religious test for entry into the country—as if someone who was secretly a terrorist wouldn't be smart enough to pretend to be a Christian in order to gain entrance. After all, masquerading one's true identity is a long-used tactic of spying and sabotage. Satan doesn't appear as a devil with horns but as an angel of light. The majority of undocumented immigrants in this country entered legally. They didn't sneak across the border because there was no wall. They had valid six-month visas. They just stayed here after their visas expired. How does a wall solve that? It just makes people feel good to think we're being big and bad to build a wall. As the teens used to say, that gets a big "Duh!" Or to quote Bill Engvall—"Here's your sign"—a stupid sign.[8] And since Obama's presidency, the net immigration from Mexico has fallen below zero.[9] Yet we trust in our mythical billion-dollar wall that will drain our budget just to maintain—and do nothing about the vast Canadian border.

Recently, a Republican who touted his Christian faith ran for Congress in my area. One of his TV ads stated, "My Democratic opponent is helping ISIS." Oh, come on. What happened to reason? Can we not disagree without demonizing each other? But aligning your opponent with Satan or ISIS (in my day it was communism) has always impacted the fundamentalist mind. That is why it crops up in political ads. Fear works.

When my fundamentalist friends buy into the fear, "Ain't it awful," the other party is a demon, or the "Antichrist" rhetoric, I make this response, quoting Scripture.

> There's a lot of fearmongering going on today. It makes big money for some to keep you scared, but my Bible tells me that **"God has not given us over to a spirit of fear, but of power and of love, and a sound mind."** (quoting 2 Timothy 1:7 KJV)

Other scriptures also come to mind: **"Fear of man will prove to be a snare**, but whoever trusts in the Lord is kept safe" (Proverbs 29:25). So I remind them, "The Bible says that fear is a snare." The word *snare* means a noose, a trap. People are scaring you because they want to entrap you and choke the life out of you, so they can manipulate you. This kind of conversation enslaves you. This is not God's way. **"The fruit of the righteous is a tree of life"** (quoting Proverbs 11:30 KJV). I quote these scriptures to myself now so as not to buy into the current liberal hysteria over Trump.

Righteous people and righteous conversations bring life, and like a tree, they keep producing life, not hate, death, and darkness. Proverbs 11:30 goes on to say that "he that winneth souls is wise" (KJV). The NIV translates this scripture as the "one who is wise saves lives." Wisdom saves lives, souls. The word *soul* here is from the Hebrew word *nephesh*, which means living beings. It refers to the seat of passions, emotions, and appetites. Our country is waging war for the hearts and passions of America—as well as for people around the world. We all, especially Democrats, need to wake up and start connecting with the better angels of our nature—our emotions that produce empathy, compassion, and confidence, not the darkness of fear, hatred, and cruelty. If we are wise, we will start saving souls.

We can keep a strong, secure nation without resorting to fear and bigotry, but Democrats must know enough about the Bible to counter insane attacks with statements that evangelicals recognize as the "Word of God." By using biblical analogies and stories, Democrats can better connect with evangelical voters and compete more effectively on Republican turf. When evangelical Christians see that we revere wisdom from the Bible, they'll have a harder time painting us as terrorists or traitors to our country.

Although I may criticize evangelicals, I want to honor them as well. It was my mother's commitment to Bible teachings that equipped me for a career in academia. I grew up watching her spend hours studying the Bible with multiple dictionaries and concordances on her lap. Between home and school, I cut my teeth on verses that said, "whatsoever your hand finds to do, do it with all your might" (meaning don't be a slacker or halfhearted); "Study to show yourself approved of God," and wisdom, knowledge, and understanding are more precious than gold. My parents gave me a lot of positive reinforcement for doing well in school, and my mom was my staunchest advocate in persuading my tightfisted dad not only to send me to college, but also to fund extracurricular activities that enriched my education. I can't say that I'm any worse off in the long run for not watching much TV as a kid in our holiness household.

I went on to complete my master's in English and my doctorate in higher education from Indiana University, Bloomington, and I became a community college administrator and teacher. I wrote and administered federal grants, bringing in several million dollars of federal funding to our then fledgling college and leading new efforts to improve student retention and achievement. We documented our successes with objective evidence to prove that our college was making wise use of these valuable resources. In so doing, I learned that the Department of Education was staffed with caring citizens like myself, who were doing their best to improve educational opportunity for all. I authored various academic publications, some with my then husband, and was committed to opening college doors for low-income and minority students and to equipping them with important reading, writing, and thinking skills. Like many young people, my passion for activism gave way to the needs of my family and my career.

Sadly, I divorced my husband in 1982. It was a long, bitter process. It created some deep family divides that last until this day. But I was thankful, because my mom, tough as nails, stood by me and helped me pay my legal bills, which were ballooning out of control as my husband kept pulling tricks and delay tactics to avoid an equitable settlement. In order to keep the costs down, my divorce attorney taught me how to do paralegal tasks, and given my doctorate in education, I readily mastered the chores he assigned. I found I enjoyed learning about the law and principles of justice and fairness. Learning the law gave me confidence at a time when I was at my worst, but my lawyer's compliments spurred me on. He would say, "I don't care what hotshot lawyer your husband just hired. I've got you; you're my secret weapon." Thanks to my extensive investigation and collection of evidence, as well as much legal research, we actually made a small piece of history, as we combined a divorce lawsuit with a tort suit against my ex, his two sisters, and his friend for conspiracy to defraud me of my share of the marital estate. I was able to prove with clear and convincing evidence how they had tried to cheat me. At one point, my husband even took one of his sisters to the bank to impersonate me on a loan for a deal he was trying to hide from me. We won the case—as Trump would say, "bigly." Afterward, my lawyer told me that I did so well that I should consider doing this full time, and so I did; at the age of 39, I went back to school and redirected my career.

I felt a bit out of place, as many of my colleagues were in their early twenties, and I was pushing forty with a small child to rear. After using a sabbatical leave for my first year, I had to finish my last two years of law school while teaching full time at my college. So I had to be disciplined in managing my time between work, family, and law school. My son went to bed every night at 8 p.m., and I'd get three hours of studying before bed. I'd listen to law lectures on tape whenever I drove around, much to the annoyance of my son, who wanted to listen to Disney stories. But the rigorous discipline forced me to be focused and intentional when I studied, for I knew I couldn't go back over it two or three more times. My mother pressured my father to agree to pay my tuition, but because I did so well the first semester, being first in my class with a high GPA, the University of Louisville gave me a scholarship for the rest of my time there. I graduated summa cum laude and valedictorian of my law school class. For nearly ten years, I held down two jobs until I became eligible to retire from college teaching and devote myself to the full-time practice of law. So it's in the spirit of an academic, civil rights activist, attorney, and my mother that I write this book.

We All Cherry-Pick the Bible

Today, "Bible-believing Christians" have no problem rejecting literalism as to passages that are now too inconvenient to follow. The Bible contains various scriptures that explain how Jezebel and other wicked harlots painted their eyes (2 Kings 9:30; Proverbs 6:25; Jeremiah 4:30; Ezekiel 23:39–41)—hence my mom's prohibition against wearing makeup. New Testament writers specifically advised women to dress modestly, not to wear jewelry, or fancy ornamentation in their hair (1 Timothy 2:9). Paul said that a woman's long hair gave her power with the angels (1 Corinthians 11: 6–10). Prohibitions widely practiced by most evangelicals of sixty to 100 years ago, which were based on literal interpretations of Scripture, have fallen by the wayside: wearing jewelry, adornment, face-painting, wearing "men's clothing" (i.e., pants), short hair, divorce and remarriage, use of alcohol, dancing, and TV watching.

Now most fundamentalists do these things, and today's churches would lose their followers if women couldn't don makeup, cut their hair, or wear pants. Shucks, now folks can go to church in shorts and flip-flops—an informality still hard for me to embrace. And with every other marriage ending in divorce, even the Catholic Church cannot hold to its strict doctrine of forbidding second marriages—based on Jesus' words in Matthew 19:9. They get around their proscription by annulling the first marriage, so that members can freely take communion after their second marriage. You pretend that you were never married the first time or that God had not properly sanctioned it. I've never quite understood how that does not bastardize your children from your first marriage. But we all play logic games and reinterpret our rules to meet current realities, and I can accept it as part of the discipline of the Catholic faith.

When I was a child and teen, mainline evangelical denominations also considered other practices of Pentecostal holiness and Catholic churches unnecessary, even inappropriate. The school I attended, which was founded and staffed by fundamentalist Bible believers, said that we modern Christians did not need actually to wash other people's feet as required in John 13:4–14. I felt silly among my peers because my church periodically held foot-washing ceremonies. I never got inspired by that, but it was designated an act of humility and ministry to another, a ceremony that reminded Christians to engage in humble service.

To the Christian denomination of my high school, however, Jesus' command to wash other people's feet was limited to that point in history when everyone wore sandals (if they even had shoes), the roads were dusty, and their feet got dirty. Thus, they sidestepped their biblical literalism to re-interpret Jesus' command as to its intent that we all be humble servants of our fellow man. And that is a reasonable extension of that command, though it doesn't invalidate

Jesus' actual words. When your feet are hot and tired, having some-one minister to them with soothing water and touch is a wonderful thing. Recently, Pope Francis washed the feet of prisoners, showing his humility and service to the despised and forgotten. He kept this ceremony relevant to the world's Catholics today.

When it comes to scriptures that require modesty, humility, and separation from worldly pleasures, the Christian Right is able to make a grand leap of enlightenment. Yet they revert to their lit-eralism when tackling issues of sexuality and reproduction, while dismissing and then ignoring all the mandates about social welfare. And, yes, we all are guilty of selectively choosing those parts of the Bible that bolster the beliefs we already hold dear, while we ignore other parts that we don't like. Most of us go through life doing this across the board. Rather than weighing the evidence on both sides of the coin, as a fair, impartial, and open-minded judge would do, we start out with a pre-judgment—like a lawyer hired solely to de-fend her client's story. Then we pick out portions of evidence that support our point of view and disregard or explain away everything else to the contrary.

If we are going to be literalists, then we must do so across the board—to be in integrity with our professed beliefs. And the minute we decide not to take the Bible literally on one point, we have made an admission that we really cannot take it literally at all. Our ac-tions speak louder than our words. When we cherry-pick our liter-alism, our fundamentalism crumbles.

My mother's independence in studying the Bible, however, made a lasting impression on me and started me on my own jour-ney toward more independent thought. Thanks to her, I realized that the same way everyone else has thought about the Bible need not be the only fair way to interpret it. Of course, be careful how you empower your children, for they will take what you give them and use it in ways you never anticipate.

As I got older and went to college, I studied the philosophy of religion, world religions, history of the multiple versions of texts, and linguistic hurdles to translations. All language is fraught with ambiguity, so the reader brings much meaning to any text, even when he is trying to render the plain meaning of words. We all approach every text, whether literary, legal, or scriptural, wearing filters—our backgrounds and biases that shape our interpretation of words. Remember, the apostle Paul acknowledged, "We all see through a glass, darkly" (1 Corinthians 13:12 KJV). All human perceptions of the divine are murky at best. We need a tad of humility, if you please.

Fundamentalists who say that they take the Bible as the inerrant Word of God don't truly believe this concept. It just comforts them to think so, for believing that the world was created in six twenty-four hour days, or that Noah and his family were the only humans on the globe saved in a flood (as opposed to a salvation of someone in their own region), or that he could have fed and housed all the animals on the entire earth for forty days, gives one a good feeling of security in an uncertain, dangerous world. And that belief is not necessarily all bad. We can read the story of Noah as empowerment in the face of overwhelming odds: "If God is for us, who can be against us?" To my point here, the reality is that all fundamentalists cherry-pick their scriptures that they take literally and those that they reinterpret with enlightened reason.

And here's another bombshell. We do not have the original texts written by the New Testament or Old Testament writers. We have copies of copies of copies of copies of copies, many times removed from the original, and there are thousands of variations in the oldest texts we do have. Think about it. They didn't have photocopiers. All writings had to be hand-copied under primitive conditions. When copying by hand under less than optimal lighting, scriveners could easily skip a line, misread a word, or even add in their own thoughts on the matter, which is proven to have occurred. So when people tell me that the Bible is error free, I say, "Yes, just tell me which of the original texts of the Bible you are relying on." This doesn't destroy the value of the Bible. If anything, it's all the more miraculous that the Scripture has retained its inspirational coherence, but it does put a damper on our absolute certainty over inerrancy. In short, I've gained access to other tools for interpreting Scripture that I lacked as a child.

Personally, I don't follow a one-scripture, literalist theology of any inspired book. Literalist one-verse theology creates dangerous radicals in all religions. Extremists in the Middle East demonstrate this fact, as well as the Westboro Baptist Church in Kansas, known for its hate speech against gays and picketing of veterans' funerals. And the new Christian Right has birthed a "Dominionist" group that is doing much wrong first by ignoring the vast weight of scriptural precedent and second by taking scriptures out of context to claim that they are supposed to take dominion over us all. Such logic then enables them to promote a political ideology that is cruel, unjust, and scary, even for many sincere evangelicals.

I advocate a literate, informed reading of all sacred texts, trying to understand as best we can the context in which they were developed—and with a tad of humility, acknowledging that the search for truth is a life-long process, not a matter of instant certainty. Yet I have written this book from the standpoint of my fundamentalist Christian background, not as an intellectual or scholar per se. And being freed from fundamentalism actually helps us to perceive the deeper moral truths running through the stories. The inspiration of God's Word is not a doctrine you give lip service to. It's the inspiration and insight, the transformation, you achieve as you read the ancient texts. That is what makes a difference.

Today, more mainline educated evangelicals, who still believe the Bible contains the inspired Word of God, understand that you have to read the Bible literately, not literally. A literate person understands poetry (and the Bible is filled with metaphysical poetry) and figurative language, as well as the evolution of human understanding (i.e., revelation) of God and just who and what God is and whose side He's on. Religious language by its nature is highly personal, emotive, and ambiguous, pointing to deeper aspects of our sense of being, purpose, and meaning. It was not intended to be scientific or a literal account of the history of the world. And knowing science alone does not give inspiration, meaning, and purpose to our lives. We have to find that elsewhere.

To understand the Bible, we have to look at the context in which certain commands and principles were given, and we have to harmonize the underlying principles with the whole, before we draw analogies to our world today. This is similar to how a good lawyer harmonizes case law. And as with case law, we understand that the unfolding of "truth" evolves, just as we see the theology of the Old Testament evolving from a tribal God, who is only on one tribe's side, to a God who loves everyone, even our enemies.

The story of Jonah is profound in that regard. Often modern readers get hung up on whether Jonah was literally in the belly of a whale for three days, not realizing that it was a literary device to get Jonah from one place to another, so they miss the profound moral lesson applicable today. God told Jonah to go preach to Israel's enemies, who had killed, besieged, and deported them. Yep, the Ninevites were the Assyrians, still feared today.[10] No wonder Jonah ran away. (What would we say of someone who said God told him to go preach to ISIS?) Then Jonah became angry with God when his country's enemies repented and showed themselves to be on God's side. Jonah would rather see his enemies killed and his prophecy vindicated than for them to be redeemed, for that left Jonah looking like a fool. The story ends with his sulking under a gourd vine because God didn't rain down fire and brimstone on his country's enemies.

The story shows that sometimes God has a plan for our enemies, and His love can turn the most ardent evildoer into a strongly righteous person. But that can't occur until God's servants are willing to have a dialog with their hated enemy. I'm not encouraging Christian ministers to go minister to ISIS, though there are Christian workers who bring food and clothing relief to ISIS war-torn areas at great personal risk to themselves. But the story of Jonah would certainly encourage us as Americans to heal our own divisions by conversing with "the others" and finding common ground. As for us Democrats, we have largely dismissed the Bible from our political thought, and as a result, we are not connecting with many Christian voters.

To interpret the Bible fairly (i.e., rationally and appropriately), we can't just lift one verse out of context and make it an absolute rule. We look at the whole in order to discern the moral principles working underneath. And the right path is not always crystal clear. For instance, we all agree on certain principles of justice. If you do the crime, you do the time. But we also know that throughout the Bible, including Jesus' gospel, mercy trumps justice. There are many hard situations, even in the Bible, where seemingly opposite results occurred as people weighed and balanced competing interests: How do I be fair but also show mercy and kindness? How do I speak the truth in love? We all tend to get angry when others rub our nose in the truth. We all have sacred cows, and we may turn vicious when someone dethrones our idols, whether it's our personal idols or our group's cherished beliefs—our dogma. Many ideals are easy to say and hard to do.

The rules and standards outlined in this book are from both the Old Testament and the New Testament. Throughout, I repeat the point that we cannot just dismiss the legal mandates from the Old Testament because we Christians are under a new dispensation. The New Testament affirms the same principles as the Old, and it affirms that we can and must learn things from the Old Testament. I grew up on the King James Version, but here is the NIV:

> All Scripture is God-breathed and is useful for teaching, rebuking, correcting and training in righteousness, so that the servant of God may be thoroughly equipped for every good work. (2 Timothy 3:16–17)

So while we may not be required to adopt Old Testament ethics, all Bible believers can and must look for what's profitable therein. If we claim to be a follower of Jesus and a Bible-believing Christian, we must give weight to scriptures throughout the Bible.

My dad used to say, "We're all ignorant—just about different things." I would add, "We're all hypocrites—just about different things." I try to remind myself of that when I hear absurdly unchristian arguments from leaders and pundits on the Right, who pride themselves on their moral superiority and tout their allegiance to their Christian faith.

Politically, the Christian Right has been hijacked by self-righteous Pharisees who, as Jesus said, wash the outside of the cup but leave it full of extortion and excess, who are like beautifully painted sepulchers that inside are filled with dead men's bones and decay[11] An example is the Christian Right's support for the Iraq War; this was hypocrisy and wickedness disguised by a show of righteousness, to use Jesus' own explanation of the figurative whitewashed tombs. The Iraq War lacked all legal and moral justification, especially since we knew that Iraq had nothing to do with the 9/11 attack on America. Yet we conjured up faulty intelligence, which was known to be weak at best and highly suspect, then rallied a coalition to invade another country, with no thought or plan of replacing its infrastructure. In essence, we became the devil in order to fight the devil. We swept Iraq's house clean of one devil (Saddam Hussein) and left it empty—only to have many more devils (al Qaeda and ISIS) move in to fill the empty void we created.[12]

I can't understand why loving Jesus means I have to be pro guns, pro war, and pro torture of our enemies. I can't make that wash. I can own that sometimes I believe and endorse things that are not moral or biblical—but when I do, I want to have the courage to admit that I'm not being "Christian" in my logic or my values.

About This Book: What It Is and Is Not

This book is an effort to help non-Christians and socially progressive Christians speak the language of the Bible to bring people together to solve some critical problems of our times. In short, it can help Democrats speak to Republican evangelicals. For the most part, I have avoided controversial social issues (such as abortion and gay marriage) in order to focus on Jesus' commands found in Matthew 25. The Bible is 100% clear in its economic and social welfare policies—and they are not supply-side Reaganomics.

This book is designed to build consensus around economic issues and social welfare principles for the entire nation. Jesus said, "Where your treasure is, there will your heart be also" (Matthew 6:21). How we spend our money tells us where our priorities lie. As an attorney, I often admonish my clients: "you keep score with the money": that is, don't get sidetracked with emotional issues and ego battles that will only run up legal bills and not help you achieve a victory at trial or a fair settlement. Our money, our treasure, and our budgets prove what's important to us in our daily lives, and the same goes for our government. If we can persuade Christians that a government that doesn't leave the poor and the sick on the margins is moral, Christlike, and good for the economy, then we've won 90% of the battle.

All too often, I've seen religious Christians say, "I may not endorse their economic policies, but I could never support a candidate who is pro abortion." Most of us agree that we should honor all living beings and that being "pro-life" is ideal, though we disagree on how that plays out in our legal system. Yet many sincere "pro-life" Christians accept a multitude of immoral, unethical, and unchristlike economic proposals from their politicians. Far too often, Republican politicians are given a pass on all issues because they simply proclaim that they are "pro-life." But Jesus didn't say that. The Bible doesn't say that. Both Old and New Testaments require the leaders of their countries to take affirmative steps to ensure that society is fair for everyone, particularly groups on the margins.

I hope this book challenges evangelical Christians to stretch just a bit and open their minds to strong scriptural evidence on certain subjects. If we purport to be disciples of Christ (i.e., Christlike people—hence the name *Christians*), then either we walk the talk, or at least we admit that the path we are on is not as close to Jesus as we'd like to imagine. As you read this book, you may be surprised, as I was, to see that parts of the Bible read like a Bernie Sanders manifesto.

All my life, I've heard my mom, a Pentecostal minister now aged 98, say, "Christians do not know their Bibles." I decided to study more in depth and see what principles we glean *if* with integrity, we examine the entire Bible as to its views on collective government action for social welfare, in particular with regard to health care and the Affordable Care Act. I make no bones about my support for the ACA or Obamacare as it is known, and I believe much of the resistance to it is illogical, contrary to clear Bible mandates, and not based on true facts about the needs of our nation.

To my Jewish or agnostic friends: This book may help you learn the standards that Christians should meet and then hold them accountable for living up to those standards. My goal is to remove the masks of piety from people who promote national policies that contradict clear biblical mandates and who disregard those mandates as mere exhortations for individual charity. I'm just tired of all the war-mongering, hate, and oppression advocated in the name of Jesus. Advocate them if you must, but after reading this book, you will see that you have no scriptural support for such cruel positions.

In this book, I'm not debating whether the Bible is the infallible Word of God. That's not the point. I am speaking from this premise: "assuming the Bible is the Word of God," or mostly so, given a few errors in translation along the way, "what should the national political standards be?" If we hope to expand the thinking of evangelical Republicans, we must do it from *their* premise, which holds the Old and New Testaments as sacred, divine authority that should guide our actions and beliefs.[13] That must be the standard against which we measure their rhetoric and conduct.

Attacking Christians as stupid and superstitious will only alienate them and drive us all farther apart. I thought Bill Maher's movie *Religulous* was funny, irreverent, and satirical, though at times disjointed. Maher presented the scientific absurdity of literal interpretations of the Bible. Thereby, he reduced faith to a literal, superstitious level in order to belittle it. He appears not to understand or appreciate the role of ancient wisdom, metaphysical poetry, metaphor, and spiritual dimensions of the human mind. Regardless, his satire will convince no one to turn against a religion they cherish. Maher can get affirmation only from those who already agree with him. Insulting people is not often the way to get them to change their minds, though, as our 2016 presidential election shows, belittling others can rally one's supporters.

While my book contains criticisms of the white evangelical culture that I grew up in, my purpose is to acknowledge the good and reclaim biblical principles that underscore my political outlook. In fact, my mother continues to this day to be the most inspirational person I have ever encountered. She began her ministry at a time when it was virtually unheard of for women to lead and teach from the Bible. Society told her that she was evil, but she persisted anyway, and eventually society caught up.

Doing the research for this book has made me proud to reclaim my biblical heritage while maintaining my progressive beliefs. I discovered amazing, insightful passages that I never knew existed, passages seldom expounded in the fundamentalist churches of my youth, but my mother's foundation of biblical scholarship kept me from throwing the baby out with the bathwater. While there are many areas on which we all may disagree, particularly about the most efficient and effective ways to achieve our goals, the basic principles of providing for the common good are firmly rooted in the Bible. And they are national mandates, not optional good works we can choose to adopt or ignore or leave to random, individual acts of charity.

In this book, I've quoted many scriptures. That's to prove my case and show that I am not just putting my own spin on the plain words of the Bible. The reality is that people don't have time to look up the passages I reference (not to mention that it's a hassle to use two books at once), so I've included the full texts here with boldface type to emphasize key phrases. If you already know these verses, you can quickly skim over them.

In this book, I use both the King James Version and the New International Version of the Bible. Some fundamentalists insist that the King James is the only reliable version. It is the version of the "old time religion" in which I was reared. As an English major who concentrated in Renaissance literature, I readily concur that the King James Version is often more eloquent. (That may be because I like Elizabethan English.) Yet I chose to use the New International Version more prominently because the grammar and syntax are easier for modern readers to understand, and I noticed that many evangelical Bible commentary websites use it as well. Where I've used the KJV, I've noted it, and the remaining citations without special identification are from the NIV.

I take the liberty of switching back and forth, mainly because some verses just feel better to me in the KJV, since that's the way I memorized them as a child. Another reason for using the KJV is that it correlates to *Strong's Exhaustive Concordance of the Bible*, first published in 1894.[14] Strong's gives definitions from the Hebrew and Greek for all key words. It is now available online and on my trusty iPad via a downloadable app, Touch Bible.[15] This may be the linguistic scholar's equivalent of paint by numbers, but it's a reputable resource for understanding the meaning of words in the Hebrew and Greek texts, a resource most accessible to us nontheologians.

I also found www.biblegateway.com to be a valuable research tool because its search engine is fast and lets you quickly see multiple renditions of the ancient texts with a mere click of a button.

In this book, I retain the traditional male pronoun for God, just to avoid jarring traditional readers and to keep from repeating nouns merely to avoid pronouns. Yes, I know that the Bible contains words for God that are feminine as well as masculine, and God is Spirit—something that transcends gender. Further, since Genesis says that God made humans, male and female, in His image,[16] one can easily say that God is the totality of male and female together. Neither one gender separately represents the complete image of God.

This book is intended to be more of a reference book than a sequential narrative, so that as issues arise, you may easily turn to specific chapters for talking points. It's organized around the four classes of people that Jesus commanded His followers to serve: the sick, the stranger, the poor, and the prisoner. While I've attempted to make it an interesting read, I realize that some people may want to consult only specific chapters for a collection of scriptures that address specific talking points. Therefore, I have purposefully repeated key scriptures under each chapter, so that the reader doesn't have to flip back and forth to find scriptural support for various propositions. Many scriptures also refer to two or three of the four groups of oppressed people at the same time, so we must revisit common passages as we address each topic.

Let me also clarify my use of the term *evangelicals*. It is easy to make sweeping generalizations that lump too many diverse groups together. And all labels are for general reference and don't necessarily apply to every member of the group. Rather, they note only major trends. On one level, any person who spreads the good news of Jesus Christ is evangelical. In this book, however, I'm referring mainly to white fundamentalist Christians (predominantly conservative Republican Protestants), who purport to believe that the Bible is the inerrant (without error) Word of God; that as God's Word, it accurately reports the factual history of the entire world; that every statement in the Bible is literally true (such as that God made the world in six twenty-four hour periods); and that it is scientifically accurate.

In general, the denominations comprising this group have viewed most progressive social movements (from abolishing slavery to allowing immigration and safeguarding Social Security, civil rights, welfare, Medicare, and women's rights) as a march toward corruption—even toward the apocalypse where we will have a one-world government ruled by the Antichrist. I'm a personal witness to this because I am a product of this culture. Such evangelicals believe it is their duty to oppose sin, especially fornication and sex outside of marriage between one man and one woman, and they have adopted one (and only one) test for all politicians—their stance on abortion rights for women.

These evangelicals are hostile to most programs of the federal government, except for the military, which despite biblical cautions to the contrary, can never be big enough or weaponized enough. They seem always to be pro guns and pro war. And their thinking is intertwined with support for states rights and deep hostility toward the federal government. I believe this stems from Civil War days—as states rights was the intellectual bulwark that upheld first slavery and then Jim Crow, for it was the big bad government that came into their homelands, upended their cherished way of life, and forced them to change. It took away their power and gave it to blacks—and now to Latinos who are invading the land. Among this group are what used to be called the Southern Christian Dixiecrats. At one time they were Democrats, but in the years since Ronald Reagan they have joined ranks with and come to dominate the Republican Party.[17]

Many black fundamentalist Christians share many of the tenets of evangelicalism, but not the anti-government ideology of their white Bible-believing counterparts. That's because they understand firsthand what it's like to be told that God supports subjugation and prejudice. They remember Jim Crow and see through today's fake news reports that lead to gerrymandering of congressional districts, stricter voter ID laws, and restricted voting opportunities in poor neighborhoods. They understand how state laws have long been used to suppress their civil rights. They also recognize the gospel of Jesus as lifting up the downtrodden, and they have rarely opposed help from the federal government. In fact, without the federal government's intervention—literally, first with Abraham Lincoln's Emancipation Proclamation and later with Eisenhower's and then Kennedy's use of federal marshals to enforce the desegregation of schools—they would have had no recourse against the abusive states' rights doctrines that barred them from educational, social, and economic opportunities. For black people, it was the federal government that stopped slavery and Jim Crow.

I also acknowledge that I am a witness only to the white evangelical culture that I grew up in—both from the very conservative fundamentalist Christian school that I attended and from the Pentecostal holiness culture of my family, as well as from interactions with friends and relatives who were Southern Baptists or from other Christian groups. I wasn't exposed to more mainline Protestants groups until I became an adult, and those groups I encountered would be classified as more moderate and progressive, but they are not fundamentalists or evangelicals as I define the latter term here.

I have been a researcher and a scholar. I have included research references in this book that document factual assertions about recent events, but I purposely do not want this book to read like an academic paper. I have also bypassed formal citation rules, opting instead to note only the hyperlinks. It makes the footnotes too long always to list the author, article title, and date, when that information is in the link itself. I have not footnoted every item of general knowledge or research that I've read, though I admit that I've footnoted more references than I first intended.

Notwithstanding my formal training, I am approaching this subject from common sense and the old-fashioned Bible lessons of my youth. My purpose is to present the Bible in ways that all can understand and let the plain wording speak for itself.

I had started this book in 2007 as I marveled at the anti-poor, anti-health care, and anti-immigrant rhetoric coming from the Republican Party, which was being supported by the Christian Right. And I was disappointed that few progressives made any references to the many scriptures that supported their policies. Yet I was practicing law full-time in two states and trying to keep up with my home, my children, and my grandchildren. I struggled to find the time to finish it, despite devoting much of my spare time to the project. Then in 2008 after Barack Obama was elected president, I assumed that our nation had turned a corner, and I felt that this work was less important, for we now understood the importance of working toward a compassionate society that cares for the sick and the downtrodden. So I set the book aside, leaving it in my computer archives as a fantasy project—maybe someday. Obviously, history has proven my hopeful assumption wrong. Alas, I've always been a bit of a Pollyanna.

I originally thought to title this book *Bible-Speak for Progressives,* because I had my own unique experiences using the language of the Bible to help people understand various moral principles that often align with Democratic policies. But I was also writing a different book on divorce, which chronicled my own journey through a hellish divorce and gave helpful tips on how to deal with similar legal challenges. I still hope to finish that book soon.

Then during the fall of 2016, my son, Stuart (no longer a hyperactive child who hated legal tapes) was speaking with me about the election. At the time, he was advising a Democratic candidate who was running in a red district. We were lamenting how Democrats in general don't use the Bible enough to justify their stances on public policy. Stuart said, "You know, Mom, there are loads of books out there on divorce, but there aren't really any books that help Democrats use the Bible for their campaigns. Maybe that should be your focus." He wanted to have a look at some of my early chapters, which were by now out of date, so he could use them in his work. "Yeah, the Democrats definitely need a book like this," he remarked later that day. "Mom, you need to get this book out there, so progressives have a resource that speaks to evangelicals. But you need a new title. *Bible-Speak* is a bit flat."

My bent is academic, not marketing. I tend to lay down the facts and let them speak for themselves. My son, on the other hand, has worked at the BBC and in the British Parliament and has written numerous political commentary pieces on international politics. And he's got more of a mind for this than I. "You need something catchier: something more controversial and more powerful. I mean, the book is basically about justifying Obama's stance on health care and other liberal causes. So pick the most controversial one and use that." We threw around some names. Then Stuart cocked his head and said, "Really, the book is about how the Bible approves of Obamacare. So why not call it *Jesus Loves Obamacare.*" We both cracked up! The title was controversial and yet catchy. "Jesus Loves Obamacare and other liberal causes"—that's what the book is about.

I decided to put my divorce book on hold and start writing this book again, but I was in no great hurry. We both thought that Hillary Clinton would win the election and the progress made in health care would be preserved. Like many, we were shocked to discover that she lost. After the election where Trump lost the popular vote by nearly three million yet won the Electoral College, Stuart insisted that we try to get this book done before the Republicans could repeal Obamacare without improving or replacing it with something better. We feared that more than twenty million Americans would just be kicked out with nowhere to go, and Stuart felt the book would lose its power if it weren't out there in time to make a difference. He agreed to collaborate and threw himself wholeheartedly into the project. We both dropped everything and worked most of the Christmas holidays and into the New Year to make this happen.

Stuart is an accomplished academic in his own right. He graduated summa cum laude from Emory University in Atlanta, with a major in religion. He earned a master's degree at the London School of Economics and a JD from Harvard Law School, where he studied under Elizabeth Warren, Elena Kagan, Alan Dershowitz, and Laurence Tribe, to name a few. What can I say? He's a chip off the old block, although he follows and is involved with day-to-day politics more closely than I.

I offered to coauthor the book with him and give him equal credit because he was such an impetus for its completion and brought my ideas current, but he insists on being listed only as a collaborator. Nevertheless, he has made crucial contributions. He fine-tuned my message, cut out unnecessary pontificating, and urged me to share more about my personal journey. He also did most of the political research, linking scriptures to current events and individual politicians (like Donald Trump, Hillary Clinton, and Elizabeth Warren). In 2007 and 2008, I had focused my examples largely on President George W. Bush and the Iraq war, which I still view as executed in bad faith, considering that Iraq had nothing to do with the September 11 attacks. Stuart ended up writing nearly 40% of the book. Yet this book is still about my journey and my voice in politics and the Bible, and as he notes, I have done most of the heavy lifting.

Stuart and I have had many and at times heated debates over what stayed in and what got excluded, what was too harsh or too soft—and also about when his academic mom started going off on intellectual tangents. "You're going down a rabbit hole," Stuart often chided. "You've got to visualize these things. Look at how it will land with people who don't know the Bible." We love our intense explorations—even when we get testy or our egos get bruised. I am grateful that I reared my son to speak his mind and debate freely in the face of any authority, even mine, all the while maintaining civility and respect. (Well, mostly. We did lose our tempers a few times.)

But being able to collaborate with my brilliant son has been a great joy and achievement that I will forever treasure. He and I are hopeful that this book makes a difference for progressive Democrats who want to find common ground with evangelical Republicans. It certainly gives us all pause to consider these issues in light of our Judeo-Christian heritage.

Why Speak from the Bible?

Regardless of our own individual religious persuasions, most people can see that the Bible is a great source of wisdom, moral principles, metaphors, and stories. In fact, even agnostic scholars recognize the Bible as the greatest book of Western civilization. Political leaders who want to work toward a more compassionate society, a society that balances economic prosperity with protections for those less fortunate, would do well to start drawing on the resources of the Bible. Many in our country are Bible believers, and if we want to communicate with them, we must use a language they understand and call on an authority that they recognize as divine.

To communicate best with others, we must speak their language. That is a given. As an English teacher, I spent years teaching inner city and rural Kentucky students that if they want to succeed in business, they must master Standard English, for the minute they use poor grammar during an interview for a position in management, they bump themselves to the back of the line. Our language, grammar, and metaphors have great impact on how our thoughts are received. We must use expressions, appeals to authority, and metaphors that ring a deep chord, build rapport, and evoke empathy from our audience. Otherwise, people will tune us out, or they just won't understand.

A large segment of our country is dominated by Bible believers. We have a better chance of persuading them to accept our policy proposals if we know the Bible's principles and use its words. The Rev. Martin Luther King Jr. changed American by using the Bible. As a trained theologian from a family of eloquent Baptist ministers, he was able to use his extensive knowledge of Scripture and his superior oratory to transform America's conscience and consciousness, for he proved again and again that white supremacists were *not* following the Bible that they so madly waved. Neither were they following the principles of the United States Constitution or any standard of human decency—though they argued that the Constitution gave them the right to serve or not serve any person for any reason. Dr. King used scriptural authority to expose the hypocrisy of Christian conservatives and to change our national conversation about race.

Evangelical Christians have also endured a fair amount of unfair ridicule—usually at the hands of secular progressives. Christians are tired of having their beliefs belittled and scorned by atheist intellectuals or comedy hosts such as Bill Maher or Jon Stewart. But Maher and Stewart are only the latest of a long line of comedians who poke fun at religious people. Rightly or wrongly, evangelical Christians feel that the secular world has demonized them for decades. So they have rallied to form their own universities that honor their biblical way of seeing the world. They flocked to Reagan, who gave them a seat at the table in a way that no previous president had, and now they swallow without question the conservative propaganda from Fox News. Many indulge in conspiracy theories from "alt right" websites, like Breitbart. Some now click only on fake news that reinforces their worldview, unaware that it is fake news. They honestly believe it's true. Consequently, for Democrats hoping to reach these groups, the Bible may be the only pathway into their consciousness.

The Democratic Party is becoming the party of the coasts. Since our coastal progressives don't need Scripture to support new ideas or programs or to develop compassion for the downtrodden, the wisdom of the Bible is forgotten. Moreover, as many young people see intolerance and hypocrisy in the evangelical Right, they have abandoned organized religion all together. We may use highfalutin words and show off our excellent education, but we are not connecting with the good Christian consciousness of the political Right. The Bible is full of justifications for government programs and much needed political reforms, but Democrats have failed to communicate the social and moral values that underpin our common Judeo-Christian heritage to red state America. The reality is that our party's values much more accurately reflect true biblical teachings than do those across the aisle.

Perhaps, wanting to outgrow the thinking of their bigoted past, progressives have thrown the baby out with the bathwater. But in trying to move past the obvious hypocrisies of the Christian Right, liberals have become elitist and closed-minded to anyone who doesn't think like they do. Rather than finding common ground with evangelicals, liberals sneer at people in the Bible belt. And Democratic politicians too often reflect this same attitude.

Moreover, many Republicans, including fundamentalist Christians, gravitate toward strong leaders who promote instant certitude and appeal to their common religious values. It's easy to say they gravitate toward authoritarianism, but it's more nuanced than that. Evangelicals are rock solid in most of their convictions. They do have strong respect for authority and an unwavering sense of loyalty. So they view indecisiveness or the liberal tendency to ponder both sides as a sign of weakness or lack of moral courage, and to a certain extent, they are right.

Democrats pass great pro-life legislation, such as the Affordable Care Act, and then they run from it. They distance themselves from their achievements, from their sitting president, and then hope the voters don't notice their cowering in the corner. But how did that work out for Democrats in 2010, 2014, and 2016? Yes, there are issues with turnout and voter suppression, but Democrats in red states and in swing states run from the very policies that are based in the Bible. Voters pick up on the fact that if you are ashamed of a law you passed, then maybe it's a bad law.

They need a dose of my mother's evangelical passion. If you know what you're doing is moral and right, nothing on this earth will make you waver from that belief, and you're not ashamed to share "the good news" with hostile audiences. Yes, Republicans spent millions (if not billions) slandering the law, but did Democrats defend the law with passion and zeal? We may have written a check to a liberal candidate or tuned into MSNBC, but did we passionately try to engage our Republican friends and neighbors? Did we speak powerfully and authoritatively? Did we use the Bible to justify our points?

Those of us more in the center or on the left need to assert that we love Jesus just as much as Franklin Graham or James Dobson—maybe more so, because we believe in walking the talk in the areas that Jesus said matter most. Being hateful, using slander and insinuation to malign people unfairly (such as in the 2004 "swift-boating of Kerry") is not Christlike, nor is it biblical. We can't stop people from being hateful, spiteful, unfair, lying, and bigoted. But we liberals need to stop letting them get away with doing it in the name of Jesus.

Once fair-minded people study the Bible, assuming they give any credence to being a Bible-believer, then they must admit certain universal moral principles that the Moral Majority has disregarded.

The question for evangelicals is not *whether* we should have universal health care for Americans but *how* we can get it done. The question cannot be how swiftly we eject aliens from our borders, but how to follow biblical commands to love the foreigners as ourselves and not afflict them by driving them out of our land.

I am not saying that all liberals should believe the Bible literally (that is a private matter of faith), but you must embrace the language of faith and embrace faith leaders who are trying to add biblical principles to the Democratic Party. As we engage with people who want to strengthen our nation based on biblical precepts, then certain conclusions are *inevitable*, for the scriptural evidence for justice in economics, politics, and law is overwhelming—not only clear and convincing, but beyond all reasonable doubt, as we lawyers say.

Others still may not like our ideas or us, but they won't so easily be conned into turning against us because of their assumptions about the Bible. Hateful people like Ann Coulter and Rush Limbaugh will keep finding other excuses to spew their venom. But we will strip away their mask of "Christianity" and expose the cruel greed and hypocrisy that drive their conversations.

The Bible has much to offer liberals to support their views. It is political malpractice for Democrats not to use the Bible to appeal to evangelical Christians in red states. That Bernie Sanders' rhetoric aligns with the Bible is not surprising. He is a Jewish man, whose consciousness was surely formed by the Old Testament. National Democrats need to marry a Bernie Sanders economic agenda with a "Nuns-on-the-Bus" religious conviction. It may seem counterintuitive for liberals, who often reject the Bible on other social issues, but Democrats must do more to prompt their politicians to think within a biblical framework if they want to improve America and find allies—and votes—in states that don't naturally go their way.

1

Matthew 25:
The Key to Progressive Policies

Having been reared as a born-again Christian, who as a child asked Jesus to come into her heart and forgive her sins, I naïvely thought that all Christians would give special weight to the words of Jesus. He is our way-shower, our model, God made flesh to dwell among us. So during the 2016 election, I posted on Facebook a gentle reminder—something that did not endorse any one particular candidate, but was drawn from Jesus' words:

> A man many Americans claim to follow laid down six criteria for being in His camp—and He gave no wiggle room: Did you feed the hungry? Clothe the naked? Give drink to the thirsty? (Half the world lacks potable water—including Flint, Michigan) Take care of the sick? The stranger? The prisoner? I'm perplexed that so many professed Christians oppose national health care and want to drive out eleven million "strangers" from our land. In the Bible, Israel was commanded repeatedly NOT to vex the stranger and NOT to drive them out of their land.

> All candidates are flawed. I'm voting for those who have a long history of advocating policies that promote Jesus' six criteria. Just letting you know my personal lodestar: Matthew 25:31- 46.

I heard back from fundamentalists, Catholics, and some of my progressive friends. The range of reactions I received struck me as surprising and comical.

Here's my homily. It forms the heart of this book and drives its purpose. All progressives who want universal health care and sensible welfare, immigration, and prison reform need to learn it by heart. It's the most important passage in the Bible that every leader ought to memorize, for it hits at the heart of the Democrats' historical platforms.

In Matthew 25, Jesus made entrance into His kingdom dependent *solely* on how we treat four classes of people. He didn't say we had to have the right theology. He didn't say we had to be pious and righteous. He didn't say we had to root out sinners from the world or live without committing any sins. He said we would be judged solely on how we treated four classes of people.

Now, you can interpret getting into Jesus' kingdom any way you like: going to heaven, aligning with Jesus' inner kingdom of the heart (since Jesus said the kingdom of heaven is within), or being in a higher circle of heaven than those "worldly Christians" who barely escape damnation. But the point is indisputable: If we want to be in Jesus' camp, if we want to be aligned truly with Him, we *must* serve the needs of four classes of people. Hence, if we want our nation to be "more Christian," then surely our nation must also do these things. And in case we didn't understand, He spelled it out for us. He gave us six criteria aimed at four groups of people. The poor received triple emphasis:

1 – CARE for the POOR
   FEED the hungry
   CLOTHE the naked
   GIVE drink to the thirsty

2 – CARE for the SICK

3 – CARE for the stranger

4 – CARE for the prisoner

This is one passage of Scripture that has virtually no ambiguity on what true followers of Jesus *must* do. It leaves little room for theologians to quibble about "how many angels can stand on the head of a pin"—that was a big debate in the Middle Ages, which represents those hairsplitting, meaningless theoretical issues that religious scholars vociferously argue.

Here's the entire passage so you can see that I'm not distorting the text.

> When the Son of man shall come in his glory, and all the holy angels with him, then shall he sit upon the throne of his glory: And before him shall be gathered all nations: and he shall separate them one from another, as a shepherd divideth his sheep from the goats: And he shall set the sheep on his right hand, but the goats on the left.
>
> Then shall the King say unto them on his right hand, Come, ye blessed of my Father, inherit the kingdom prepared for you from the foundation of the world: **For I was an hungred, and ye gave me meat: I was thirsty, and ye gave me drink: I was a stranger, and ye took me in: Naked, and ye clothed me: I was sick, and ye visited me: I was in prison, and ye came unto me.**
>
> Then shall the righteous answer him, saying, Lord, when saw we thee an hungred, and fed thee? or thirsty, and gave thee drink? When saw we thee a stranger, and took thee in? or naked, and clothed thee? Or when saw we thee sick, or in prison, and came unto thee?
>
> And the King shall answer and say unto them, Verily I say unto you, Inasmuch as ye have done it unto one of the least of these my brethren, ye have done it unto me.
>
> Then shall he say also unto them on the left hand, Depart from me, ye cursed, into everlasting fire, prepared for the devil and his angels: **For I was an hungred, and ye gave me no meat: I was thirsty, and ye gave me no drink: I was a stranger, and ye took me not in: naked, and ye clothed me not: sick, and in prison, and ye visited me not.**
>
> Then shall they also answer him, saying, Lord, when saw we thee an hungred, or athirst, or a stranger, or naked, or sick, or in prison, and did not minister unto thee? Then shall he answer them, saying, Verily I say unto you, **Inasmuch as ye did it not to one of the least of these, ye did it not to me. And these shall go away into everlasting punishment: but the righteous into life eternal** (Matthew 25: 31–46 KJV).

In this passage, Jesus explains how He will tell His true followers from the imposters. When He comes into His kingdom in His
glory, He will separate His true followers, His sheep, from those
who are *not* of his flock, whom he likened unto goats.

Jesus accepts the sheep into His kingdom because He was hungry, and they gave Him meat. He was thirsty, and they gave Him
drink. He was naked, and they clothed Him. He was a stranger, and
they took Him in. He was sick, and they cared for Him, and He
was in prison, and they provided for Him.

> And the people said, "Well when did we see You, Lord hungry,
> thirsty, a stranger, naked, sick, and in prison?" Jesus answered:
> "Inasmuch as ye have done it unto one of the LEAST of these my
> brethren, ye have done it unto me."

Conversely, who were the goats, those Jesus rejected? Those
who gave no food to the hungry, no drink to the thirsty, no clothing to the naked, and no care for the stranger, sick, or imprisoned.
And when His fake followers protested that they had never done
that to Jesus directly, He said, "Inasmuch as ye did it *not* to one of
the *least* of these, ye did it not to me."

Nothing in this passage requires people to have a certain profession of faith, to say the magic words, or to be "theologically correct." Rather, they just have to do these six things. That is the sole
test of their alignment with Jesus, their ticket to remain with Him.
This passage clarifies that actions count more than pious words—or
our fancy opinions and beliefs.

Jesus didn't make meeting these basic needs of people conditional on the merit of the recipient. In fact, he said, do it unto the
least of these. In the ancient text, the word *least* means the smallest
in size, in amount, in importance, in authority, in rank, excellence,
and estimation of people.[18] The word's meaning includes the concept not only of little ones (children who are small in physical stature), but also of the lowest levels of society: those who are the least
in importance, rank, power, and social esteem—those we call
worthless dirtbags. No wonder Christians who take Jesus seriously

become like Mother Theresa, working among the poor, the discards, and the untouchables.

One more thing. The term "visit the sick" or "visit the prisoner" does not mean to drive by, wave, and say howdy. In the Greek, the word *visit* means to see after them in order to care for them, to provide for them. So we don't get to be righteous merely by making a social call and wishing others well or merely praying for them. Both the KJV and the NIV use the word *visit*, and the New Revised Standard Version (NRSV), which is also used by conservative Christians, uses the term *care for*. Regardless of our translation, *Strong's Concordance* defines the meaning from the ancient Greek.

In other passages, Jesus repeated the same assertion that not everyone who pays lip service to being His follower will enter His Kingdom.

> **Watch out for false prophets. They come to you in sheep's clothing, but inwardly they are ferocious wolves.** By their fruit you will recognize them. ... Every tree that does not bear good fruit is cut down and thrown into the fire. Thus, by their fruit you will recognize them. **Not everyone who says to me, "Lord, Lord," will enter the kingdom of heaven, but only the one who does the will of my Father who is in heaven.** (Matthew 7:15-16, 19-21)

No doubt, both sides will claim that the politicians from the opposing side are the false prophets and wolves. Yet lip service and name-calling do not rule the day. Only actions reveal which leaders are following Jesus' commandments. Those who do not do the things Jesus commanded are false prophets. In Matthew 25, Jesus left no doubt as to what constituted the "will of His Father": serving the poor, the sick, the stranger, and the prisoner. This book demonstrates that the Bible provides a strong foundation for government programs to serve the rejected, needy, and lowly.

For too long, Democrats have withdrawn from the religious sphere, for fear of being attacked over social issues, such as abortion and gay marriage. But even if Democrats don't think they can win direct votes of white evangelicals, they need to urge evangelicals to find common ground for compassionate economic causes. Democrats can use the Bible to bring moderates and conservatives together to do something about health care, poverty, immigration, and prison reform. By using Bible verses and stories, we are not trying to proselytize for a religion. We are merely acknowledging our common Judeo-Christian background and building a bridge to evangelical Christians.

Of course, reminding others of Jesus' words does not guarantee immediate conversion. In my Facebook venture into promoting Matthew 25, I got only two "likes" from my many fundamentalist Bible-believing friends, some ruffled feathers, defensive arguments, which I discuss in the next chapter, and evasive comments like "We are just supposed to show the love of Jesus to everybody." The vast majority of support for the proposition came from my progressive friends who are Catholic or non-church going. One Bible-believer did say, "You made a few good points, but...." I realize that when we are commenting quickly, we don't always say what we mean, but this remark hit me as hilarious. Think about it. The words of our Savior, the one we say is "the Way, the Truth, and the Life," the one we pray to and seek to emulate, merely provide a few good points—among the wide range of all other good thinking that might inform our voting. To me, if I am a Christian, the words of Jesus should be treated as controlling authority—not merely a nice opinion among many others.

2

Debunking the Myth
That the Bible Only Endorses
Small Government

In 2009 I was discussing Matthew 25 and Jesus' command to serve four classes of downtrodden people (the poor, the sick, the immigrant, and the prisoner) with a right-wing Christian friend. The first words out of her mouth were, "Well, Jesus wasn't speaking about governments. He was speaking to us personally. We should do these things through private charity and the church, not through the government."

I looked at my friend slack-jawed in disbelief. Soon as she said it, I think she felt how silly her argument was, but her pride wouldn't let her back down. I reminded her that she participated in anti-abortion activities so that our nation would be more "Christian," and that is fair, so why wouldn't she support a national health care initiative, which would cause our national policy to reflect Jesus' command? She didn't budge. She hates our government doing most anything, except the military. She herself has lived most of her adult life with a military pension and free health care, at the taxpayers' expense, but she doesn't want the government funding other people's health care. I totally honor our military, endorse all the support our service people get, and want them to have even more, but I can't compute why poor people should be denied basic food and health care in a country as rich as ours. On C-Span I have

51

heard conservative groups echo my friend's argument. In fact, they encourage their members to do more private charity in order to fend off the need for government programs. And I got this same response from a fundamentalist Christian to my Facebook posting about Matthew 25.

This is the biggest contradiction I see among today's evangelical Christians. They want national policy to condemn and forbid individual moral "sins" (so they want to legislate against abortion, gay marriage, and even access to birth control), but they recoil from any sort of national policy that promotes the health or well-being of the nation. To them, it is an anathema, and they refuse to acknowledge the contradiction in their thinking: "I will force you to bring a child into this world, but I won't give you a dime to support it once it's here." That offends any rationale for being "pro-life." The Bible is full of commandments for people to help the poor and the sick, and in the Old Testament, as we shall soon see, it was the national law. And nothing in Jesus' words prohibited people from collectively doing what He asked.

Maybe the difference is that a prohibition doesn't appear to cost money. I'm not increasing the budget if I forbid something (though there is a huge cost if you put enforcement teeth into your prohibitions). Prescriptions (the affirmative duty to act), however, cost money, time, and effort. Prohibitions seem cheap, as we can sit back in our armchairs and forbid others from doing what we don't like. It's ironic that between liberals and conservatives our "personal freedom" arguments flip-flop on these issues. Progressives want to keep the government out of women's wombs and everyone's underwear, while conservatives want to keep the government out of our pocketbooks. Well, as we lawyers often say, the pocketbook is the most sensitive part of the human anatomy.

Conservative Christians further ignore the contradictions in their logic. Even if Jesus' words do not mandate health care as modern law, surely such policies are still consistent with Jesus' commands. The mere act of a secular government's performing a Christlike service does not make that service inherently evil or immoral.

Where in the Bible does it say that governments are bad when they follow biblical values? Would we want a government that always did the opposite of Jesus' moral imperatives? If the Bible encourages certain good conduct (like not stealing, not murdering, or caring for the sick, poor, and oppressed), what rationale prohibits any government from adopting such good conduct in its laws and programs? What could be wrong with that, so long as we have followed our constitutional and legislative processes fairly to enact such laws?

We are a government of the people, by the people, and for the people. Our government is not some foreign occupying power. It is we—our elected officials who enact laws and programs that employ our fellow citizens for the common good. Unlike the people of the Bible, we have a resource to use to help achieve the commands of Jesus—our democratically elected government. Among the six purposes stated in the preamble to our Constitution, we read, "We the People of the United States, in Order to ... promote the general Welfare, ... do ordain and establish this Constitution for the United States of America." One purpose of our Constitution is promoting our general welfare. So why shouldn't we use our voting power (this resource in our hands) to demand that our political leaders create an economic system that reflects the compassion of biblical principles? But such arguments land on deaf ears. Why? Because revering the Bible is a charade, which makes Christians feel good to mouth. The real god running the show is Mammon.

Had I done more research at the time of my discussion with my right-wing friend, I would have been able to pinpoint numerous examples from the Bible that proved that these issues were government mandates. The Law of Moses started it all, and Jesus, being a Jew and a rabbi, was speaking in the context of upholding the principles of His legal heritage.

Many scriptures establish that we have a moral duty to require our government to act on behalf of the poor and oppressed. From Moses to King David, King Solomon, Isaiah, Ezekiel, Amos, Zechariah, and Malachi—again and again, God told the rulers, the princes, and the "shepherds of the nation" to do right by the poor—and even the stranger, those pesky "illegal aliens" we love to hate. These were not supply-side tax incentives or matters of personal conscience. They sprang from the laws established by Moses, their very constitution, if you will. Democrats have not done enough to call out Republican hypocrisy on this point. And the Bible supports government intervention for infrastructure programs when the well-being of the nation is at stake (but that's the topic of another book).

The statutes and commandments, the legal authority of the Hebrews, specifically required everyone to make provisions for the poor and the immigrant. Their laws impinged on private property and commerce to make sure that poor people and immigrants could get food. We will review later in detail these passages from four books of the Torah—Exodus, Leviticus, Numbers, and Deuteronomy—and from the prophets, who decried their nation's apostasy from those commandments laid down when their country was first formed. But for now, let's review a few that specifically address government.

Ezekiel spoke directly to this point, arguing that the leaders, the rulers of Israel and other nations, had a duty to care for the sick and the poor, and he castigated them harshly for disobeying the Law of Moses. Ezekiel lived and prophesied around 600 BC. Having grown up in Jerusalem and having served as a priest in the temple, Ezekiel witnessed the deterioration of his own country's leadership, and then he was taken into captivity along with Judah's King Jehoiachin by the Babylonians under King Nebuchadnezzar II. Hence, he lived under two different governments.

Early on, Ezekiel declares how far Israel as a nation had fallen from God's legal standards, and he indicts Israel for her transgressions. He foretells Israel's doom, for she has turned God's just laws into wickedness, more so than the other nations around her.

> This is what the Sovereign Lord says: This is Jerusalem, which I have set in the center of the nations, with countries all around her. **Yet in her wickedness she has rebelled against my laws and decrees more than the nations and countries around her. She has rejected my laws and has not followed my decrees.**

Therefore this is what the Sovereign Lord says: You have been more unruly than the nations around you and have not followed my decrees or kept my laws. You have not even conformed to the standards of the nations around you.

Therefore this is what the Sovereign Lord says: **I myself am against you,** Jerusalem, and I will inflict punishment on you in the sight of the nations. (Ezekiel 5:5–8)

One may assume that Ezekiel's wailings are only about idol worship and have nothing to do with government action, but by chapter 22, he details which laws the nation's leaders have broken: those regarding the poor and the stranger (the foreigner dwelling among them, i.e., the immigrant). And he explains that their wickedness comes about because of greed.

See how **each of the princes of Israel** who are in you uses his power to shed blood. In you they have treated father and mother with contempt; in you they **have oppressed the foreigner and mistreated the fatherless and the widow.** You have despised my holy things and desecrated my Sabbaths.... **In you are people who accept bribes to shed blood; you take interest and make a profit from the poor.** You extort unjust gain from your neighbors. And you have forgotten me, declares the Sovereign Lord.

I will surely strike my hands together at the unjust gain you have made and at the blood you have shed in your midst. (Ezekiel 22: 6–8, 12–13)

Her officials within her are like wolves tearing their prey; they shed blood and kill people to make unjust gain.... The people of the land practice extortion and commit robbery; **they oppress the poor and needy and mistreat the foreigner, denying them justice.** (Ezekiel 22:27, 29)

Ezekiel proves that God's Word was addressing national policy and government behavior. There's no doubt that he is speaking to the rulers, the governors of the entire nation, since he repeatedly used the phrase "princes of Israel." Ezekiel did not advocate giving the rich a tax break and letting it trickle down. He blasted them for oppressing the poor and the stranger, which violated Hebraic law.

By chapter 34 Ezekiel's words read like articles of impeachment against the nation's leaders, as this prophet rehearses their oppression and wickedness.

> The word of the Lord came to me: "Son of man, **prophesy against the shepherds of Israel**; prophesy and say to them: 'This is what the Sovereign Lord says: Woe to you shepherds of Israel who only take care of yourselves! Should not shepherds take care of the flock? You eat the curds, clothe yourselves with the wool and slaughter the choice animals, but you do not take care of the flock. **You have not strengthened the weak or healed the sick or bound up the injured.** You have not brought back the strays or searched for the lost. **You have ruled them harshly and brutally.**'" (Ezekiel 34:1-4)

By now, Ezekiel has shown the rulers' wickedness against three of the four classes of people that Jesus commanded us to help: the poor, the foreigner, and the sick. Note the phrase "shepherds of Israel." In no way can this be construed as the people who were actually herding sheep in the fields. The shepherds of Israel were the leaders—those men in positions of power, those who controlled the policies and practices of the nation.

The vast majority of commentators agree that Ezekiel is referring to political leaders as well as to religious and business leaders—anyone in a position of rule and authority over others. So who would be the princes of America, or our national shepherds? Our political rulers establish and enforce our laws as well as provide for the common good, while our religious leaders guide the moral and spiritual lives of their parishioners, and our CEOs and corporate directors control the livelihoods of their employees. If such leaders had moral and legal imperatives in biblical times, then surely they do so now—if you believe that the Bible should influence all aspects of our lives, and therefore must play a strong role in guiding Christian efforts to guide national policy.

Later in this same chapter, Ezekiel repeats his indictments of leaders and promises God's punishment for acting like stronger cattle that butt with their horns, shoulders, and backsides to drive out the weak and sickly.

Because you shove with flank and shoulder, butting all the weak sheep with your horns until you have driven them away. (Ezekiel 34:21)

This prophecy still stands as a moral indictment of the misapplication of Darwinian evolution to social policy, a now popular libertarian doctrine that says it's every man for himself, only the strong should survive, and the weak and inferior need to die off. That's natural selection. It's really an age-old debate: am I my brother's keeper? I can understand atheistic thinkers, like Ayn Rand, when they oppose taking care of the poor and weak, whom they deem inferior and lazy. But how they enticed the Christian Right into believing such Darwinian rubbish stands as the greatest con of all.

Although Ezekiel was perhaps the most vocal in railing against the politicians of his day, he was not the only Bible writer to do so. Psalm 72 is classified as a "royal psalm." Recited by the priests and the people, royal psalms were praises to God and His anointed king, and they enshrined the duty of the king.[19] Psalm 72 clearly establishes that the king's top priority is to do right by the poor and those in need. Again, this was not a plan for King David to give tax cuts or incentives to the rich of the land to let their riches trickle down to the common folk. The king had an affirmative duty to act on behalf of the least of his people.

> **Give the king thy judgments**, O God, and thy righteousness unto the king's son. He shall judge thy people with righteousness, and thy poor with judgment. The mountains shall bring peace to the people, and the little hills, by righteousness. **He shall judge the poor of the people, he shall save the children of the needy, and shall break in pieces the oppressor.** (Psalm 72:1–4 KJV)

The Hebrew word for *judge* doesn't mean simply to pass judgment on poor people—as in assigning fault, blame, and punishment. Rather, it means to defend, litigate, or advocate on their behalf. That's likely why the NIV frequently translates the expression as "to give justice to." Keep in mind that they didn't have hired lawyers back then, and the people came directly before the leader or king to plead their cause, so administering the law in a just manner was critical to good government.

But even without debating the meaning of the Hebrew word translated *judge*, the king (the government) had an affirmative duty to save poor children and to break the "oppressor." It doesn't take a tree-hugging New Age theologian to see the implications of this principle for our modern system. If large financial institutions are oppressing the public, God says break them into pieces! The Bible makes numerous other references to the oppression of the poor by the rich.

As a roaring lion, and a ranging bear; so is a **wicked ruler over the poor people.** (Proverbs 28:15 KJV)

As a hungry lion looks for prey, so a wicked ruler seeks to devour the poor, seeking only to satiate his hungry greed. This chapter goes on to attack the moral failings of cowardly men who seek power, but the message is clear. Wise and just rulers help the poor in society; they don't attack or vex them.

Whoever oppresses the poor shows contempt for their Maker, but whoever is kind to the needy honors God. (Proverbs 14:31)

If the people are suffering and dying, the king is not doing his job, and he is *not* following God's law. If our president and our members of Congress, whom we elect, stand by and let millions of our brothers and sisters get sick and die, because our broken health care system refuses to treat their preexisting conditions, then God is not pleased. The promise of the Bible is that God will destroy the nation that allows this to happen—and maybe that's because such a nation sets in motion a chain of events that cause it to implode.

It keeps getting better (or worse, depending on your point of view). Even more poignant are the words of King Lemuel, which outline the duties of a king (the ruler). He acknowledges that these are kingly duties that his mother taught him (Proverbs 31:1). So often do our mothers pass down principles of empathy, fairness, and compassion!

Speak up for those who cannot speak for themselves, for the rights of all who are destitute. Speak up and judge fairly; **defend the rights of the poor and needy.** (Proverbs 31:8–9)

These are the duties of the ruler: to speak up for those who have no voice and for those who are disadvantaged—whether physically, economically, educationally, socially, or legally.

The Prophet Isaiah lived around 700 BC. A forerunner to Ezekiel, he also condemned the governors of his day for doing wrong by the people of Israel. The early chapters of the book of Isaiah enumerated the transgressions of the nation and attacked those in power over their greed, corruption, and failure to defend the poor.

> Your silver has become dross, your choice wine is diluted with water. **Your rulers are rebels, partners with thieves; they all love bribes and chase after gifts. They do not defend the cause of the fatherless; the widow's case does not come before them.** Therefore the Lord, the Lord Almighty, the Mighty One of Israel, declares: "Ah! I will vent my wrath on my foes and avenge myself on my enemies. I will turn my hand against you...." (Isaiah 1:22–25)

Wow! Sounds like God likes campaign finance reform. Would He condemn the *Citizens United* Supreme Court decision that has allowed unlimited corporate donations to flow into our political campaigns? But we'll leave that for another day. The point is that Isaiah didn't just censure individuals. He condemned the "rulers" of Israel, the politicians. He said they were rebels and partners with thieves. Given that they were rich, it's highly unlikely that they were hanging around with literal thieves, who burgled homes at night. It's obvious that those who sought to ingratiate themselves with the rulers of his day were thieves in the sense that they engaged in unethical business practices and exploited the poor to amass wealth.[20]

Ezekiel and Isaiah could be preaching to the 115th Congress. Although America has no royal lineage by bloodlines, it certainly has rulers. The "princes" of the United States include our governors, senators and members of Congress. Congress has an approval rating lower than 20%, in part because it seems to do little beyond squabbling. Congressional Republicans obstructed Obama at every step, even when he promoted his opponents' ideas, so one could view them as "rebels"—not to mention the rudeness one Republican displayed during Obama's address to a joint session of Congress, as he yelled out, "You lie." This was a disrespectful gesture unprecedented in modern American history. And despite passing little legislation of substance, they raise money from rich and powerful interests—potentially the thieves Isaiah was referring to—all the while campaigning for their own reelections. This is fairly true of both Democrats and Republicans.

And if you still have doubts that the prophets are addressing governments, consider this passage:

> **Woe to those who make unjust laws, to those who issue oppressive decrees, to deprive the poor of their rights** and withhold justice from the oppressed of my people, making widows their prey and robbing the fatherless. (Isaiah 10:1–2)

Who can make unjust laws and unrighteous decrees? Only rulers who have the power of government, as well as CEOs and corporate directors who have the power to make decrees for their companies that oppress poor laborers and make contracts with foreign entities to buy goods made from near slave labor. This is a warning our Congress should take to heart. It's wicked to write laws that harm the poor and oppressed. Yet Republicans hated the formation of the Consumer Financial Protections Bureau, the only government watchdog that has authority to expose how poor and average citizens are being oppressed and defrauded by financial services companies—which it recently did by stopping the abusive practices of Wells Fargo.[21] As a progressive, I see Republican intransigence around raising the minimum wage as equally oppressive. Blocking good legislation is just as evil as passing bad legislation. It's not consistent with biblical teachings.

Now, you can see how the Bible is beginning to sound like a Bernie Sanders manifesto—particularly on Wall Street reform. The Bible leaves no ambiguity. Rulers who oppose helping those in need are violating God's laws.

The Lord takes his place in court; he rises to judge the people. The Lord enters into **judgment against the elders and leaders of his people**: "It is you who have ruined my vineyard; **the plunder from the poor is in your houses**. What do you mean by **crushing my people and grinding the faces of the poor?**" declares the Lord, the Lord Almighty. (Isaiah 3:13–15)

Isaiah not only condemned the rulers of Israel explicitly, but he also made a wider allegation toward the wealthy—the "job creators" that Republicans seek to protect. If rich business owners were beating the people to pieces and grinding the faces of the poor, God was not happy, and God certainly wasn't going to give them a tax cut. Advocating for the rights of the poor and the workers in our politics is far from heretical thinking for followers of the Bible. It is a central tenet, so government action to do good and help the dispossessed is also biblically justified.

In a position of influence, the prophet Daniel urged Nebuchadnezzar, king of Babylon, to use his political power directly to help the poor.

Wherefore, O king, let my counsel be acceptable unto thee, and **break off thy sins by righteousness, and thine iniquities by shewing mercy to the poor;** if it may be a lengthening of thy tranquility. (Daniel 4:27 KJV)

The way for this earthly ruler to obey God's will and make amends for past transgressions was to show mercy to the poor. It's true that showing "mercy to the poor" can come in many forms. Regardless, the king had a duty to act, which by its very nature is government intervention. And, as this book continues to show, the Bible clarifies that mercy to the poor was demonstrated by affirmative national laws that included direct taxation of the more wealthy in order to provide for "the least of these." Because most people of faith accept the Bible as a source for moral guidance, we forget that in ancient times it represented national law for the Jews. The Torah (the first five books of the Bible) was, and still is, viewed as divinely dictated to Moses, who wrote it down as a source of law for Israel to follow.

Old Testament Taxation on Wealthy Property Owners

Most are familiar with the concept of the traditional tithe of 10%, but fewer are aware of the many details surrounding tithes that change our understanding of their giving requirements. Hebraic law required social welfare for the poor, and it impinged on private property rights to do it. Here's a fact you don't hear much from evangelical Republicans: In the Bible, only those who owned land and farm animals were required to tithe, so it really was a flat tax—on property owners. Only property owners tithed on their crops and on their herds and flocks (every tenth animal was given in tithe).

> **A tithe of everything from the land,** whether grain from the soil or fruit from the trees, **belongs to the Lord**; it is holy to the Lord. Whoever would redeem any of their tithe must add a fifth of the value to it. Every tithe of the herd and flock—**every tenth animal** that passes under the shepherd's rod—**will be holy to the Lord.** (Leviticus 27:30–32)

Common laborers who did not own land did not pay tithes. You had to be a more affluent property owner before you owed a tithe. Hired laborers, those who eked out their day-to-day subsistence, were not required to tithe, only those who owned land, herds, and flocks.

Leona Helmsley famously said, "Only the little people pay taxes." She went to jail shortly thereafter. But according to God's law, it's the opposite: only the rich pay taxes. So how do we square this principle with Mitt Romney's disdain of the 47% low-income people in this country (the so-called "takers") who don't pay federal income taxes? If you want to "believe the Bible literally," then we have to look literally at the full amount of taxation paid (potentially up to 40 or 50% as we shall soon see) and consider that these taxes were levied solely on owners of land and livestock. This would make for some uncomfortable talking points for our politicians, including many Democrats.

I'm not saying that the Hebrew laborers never paid any tithes or taxes in biblical times. They all gave additional offerings, and some mandatory rituals had options for the poor to provide alternative, inexpensive offerings. And when the Jews were conquered, they had to pay their taxes to the conquering authority, such as Rome ("render unto Caesar what is Caesar's"). But these are facts that progressive Democrats need to know when debating Republicans on the size of government and taxation, and this should inform our politics if we want to put the Bible at the center of our policy making. In fairness, some Republicans, including Marco Rubio, have at times supported the earned income tax credit and other tax credits to help ease tax burdens on the working poor, but we need to ensure that such programs don't "rob Peter to pay Paul" by gutting Obamacare and other vital social programs. The Bible gave tax relief to workers and levied the higher burden on the wealthy, yet few Democrats make this argument in public. But hold on. It's about to get really intense as the Bible pushes all our hot buttons.

The Torah Required Landowners to Leave Parts of Their Harvest in the Fields for the Immigrants and the Poor to Collect

> And when ye reap the harvest of your land, **thou shalt not wholly reap the corners of thy field, neither shalt thou gather the gleanings of thy harvest**. And thou shalt not glean thy vineyard, neither shalt thou gather every grape of thy vineyard; **thou shalt leave them for the poor and stranger**: I am the Lord your God. (Leviticus 19:9–10 KJV)

So in Old Testament times, if your land were a perfect square, you'd be allowed only to harvest the portion inside the circle. The corners were left for the poor and the immigrants. Since I was an English major, I asked my grandson who is in engineering school to figure the math (πr^2 and all that). He says that if a circle lines up with the sides of a square, as in the diagram below, the corners comprise 21.5% of the square. Of course, landowners back then may have played games to cut back on the size of a "corner," but regardless, as you can see, it was a sizeable chunk of land.

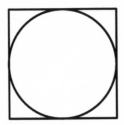

Thousands of years ago, the economy and welfare of the nation revolved around farming. Those who owned the land could control it, and landowners had few restraints on their authority. Survival required that harvested crops be stored for later use for times of drought, winter, or famine. So when God created a law whereby native Israelites were forbidden from harvesting the crops in the corners of their fields but were required to leave them for the poor and the stranger (the foreigner) to gather, that likely infuriated many. God required you to "dip into your own pocket" to pay for a moral mandate—exactly the opposite of what many Republicans would have you believe.

The Jews were also forbidden from fully harvesting all their crops. Those of us who garden know that when you go through and reap your harvest the first time, you easily overlook many fruits, and some ripen later after the main group. Biblical law forbade landowners from going back the second and third time to pick their harvests clean. That's what *gleanings* means. This second and third harvesting was left for the poor and the stranger (the foreign immigrant). So they didn't just get the corners; they also got access to your main field after you had reaped your first harvest. This law was another government imposition on private property rights. In case people missed it the first time around, the Bible repeats the commandment.

> When you reap the harvest of your land, **do not** reap to the very edges of your field or **gather the gleanings of your harvest. Leave them for the poor and for the foreigner residing among you.** I am the Lord your God. (Leviticus 23:22)

What an outrage to the job creators of the day! Those lazy poor people and invasive foreigners did not help you plant your seeds and nurture your crops. They didn't own the land. They were taking a free ride on your capital. But still, you had to leave parts of your crops on your land for them, "thus saith the Lord."

Imagine what Republicans would say today if Obama had proposed something similar: what if we had to set aside a certain percentage of US crops (or income) to feed the hungry and help immigrants? Would Republicans congratulate him for following God's law, or would they castigate him for cuddling up to "ISIS sympathizers"?

In ancient times, there were no banks or paper currency. A few places in the world used gold and silver, but during these times, people mostly bartered crops for other goods. So if you were forbidden from harvesting all of your crops, then you lost the ability to trade those crops for other items. In essence, the Lord was requiring the Israelites to pay taxes to the poor and to immigrants.

Whew... That's heavy, but it's the truth, if you view the Bible as God's inspired Holy Word. The same law is recorded in Deuteronomy 24:19–21.

> When you are harvesting in your field and you overlook a sheaf, do not go back to get it. **Leave it for the foreigner, the fatherless and the widow**, so that the Lord your God may bless you in all the work of your hands. When you beat the olives from your trees, do not go over the branches a second time. **Leave what remains for the foreigner, the fatherless and the widow.** When you harvest the grapes in your vineyard, do not go over the vines again. **Leave what remains for the foreigner, the fatherless and the widow.**

This is incontrovertible evidence that God dictated national laws that required God's chosen people to leave part of their earned wealth, their resources, for the stranger (the foreign immigrant, the "illegal alien") and the poor. As a gardener, I can see how this gleaning prohibition would cause them to lose at least 20% of their crops, likely more. And this was in addition to the 10% tithing that they did to the priests and the third year tithe, which we shall review shortly. So the notion that the government should never be allowed to take more than 10% of your earnings is not in the Bible at all. You can advocate that as a policy in alignment with the philosophy of Ayn Rand, but not in the name of Jesus.

I would also be remiss if I didn't point out that obviously the strangers and poor had to work to get the bounty from the lands of Israel. God didn't command the Jews to harvest the crops and give them directly to the immigrants; the immigrants had to get out and harvest it themselves. That's fair. Democrats should be willing to bring accountability and personal responsibility to the government programs they propose. New programs must be fair to those who receive them and fair to those who pay for them.

Democrats should embrace amendments to social services to ensure that able-bodied recipients are out there working and contributing. But in today's political climate, I don't see that Republicans are trying to tweak government programs to ensure that recipients are working appropriately. The rhetoric coming from Trump and the "alt right" is nasty and racist, demonizing immigrants. That is the opposite of God's teachings. Period.

Here was a legal provision for social welfare so that everyone, whether he owned fields or not, could harvest food, not go hungry, and store up some grain. Some Christians might argue that Jesus reformed this law, making it unnecessary, but everything Jesus commanded in the New Testament required more effort and sacrifice than the original Hebrew Bible, not less. Jesus never said, "Forget the law on giving to the poor; we need supply-side economics for the 'harvest creators' in society. We don't want to kill the incentives of farmers to work the land or give the poor an incentive to stay poor." Whether you were a job creator or an undocumented stranger, God's law made provision for you.

I accept that in today's global environment, it would be impossible to apply these laws literally. A farmer in Indiana who left the corners of his fields unharvested would not help a poor hungry person in Idaho; crops would rot before anyone could gather them.

But the broader point is worthy of consideration: there were legal provisions for the immigrant and the poor enshrined in national law. These were taxation and government top-down mandates—things that Republicans rail against when Democrats propose anything similar.

Property Owners Were also Commanded to Tithe Not Only to the Priests (i.e., the Church), but also to the Immigrant and the Poor Every Third Year

The word *tithe* means a tenth. Yes, the Israelites had a second national law that provided for social welfare for the poor and the stranger. It was a special tax, if you please, every three years, and that doesn't include the costs paid to the king, his princes, and his armies.

> At the end of every three years, bring all the tithes of that year's produce and store it in your towns, so that the Levites (who have no allotment or inheritance of their own) and the foreigners, the fatherless and the widows who live in your towns may come and eat and be satisfied, and so that the Lord your God may bless you in all the work of your hands. (Deuteronomy 14:28-29)

> [Then you shall declare before the Lord] "So the Lord brought us out of Egypt with a mighty hand and an outstretched arm, with great terror and with signs and wonders. He brought us to this place and gave us this land, a land flowing with milk and honey; and now I bring the firstfruits of the soil that you, Lord, have given me." Place the basket before the Lord your God and bow down before him. Then you and the Levites and the foreigners residing among you shall rejoice in all the good things the Lord your God has given to you and your household. **When you have finished setting aside a tenth of all your produce in the third year, the year of the tithe, you shall give it to the Levite, the foreigner, the fatherless and the widow, so that they may eat in your towns and be satisfied.** Then say to the Lord your God: "I have removed from my house the sacred portion **and have given it to the Levite, the foreigner, the fatherless and the widow, according to all you commanded.** I have not turned aside from your commands nor have I forgotten any of them. (Deuteronomy 26:8-13)

Again, I've quoted the KJV and the NIV, so you can see that I'm not playing games with different versions. The stranger was the foreign immigrant. This tithe to the poor and immigrants was an *additional tithe* above and beyond the 10%, which is the commonly known "tithe" that went to Hebrew priests (ordained ministers) and the other Levites (the church workers). This additional tithe was to be shared among the Levites, foreign immigrants, and the poor. It was not a subtraction from the Levites, who depended on their annual 10% for survival. Otherwise, the tithe to the foreigner and the poor would have been paid only by the Levites from their meager share.

This third year tithe was collected and stored in towns and distributed by the Levites, the "government officials" in the Hebrew theocracy. Hence, there was a centralized collection system for distributing resources to the needy.[22] Obviously, since this tithe was stored in central collection points, the poor and the foreigner did not directly have to pick or glean it. The harvested produce was shared with them. This was welfare they did not work for.

Also, few people realize that Hebraic law also included a biennial "festival" tithe (another 10% of the remaining 90%) that was paid once every two years. This was in fact to make provision for a celebration for the nation of Israel. And everyone enjoyed the festival—the donors, the poor, the immigrants, and the priests.

Few Christians realize that Hebraic law had three different tithes: the annual tithe, the biennial festival tithe, and the triennial poverty tithe. See Leviticus 27:30–33, Numbers 18:20–21; Deuteronomy 12:17–18; Deuteronomy 14:28–29. The total tithe burden was not 10 percent, but more like 22–23% when you average them out.[23]

This is likely surprising to most church-going people who've always heard their tithe is 10%. The online Jewish Encyclopedia states as follows:

> According to the Rabbis, the Books of Numbers and Deuteronomy are complementary to each other...; consequently there can

be no contradiction between them. Thus there were three kinds of tithes: (1) that given to the Levites as stated in Num. xviii. 21 *et seq.*, and termed "the first tithe" ("ma'aser rishon"); (2) the tithe which was to be taken to Jerusalem and there consumed by the landowner and his family, and which was termed "the second tithe" ("ma'aser sheni"), it being taken from what remained after the first tithe had been appropriated; and (3) that given to the poor ("ma'aser 'ani"). Therefore two tithes were to be taken every year except in the seventh year: Nos. 1 and 2 in the first, second, fourth, and fifth years; Nos. 1 and 3 in the third and sixth years.[24]

This calls into question Ben Carson's proposition of a 10% flat tax because, as he said, "it was the biblical way." Carson's sloppy Bible scholarship affirms my mom's saying, "Christians just don't know their Bibles." If we're being biblical, we would propose at least a 22% flat tax, and once we add in the 20% lost from the corners of the field and the gleanings, the effective tax rate may be even higher, potentially in the range of 45 percent.

God's law made provision for the poorest in society and the immigrants, so they, too, could be "filled." If God's law mandated tithing to the "least of these," how much more would Jesus Christ ask from His people, particularly those in the United States, which is the richest and most powerful nation on earth? In America, we take for granted how abundant our nation is, because many of us have never lived in countries that lack natural resources or rich farmland. As a nation, we've forgotten that our forefathers were once foreigners here. They were oppressed in Europe and moved to find a new life in America—with no invite from the Native Americans. So how can Christians of good conscience endorse hateful and divisive rhetoric against immigrants, when God's law made taxation provisions for them?

In our current political debates on welfare and the size of government, Republicans are correct to warn us to "live within our means" and be wise stewards of the taxpayers' money. But often, they say that the government can't afford social programs, because they require unjust levels of taxation. When we sum up the Hebrew tax burden on property owners, however, our tax rates seem fairly small:

10% annually for the Levites (who ran their government in a theocracy)

10% every third year as the poverty tithe

20% (approximately left in the corners of the fields)

10–20% left in the fields for the gleanings and walk-on pickings

Some years, this could add up to 50%, and these are just approximations. I leave it to rabbinical authorities to sort out the precise math, since the corners and gleanings could be fluctuating numbers, and I haven't processed the festival tithe that occurred every other year, partly because the tither himself got to enjoy the benefits of this tithe.

Regardless, the plain wording of the Scripture fairly well nixes Carson's idea of a 10% flat federal income tax as the biblical way.[25] If we're being biblical, we would propose at least a 30% flat tax, in order to be in integrity with the "corners and gleanings of the field" and the third-year poverty tithes. I'm not advocating a flat tax of 30% as ideal or God's law. I'm just saying that Democrats need to know these scriptures if they want to convince evangelicals that paying a bit more in taxes to provide for social programs is consistent with the Bible, nor should Christians fall for the 10% flat tax as the Bible's way.

So there you have it, progressives—proof positive that God's commandments gave the rulers of God's nation an affirmative duty to care for the sick, the poor, and the immigrant. This book repeatedly shows how the Bible—from the Torah, to Psalms, Proverbs, Ezekiel, Jeremiah, Isaiah, Zechariah, and Malachi, on to Matthew, Acts, Hebrews, James, and even into Revelation—endorses government action and collective efforts for many progressive causes.

Some may argue that the Old Testament prophets were speaking only about the future, foretelling a time when God will come back to set the world aright and judge everyone. Consequently, they may argue, there is no need to worry about programs for the poor in the present day, for God will fix everything in the hereafter. But that does not fly. The prophets called the rulers to act now, to change their conduct on earth immediately. They did pine for a perfect age and proclaimed a vision of redemption when these inequities would cease. Yet their vision of the future did not negate the clear mandate to do right in the here and now. The prophets' words gave practical instructions for leaders. And God's law given to Moses mandated taxation, restrictions on private property, and redistribution to the poor.

If we seek to follow God's commandments and inject Judeo-Christian principles into our politics, we must consider how numerous Old Testament prophets judged the rulers of their day and apply those principles rationally to modern politics. Democrats have been hesitant to do this, and they've lost the opportunity to find common ground with a large section of the Republican base.

Government Duties under the New Testament

Sometimes Christians negate or ignore parts of the Old Testament that they don't like. True, we all do that, given that there are draconian laws that modern people can't and shouldn't follow. Consider, for example, prohibitions against eating shellfish, wearing garments made from two different materials, or stoning people for committing adultery or blaspheming our deity. But the themes of helping the poor, welcoming the immigrant, campaigning against oppressive rulers, recur often and are as relevant to today as to the ancient world—even more so because we have more resources to share.

The Old Testament prophets are fierier in condemning their rulers than the New Testament saints were. But the New Testament writers recognized the Old Testament as part of their controlling authority. Remember: **"All scripture is** given by inspiration of God, and **is profitable ... for instruction in righteousness..."** (2 Timothy 3:16-17 KJV). No evangelical can deny that the Old Testament contains wisdom for everyone in authority—senators, governors, and members of Congress, as well as business leaders who rule specific companies and pastors who have authority to set moral standards in the minds of their parishioners.

As a studied rabbi, whose knowledge of Judaic law and scriptures astounded everyone, Jesus would have known all the passages quoted above, for He spoke in the context of the Old Testament law and prophets. Early on in His ministry, He went to Nazareth, stood up in the synagogue, and read aloud nearly verbatim the famous passage from Isaiah 61:1-2:

> He went to Nazareth, where he had been brought up, and on the Sabbath day he went into the synagogue, as was his custom. He stood up to read, and the scroll of the prophet Isaiah was handed to him. Unrolling it, he found the place where it is written: "The Spirit of the Lord is on me, because **he has anointed me to proclaim good news to the poor. He has sent me to proclaim freedom for the prisoners and recovery of sight for the blind, to set the oppressed free,** to proclaim the year of the Lord's favor." (Luke 4:16-19)

Jesus then shocked His audience by proclaiming, "This day is this scripture fulfilled in your ears" (verse 21 KJV). In fact, many of Jesus' sayings were quoted not only from the Torah (Genesis, Exodus, Numbers, Leviticus, and Deuteronomy), but also from Psalms and from the prophets Isaiah, Jeremiah, Hosea, Micah, Zechariah, Daniel and Malachi.[26]

Some right-wingers may yet cling to the now demolished argument that since Jesus' first coming was a "reform" of the law, we should only help the poor individually, not through our government. Yet that argument dissolves in the face of any fair review of the scriptural evidence presented in this book—apart from my commentary. If anything, Jesus always demanded that people do more than what the Old Testament law required, not less. He elevated the moral commands of the Old Testament to higher, even more difficult, standards. For instance, when Jesus spoke of the commands not to commit adultery or murder, He pointed out that lustful and hateful thoughts were part of the same sins, so the mere thoughts themselves should be avoided. It's illogical to claim that Jesus' commandments to help the poor invalidated the older Hebrew statutes that required government intervention and set a national standard for all to obey. All of Jesus' commands were given in the context of upholding His Jewish heritage.

During the time of Jesus and the early Christian church, Israel was occupied by the oppressive Roman Empire. One false move or protest against Caesar could land you in jail or get you crucified. When the Old Testament saints had the freedom to lambast their government and get away with it, they did. The early Christian church had far less latitude than the ancient prophets. Jesus knew that the Pharisees were constantly trying to trick Him into saying something that would get Him in trouble with the Romans, so He often spoke in riddles and parables—not to mention that storytelling is a great way to penetrate people's hardened consciousness.

Early Christians Practiced Wealth Redistribution

Early Christians, often a secretive, underground minority under severe persecution, could not openly castigate Rome, but they built their own small communities on Old Testament principles that Jesus affirmed. Early Christians were required to engage in severe economic sacrifice—something unheard of today. By their conduct we know them. Joining the early Christian church in Jerusalem meant you were required to sell all of your earthly possessions, *literally*, and practice wealth redistribution. A righteous prince could still be wealthy during the days of the Old Testament, so long as he tithed to the temple and to the poor and immigrant every third year. Early Christians made no such provisions. Rich people who joined the church sold all their possessions and gave them to the apostles to distribute among the group.

> And the multitude of them that believed were of one heart and of one soul: neither said any of them that ought of the things which he possessed was his own; but they had all things common. And with great power gave the apostles witness of the resurrection of the Lord Jesus: and great grace was upon them all. **Neither was**

there any among them that lacked: for as many as were pos-
sessors of lands or houses sold them, and brought the prices of
the things that were sold, And laid them down at the apostles'
feet: and distribution was made unto every man according as
he had need. (Acts 4:32–35 KJV)

Although many of today's powerful evangelicals may not discuss this historical fact, it remains in black and white in Acts 4:32–
5:11. That will end anyone's desire to recreate the original Jesus
church. Some people, who want us to take the Bible literally when
it comes to the earth being 6,000 years old, suddenly want to have a
more symbolic interpretation when they see this passage: "That was
for then; we cannot take such scriptures as literal commandments
for today." Regardless, the early Christian economic model was di-
ametrically opposed to today's Republican/Ayn Rand model of
trickle-down economics.

The Apostle Paul Protested against Injustice and Stood Up for His Civil Rights

The example of the apostle Paul in the book of Acts, chapters
16 to 27, is even more instructive as to how Christians should interact with their government leaders to assert the cause of justice. Paul
vigorously and publicly asserted his rights as a Roman citizen.[27]
Many people have taken Paul's admonitions in Romans 13:1–7 to
conclude that the Bible teaches submission to the status quo: "We
are not to fight earthly corruption below but must look for our
reward in heaven, for the apostle Paul told Christians to obey those
in authority who ruled over them, and he acknowledged that God
sets earthly rulers in place for our greater good." Unfortunately,
such logic justified the divine right of kings and Christian cooperation with the Nazi government in Germany or with apartheid laws
in South Africa. This was preached to me when I participated in
civil rights marches in Louisville. We are not supposed to get entan-
gled with straightening out earthly kingdoms, for our kingdom is
not of this world.

In the last few decades, however, evangelicals have rejected this doctrine as they learned to flex their power and gain clout with politicians. Of course, other theologians have explained the context in which Paul was speaking; they assert that he was speaking of just laws that impose reasonable restraints to curb bad behavior. Regardless of how we interpret Romans chapter 13, the book of Acts shows that Paul took advantage of his legal rights and spoke up to the rulers of his day. Surely, Paul was not being a hypocrite who preached one way and acted another.

At Philippi, Paul and his companion Silas were arrested for disturbing the peace after he converted a slave who was a sorceress and made money for her owners by telling fortunes. This was a form of divination that the Old and New Testaments condemn. Obviously, her owners were furious when their gravy train dried up, so they riled up a mob against Paul. After the officials beat, jailed, and chained him and Silas, the officials realized they had screwed up because Roman citizens had rights under laws that shielded them from such cruel punishment. When the guards came to release them secretly, Paul refused to leave. He made a public fuss about the wrongs they perpetrated on him:

> They beat us publicly without a trial, even though we are Roman citizens, and threw us into prison. And now do they want to get rid of us quietly? No! Let them come themselves and escort us out. (Acts 16:37)

The officials met Paul's demands, humbly trying to appease him and asking him to leave. When you realize you have stepped in manure, you want to bury it as soon as possible. Covering over mistakes and hoping everyone will forget are longtime tactics of politicians. Later, Paul did leave the city, but only on his own time schedule (Acts 16:38-39).

At Jerusalem, once again the Jews, his fellow countrymen, riled up a mob against Paul, as they falsely accused him of sedition and defiling the Temple. When the local officials came to arrest him, they realized that the charges were questionable. But because of the mob, they took him into protective custody; still, they allowed him to address the crowd. The crowd listened quietly until Paul said that God had spoken to him to minister to the Gentiles. Then, their prejudice against foreigners took over, and they immediately began to chant for his death (Acts 22:22). In an effort to appease the mob, the commander ordered Paul to be flogged. The reaction of Paul's fellow Jews, his religious brethren—since Paul himself was a Jew—draws eerie parallels for today. Religious people will let you talk about God until you challenge their innate prejudices and ask them to love those they hate.

As his civil rights were violated again, Paul stood firm and reminded the officials that their treatment of him was illegal. This alarmed the commander who realized he could be in serious trouble for mistreating a Roman citizen. Thus began a long story of legal proceedings and government entanglement, as Paul was transferred from one jurisdiction to another because no one knew what to do with him. And the story shows politics at work. The officials knew the charges were bogus, but they were under intense pressure to punish him.

Before every tribunal in his elaborate appeal, Paul spoke truth to power, and he stood up for his rights under the law—even though he knew that God would work his tribulations for good and these transfers allowed him to preach the gospel in new venues. His religion did not make him passive and submissive to injustice. He spoke up and spoke out against the injustice perpetrated upon him, and he vigorously mounted his defense with technical objections that only competent lawyers would think to make: insufficient charges, lack of proper complaining witnesses, lack of evidence, and improper venue (Acts 24). Although the system was rigged against him, Paul went down protesting every step of the way, and he left a legacy for us to follow, which eventually changed the world—naturally and spiritually.

As this book repeatedly shows, there is plenty to demonstrate that the New Testament is compatible with government's playing a role to provide for the poor and the sick and for Christians to kick up a fuss about injustice. Further, the fact that New Testament writers abstained from the revolutionary rhetoric of Isaiah, Jeremiah, and Ezekiel doesn't mean that they endorsed supply-side economics. They did the opposite, in fact. While not openly decrying oppressive governments, the New Testament leaders did not abandon the moral commandments of the Old Testaments.

Most biblical scholars posit that the text of the book of Revelation was written around AD 90–95, two decades after 60,000 Roman soldiers stormed Jerusalem, destroyed the great temple, massacred a million Jews, and left the city in ruins after the Jews had attempted a revolt.[28] Many scholars have noted that Revelation is an attack on the Roman Empire, which dominated the region then.[29] In fact, it is seen as a politically subversive text, since the number 666, the symbol for the mark of the beast, was a code for spelling the name of Nero (hence, all Caesars).[30] And the Romans, particularly Domitian, the Caesar from AD 81 to 96, had actually committed many of the horrible crimes of the Beast and the Antichrist.

The Caesars proclaimed themselves to be gods. At the time, people could not buy or sell in the market without first burning incense to, and hence worshipping, Caesar. Then they put the ash from the incense on their hands and foreheads to prove that they had performed their proper obeisance to the god Caesar (the mark of the beast). Obviously, that created a real dilemma for Christians who needed to buy food for their families yet could not in good conscience even pretend to worship Caesar.[31] Hence, there is plenty of protest literature in the Bible—along with passages advocating law and order. No one wants chaos and anarchy.

Christians may have been unable to overthrow Rome in the first century, but they consoled themselves with the vision that Jesus would one day come back and finally overthrow the oppressive regime and rule justly throughout all eternity. I state the history behind the book of Revelation not to argue that it lacks religious merit but to show that Revelation isn't only about sending people to heaven or to hell; it's also about envisioning a just government that works for God's people forever.

We are free to disregard early Christian practices (and I'm not signing up to give away my wealth to a pastor to redistribute), but it seems that we could, at least, acknowledge that this was the economic model of those Christians who were closest in time to Jesus and who were the more likely than any other group to have understood His message: they gave away their wealth and demanded justice from the government. So how can anyone argue in good conscience that Jesus condones only small government that favors tax cuts for the rich? It's absurd. No one wants waste and inefficient administrative systems. The point is not the size of government but the effects of government. We Democrats should help champion all efforts to cut wasteful, ineffective spending.

I remember when the "do it personally but not by the government" argument was used by white conservative Christians to oppose the civil rights movement. Those I heard speaking up for the status quo prefaced their comments by saying that individually, we all should be kind to our "colored folks," but we should not force other people to mingle with those they dislike. They argued, "If I own a business and don't want to serve black people [often referred to as *colored* or *Negroes* or worse], that's my constitutional right. You would be infringing on my personal freedom to force me to associate with other people against my will."

In the 1950s and '60s the common response of the white, evangelical Christian community was that we should not push to change this world, but we should wait for God to change the hearts of people. While upholding the status quo, these blind but well-meaning people insisted that they actually loved "the coloreds" just as much as anyone else. Yeah, right—just not enough to suffer inconvenience, respect their basic human rights, or learn about the atrocities they suffered. A fairly accurate presentation of the excuses for objecting to civil rights can be found in recent movies that recount the struggle for the passage of civil rights laws, like *The Butler*, *Selma*, *Loving*, and *All the Way*.

Many people may not recall from one of Jesus' parables that before the Good Samaritan encountered the wounded traveler along the road, a temple worker and a priest passed him by on their way to fulfill their religious duties in the temple, pretending not to see the bleeding man's dire circumstances. That's how I viewed many in the white evangelical community in the 1950s and '60s. They too put on blinders and ignored the bleeding of their neighbors, as they rushed off to church every Sunday. Like the Levite and the priest in Jesus' parable, they pretended not to see the wounds and bleeding of their "neighbors."

The mythology, however, that the big bad government should not make laws that require respect and equal treatment of people in public venues or engage in efforts to care for the sick, the poor, and the immigrant is a silly doctrine promulgated by Ayn Rand and long touted by libertarians. It is nothing but social Darwinism (the very doctrine that Republican Christians claim to oppose). My own state's senator, Rand Paul (and his father Ron Paul) proudly revere this author and have publicly admitted so.[32]

Ayn Rand's philosophy rings through Rand Paul's recent words:

> There's a difference between charity and taxation and, sure, I have a great deal of sympathy and I have helped through our church with helping refugees—that's charity and something you give voluntarily. But to say, "Oh, we are going to bring them here and put them on welfare," well, that's not charity, that's not humanitarian, that's you saying, "Oh, it's great to give somebody else's money." Give of your own money. [33]

Senator Paul has the same attitude toward hungry senior citizens. They should look to private charity, and the government owes them nothing.[34] Such ideas are fair game in the free market-place of ideas—for whoever is gullible enough to believe them. But they come up against the Bible, and Rand Paul professes to be a devout Christian. On an individual level, he has done admirable pro bono ophthalmology work; he just wants to block any systematic plan that would meet the eye care needs of all. Woe unto glaucoma patients who don't live in an area where physicians volunteer free eye care.

Here's the problem with private charity to solve these problems: it's random, piecemeal, and inefficient, yet it beguiles us into thinking we have satisfied our duty. We all know the story of the little boy at the edge of the ocean, throwing starfish back into the sea. Yes, he was only making a miniscule difference overall, but to those few starfish he saved, it was everything. And to those relatively few fortunate recipients, private charity makes a world of difference. The charity that churches and private groups do is wonderful, inspiring, and amazing, and they deserve our praise and support.

Private charity is like love and garlic—you can never have too much. But at best churches are serving only a portion of those in need, and each charity is reinventing the wheel to get its own infrastructures in place to deliver services. I believe in government and private nonprofit partnerships. We've seen them make a world of difference. President Jimmy Carter did that to virtually eliminate the scourge of the guinea worm in Africa. President Bill Clinton did that to bring AIDS drugs to impoverished Africans. But private charity alone can't get the job done, any more than private charity can maintain our roads or garbage service.

As an intellectual, I can appreciate Ayn Rand's "good points" in her philosophy of objectivism and her firsthand experience with the cruelty of Russian communism. I believe in science, which is sometimes wrong but self-correcting over time. I believe that evaluations of all actions in any sphere must be based on objective evidence and measurable results—not just feel-good thinking. In college, I studied the American philosophy of pragmatism, which states that a thing is known or "real" only when based on its observable, measurable results—something Jesus said 2,100 years ago: "by their fruits, you shall know them." But Ayn Rand's premises are flawed, as she makes sweeping generalizations about government programs and their lack of quality standards or accountability. She portrays dramatically one example of a government program where sloppy workmanship proved disastrous, and then she generalizes that one example as being true for all public projects. Ayn Rand's premise assumes that all public projects are like buildings in China that have

collapsed and killed many citizens because they were poorly con-
structed.[35] But these calamities come from corruption and greed,
which too often invade both the private and public sector. A simple
Google search shows many articles about similar instances around
the world, including in America.

If you don't believe me, check out the story of the Beverly Hills
Supper Club, something we Kentuckians painfully remember.[36]
When a fire swept through a popular nightclub in 1977, 165 people
died, and 200 were injured. This disaster sprang from private enterprise unfettered, which subjugated safety to profit. At the time,
building codes and inspection requirements were woefully lacking.
Now, with the help of our majority Republican legislature, Kentucky's new far-right Republican governor appears to be well on his
way to rolling back regulations to the good old days, when there
was little oversight over building codes and regulations. Indeed,
why should we shackle our good entrepreneurs and real estate de-
velopers with these pesky building rules?[37]

Would Conservative Christians Argue that the Government Should Not Be in the Business of Providing Clean Water?

The disdain of government leads to arrogance, which leads to
destruction. (We'll consider Bible verses about this later.) Consider
the arrogance of the Republican administration and legislature in
Michigan, which first passed laws that allowed the governor to ap-
point emergency managers to take over municipalities and bypass
locally elected officials whenever a town was running a deficit. So
when the poor community of Flint was in fiscal trouble, the hot-
shots came in and decided to save money by taking the town's water from the nearby Flint River rather than from the more expensive Lake Huron via Detroit, which was farther away. They were
warned not to do this without installing special water treatment
equipment because the river water was corrosive. But such expensive treatment would have unraveled the cost savings. And when
you disdain science and assume that all restraints on your plans are

some sort of liberal conspiracy, why should you listen? Of course, they poisoned the water for tens of thousands of residents, as corrosive chemicals in the river water leached lead from the city's old water pipes and sent contaminated water right into the residents' taps.

As a result thousands of children and residents now have lead poisoning, which causes lifelong illness and irreversible brain damage,[38] and the water is unsafe to drink. But first, state officials denied the problem and stonewalled remedial efforts.[39] Then, when the damage could no longer be hidden, this governor, who orchestrated the entire plan of government management that created the calamity, then begged President Obama to declare Flint a disaster area so that federal tax dollars could bring relief and clean up his mess. Even the Republican Congress in Washington dragged its heels in offering federal aid to this poisoned town, since now the entire water system must be dug up and replaced.[40] The result of such arrogance is the very kind of big government bailout that Republicans decry, yet it was a bailout that their policies unnecessarily required.

At least, no one argued that giving these people clean water was a matter of private charity because our government would be fulfilling one of Jesus' commands. But the same logic applies to health care. We just take clean water for granted, so it never occurs to us to adjust our thinking. Clean water is needed in order to live and contribute to society: health care is needed in order to live and contribute to society.

Just as only the government can ensure that we all have safe drinking water, only the government can adequately insure the common good for our society. Today, we have resources and abundance unimaginable in Bible days. And we can vote. We all have resources that we can aim toward our collective good. The Bible commands us that whenever we have the resources to help others, we must do so: "Withhold not good from them to whom it is due, when it is in the power of thine hand to do it" (Proverbs 3:27 KJV). Not convinced? Try these New Testament scriptures:

If anyone, then, knows the good they ought to do and doesn't do it, it is sin for them. (James 4:17)

Make sure that nobody pays back wrong for wrong, but always **strive to do what is good for each other and for everyone else.** (1 Thessalonians 5:15)

From everyone who has been given much, much will be demanded; and from the one who has been entrusted with much, much more will be asked. (Luke 12:48)

Christian denominations universally agree that we should be good stewards of all the resources we have received—whether they are material wealth, gifts, special abilities, or opportunities. When we stand before our Maker (whether in our own conscience on our deathbeds or at the day of judgment), how can we explain our squandering an opportunity to enable our government to follow Jesus' commands to aid the poor, the sick, the stranger (immigrant) dwelling among us, and the prisoner? In America, we have an opportunity and a responsibility not to hamper and obstruct good government. We have the opportunity to make sure that our government provides for our safety and the common good.

Franklin Roosevelt noted that "The test of our progress is not whether we add more to the abundance of those who have much; it is whether we provide enough for those who have little." And a few decades later, Vice President Hubert Humphrey elaborated on this thought—in the spirit of Jesus' words: "The moral test of government is how it treats those who are in the dawn of life, the children; those who are in the twilight of life, the aged; and those in the shadows of life, the sick, the needy and the handicapped."

And here's a wise word for those of us who feel we are beating our heads against a wall, fighting for justice and compassion:

Let us not become weary in doing good, for at the proper time we will reap a harvest if we do not give up. Therefore, as we have opportunity, let us do good to all people, especially to those who belong to the family of believers. (Galatians 6:9–10)

According to the Bible, when it's in our power to do good, we must do it. If God hates it when the rich oppress the poor, then it makes no sense to insist that we should never vote for government laws that restrain the rich from oppression or that require them to contribute more to others. Such thinking violates clear biblical mandates. Remember, also, that the vicious ire in the 2016 election about raising taxes was over a 3% increase for the wealthiest Americans. No one advocated early church economics. No one advocated a return to the 1950s when the wealthy were taxed at 90% of their income—though their effective tax rates were lower (around 70%), but still high enough to make us all cringe.[41]

At the very least, evangelical Christians who protest abortion and gay marriage and seek to use the power of the federal government to regulate individual morality must also advocate for increasing services for the poor, the sick, the immigrant, and the prisoner—but only if they wish to retain integrity in their commitment to being biblical. Installing restraints on greed and excess is what Jesus and the entire Bible stand for

3

Jesus Loves Obamacare!

I was sick ..., and you did not look after me (Matthew 25:43).

In 2007, I saw Michael Moore on *The View*, as they were discussing health care reform. Moore had recently released his documentary film, *Sicko*, in which he pointed out the corruption in the health insurance industry and how these companies often left people to die and refused to pay for treatments for the slightest reasons. He presented solid evidence that America's health care is more expensive yet inferior to that in many other Western countries, which cover all of their citizens who, in turn, have longer life expectancies. The guest co-host that day was a well known born-again Christian, Star Parker, a beautiful, tall, sleek African American with long braids and a powerful demeanor. Her attire, however, did challenge my own holiness upbringing and "dress for success" training, since she wore a low cut sleeveless blouse that flaunted her exposed bosom, torqueing my notions of a modest, godly woman.

To the accusation that nationalized health care would be "socializing medicine," Moore responded first by recounting Jesus' command to take care of the least of these, including the sick. Then he asserted, "We shouldn't be calling it socialized medicine. We should call it Christianized medicine; it's to help everyone."

Star Parker immediately quipped, "He didn't say, 'Go into your neighbor's pocket and make them do it.' He said, 'Individually you should do these things.'" Moore tried to explain that whatever Jesus

85

tells us to do, as Christians we all should collectively do it.[42] But interrupting him, Parker hammered back, "No, He did not say that."

I almost jumped out of my seat in excitement. First, Moore gave a brilliant response: no, we are not socializing medicine; we are *Christianizing* medicine—a sound bite that Democrats should adopt. Second, I saw that Parker was distorting the text. "That's not in the scripture," I shouted at the TV. "You misquoted Jesus!" Parker added words to the Bible in order to justify her position. Jesus did not address the logistics of how we get it done, and He imposed no such limitations on enacting His commandments. He never said, "Do it individually but don't band together to do it as a group." Jesus never condemned secular efforts to do the good that He required.

Unfortunately, Moore wasn't able to call Parker out on her misrepresentation of Jesus' words. My guess is he did not have a strong recall of the scriptures. Plus, when all the women started talking loudly over each other, he was drowned out. The next day, Moore explained the scripture more coherently, though he never referenced Matthew 25. And he acknowledged that he was relying on his memory of Bible lessons taught by the Catholic sisters at his school.[43]

In *Sicko*, Moore pulled some surprising stunts to make his point, and he cited a lot of statistics and facts and brought them alive to hold a viewer's interest. He took a group of sick 9/11 responders to the Guantanamo base in Cuba to get free treatment that they were denied in the US because their health insurance denied them coverage. He pointed out that the prisoners, who were suspected terrorists, were getting better health care than these firefighters, who risked their lives to save others. He also dared to show how the Cuban health care system ranked alongside and in some areas surpassed ours (America ranked 37th, while Cuba was 38th).

Of course, that inflamed many conservatives who feel it treasonous for an American to state that any communistic country could do anything nearly as well as we. Many Americans believe that any criticism of our government's policy is unpatriotic. Witness the backlash against the Dixie Chicks, who tanked their lucrative music career by criticizing President Bush for taking us to war in Iraq.

Watching that free-for-all discussion on *The View* motivated me to take up this book, with the words of my mother ringing in my ears: "Christians don't know their Bibles." Then, barely two years later, a conservative friend "Polly-parroted" to me the same talking points that Star Parker barked—leaving me in awe of how Republicans are able to harmonize their message and hammer it home among their followers. In essence, this argument is, "How dare you dip into my pocket to follow Jesus' commandments!" The argument is absurd on its face, and it lacks any scriptural basis. But because a large segment of the evangelical community believes it, it can be daunting to confront. Yet it can be overcome—if progressives learn the right Bible verses.

I wonder what Star Parker would make of the story of the early church in Acts chapters 4 and 5. At that time, being a Christian meant that you sold all your property and gave it to the church to distribute among all according to their need. That was pure socialism—an economic system none of us desire. Then two people disagreed with the rules, yet they wanted to be part of the Christian community. Ananias and his wife Sapphira sold their property, but they gave only half to the apostles and held back the remainder for themselves. So they lied to the apostles about what price they obtained for their land.

> Then Peter said, "Ananias, how is it that Satan has so filled your heart that you have lied to the Holy Spirit and have kept for yourself some of the money you received for the land? Didn't it belong to you before it was sold? And after it was sold, wasn't the money at your disposal? What made you think of doing such a thing? You have not lied just to human beings but to God." When Ananias heard this, he fell down and died. And great fear seized all who heard what had happened. (Acts 5:3–5)

The same fate befell his wife Sapphira as she too lied when Peter confronted her (Acts 5:9–11). The notion of "You can't dip into my pocket to follow Jesus' commandment," brought damnation and death to this couple. And the other Christians understood the lesson, as "great fear came upon them": you could not begrudge or withhold a portion of your money from the collective good; you had to surrender it all. So I'm not sure how people can advocate the notion that raising taxes ever so slightly on the rich to pay for health care is somehow not in keeping with biblical principles. If you take the Bible literally, the proposals of government-run health care advocated by Bernie Sanders don't go far enough!

In 2007, conservatives accused Moore of sloppy data management and distortions, yet CNN's Sanjay Gupta admitted on *Larry King Live* that Moore's points in the movie were essentially true.[44] America's health care system was broken. Having studied statistics (only because it was required for my doctoral degree), I understand that we can find seemingly contradictory data because unknowingly we compare apples and oranges, and even government reports vary. Regardless of which data source is used, however, certain basic trends are clear: American health care costs more and gives poorer results compared to most western European countries, yet the health insurance industry and its excessively compensated executives rake in astronomical profits. We can quibble about specific numbers, but the essential facts are irrefutable.

Recent studies show that *Sicko* was right on the mark: We still fall far behind in health care, and the rank of thirty-seven has substantial support.[45] A report by U.S. News and World Report stated that:

> The Social Progress Index 2014 rates the U.S. as 70th among 132 nations in health and wellness. A 2013 Institute of Medicine report titled "U.S. Health in International Perspective: Shorter Lives, Poorer Health" ranks the U.S. near last among 17 high-income nations in several categories ranging from infant mortality and low birth weight to life expectancy. The Commonwealth Fund analysis also ranks the U.S. last among seven nations in health care. The U.S. ranks worst among 16 developed countries in preventable deaths, according to a 2011 study published in Health Policy. There are some bright spots: Survival with some

cancers (cervix, breast, prostate) is better in the United States, but this may be because of better screening.[46]

Democrats need to go to faith leaders and ask, "What can we do to bring Christ into the health care industry? Is it okay if we, as citizens of the richest nation on earth, stand by and let thousands of people die, because they can't afford expensive operations or new medicines? Would Jesus be pleased with that?" They are not going to change their beliefs on abortion or gay marriage, but they may begin to embrace health care reforms when we meet them on their turf. The key is not to convince Republicans to agree with progressives on every issue, but to use the Bible to map out common ground on key economic proposals relating to those who are marginalized.

We've already reviewed how Ezekiel censured the shepherds of Israel because they had "not strengthened the weak, healed the sick, or bound up the injured" (34:1-4). Yet Ezekiel ended his proclamation with hope that God would punish the bad rulers (the "fat cats" in charge) and restore His people with food and with healing:

> I will feed my flock, and I will cause them to lie down, saith the **Lord God**. I will seek that which was lost, and bring again that which was driven away, and **will bind up that which was broken, and will strengthen that which was sick**: but I will destroy the fat and the strong; I will feed them with judgment. (Ezekiel 34:15-16 KJV)

So much for the argument that healing the sick is just a private matter and not for the leaders of a nation. If the leaders hadn't known they had a duty to make available health care for their citizens, the prophet would not have railed against them for their failure. Nowhere in the Bible are people indicted for failure to take action, unless they knew they had a duty to the contrary, and here the duty was to address the needs of the sick. Ezekiel was lambasting government for its refusal to help the most vulnerable in society and for practicing the philosophy that only the strong should survive and the weak should die off.

How applicable is Ezekiel 34 to our modern system? Before the
Affordable Care Act, if a lower or middle-income family with no
insurance got sick, we as a society did little to help them. The rulers
of our land, our governors, senators, and congressional representatives, refused to help. They might say a prayer for them or hope
that they improve, but the sick and injured were left to the cruel
mercies of the insurance industry, which with impunity could deny
someone coverage for a preexisting condition, deny them coverage
if they hit a lifetime limit, and sometimes, deny claims for no good
reason at all. If you doubt this, run a Google search on bad faith
claims against health insurers. And ask doctors, who will also tell
you that insurance companies can take months to process reim-
bursements.

Born nearly thirty years before Ezekiel, the prophet Jeremiah
proclaimed similar sentiments. Some scholars believe that Ezekiel
was familiar with the prophecies of Jeremiah (having either heard
or read them), but the Bible doesn't actually say. Regardless, there
are common themes that stream through both books. Like Ezekiel,
Jeremiah was decrying the national state of affairs, as Israel had been
taken captive:

> **Is there no balm in Gilead? Is there no physician there?** Why
> then is there no healing for the wound of my people? (Jeremiah
> 8:22)

> Have you rejected Judah completely? Do you despise Zion? **Why
> have you afflicted us so that we cannot be healed?** We hoped
> for peace but no good has come, for a time of healing but there is
> only terror. (Jeremiah 14:19)

> "But **I will restore you to health and heal your wounds,**" de-
> clares the Lord, "because you are called an outcast, Zion for
> whom no one cares." (Jeremiah 30:17)

The health of the country is a matter of urgent concern for rulers. It's not a guideline that people can ignore when it's inconvenient.

In biblical days, scientific medicine was nonexistent. As a result,
many people believed that plagues and diseases were a sign of sin or

a failure of the people to follow God's law.[47] But even though most people today would reject the notion that an outbreak of disease is a direct punishment from God, the premise regarding health care still applies: if sickness among the masses was seen as a result of rulers' disobeying God's will, then rulers who provide for the health for their people are acting in alignment with God's will. If God brings health and healing, then if we are to be like God, we too must bring heath and healing. The nation's health and well-being should be a priority for its rulers.

Throughout the Bible, healing and health are signs of being on God's side and receiving His blessings. Rulers who ensure that their people have good health are in alignment with God's Word.

> Then they cried to the Lord in their trouble, and he saved them from their distress. **He sent out his word and healed them**; he rescued them from the grave. Let them give thanks to the Lord for his unfailing love and his wonderful deeds for mankind. (Psalm 107:19–21)

> The Lord builds up Jerusalem; he gathers the exiles of Israel. **He heals the brokenhearted and binds up their wounds**. (Psalm 147:2–3)

When Israel was first formed as a nation, after gaining her freedom from Egyptian slavery, the vision of the Promised Land (an ideal state) was living in harmony with God and being blessed with abundant food and health. God promised the nation, "Ye shall serve the Lord your God, and he shall bless thy bread, and thy water; and **I will take sickness away from the midst of thee**" (Exodus 23:25 KJV). This was a vision for national prosperity and good health for all citizens.

In his speech outside the Judiciary Committee in 2007,[48] Michael Moore noted that Muslims and Jews support the proposition that the entire society needs to care for the sick. That got me thinking. Why? Because both of these religions revere the Old Testament. Why is it that Jewish people are not contending, "Only take care of the sick individually, not collectively"? Because they know their Bible (and many Jews know the New Testament better than some Christians). This is not disputed in modern day Israel, which instituted universal health care in 1995. Evangelicals give lip service to honoring Israel. They pray for the peace of Jerusalem and tend to endorse unquestioningly all of Israel's decisions. Despite facing threats from terrorism, Israel ranks eighth in the world for life expectancy, whereas the US ranks twenty-sixth.[49] So why can't we follow Israel's lead on health care?

Evangelical Christians are supposed to revere the Old and New Testaments, and there are still more biblical passages that bolster our collective responsibility to heal the sick. During His entire earthly ministry, Jesus was known for healing the sick. That is what He stood for: the end of disease and the end to physical and mental suffering. It would take us pages to recount each story where Jesus healed the sick. But the next passage sums up His ministry.

> And Jesus went about all Galilee, teaching in their synagogues, and preaching the gospel of the kingdom, and **healing all manner of sickness and all manner of disease among the people.** (Matthew 4:23 KJV)

More importantly, He established a legacy and command: He empowered His disciples to heal all manner of diseases.

> And when he had called unto him his twelve disciples, **he gave them power** against unclean spirits, to cast them out, and **to heal all manner of sickness and all manner of disease.** (Matthew 10:1 KJV)Jesus' disciples followed suit and were known for their healings. Even Peter's shadow passing by had healing power (Acts 5:14-16). And Paul, after his conversion, likewise worked many healings (Acts 9:11-13). The elders of the church were directed to minister to the sick (James 5:14). Early Christian history is replete with examples of how the Christians tended to the sick when others, fearful of catching contagion, would leave them to die. In fact, some writers credit Christians for changing the callous attitude of the Romans toward the sick and dying.

The totality of Scripture establishes an irrefutable correlation: being on God's side brings good health, and people are healed. So if your nation has fewer people getting sick, then your leaders are following God's commandments. If more people are getting sick, then something is wrong. If Jesus commanded His followers to heal the sick, and the Old Testament prophets declare that rulers must take action to help the poor and the sick, then you don't need a master's degree in divinity to see that the Affordable Care Act is consistent with biblical teachings. Today, over 70 percent of Americans identify themselves as Christians. Since we have the power to heal all manner of disease, which was unimaginable 2,000 ago, shouldn't we use our power, including our vote, to effect the healing vision of the gospel?

As we saw earlier, we have a duty individually to do everything in our power to heal the sick and take care of the least of these. But one individual cannot stop a sick person from being denied insurance due to a preexisting condition. Visiting a cancer patient in the hospital is a kind deed, but pushing the "princes of Israel" to ensure that such a sick person receives necessary treatment is truly following Jesus' commandment. Voting, lobbying Congress and state legislators, lifting our voice, and supporting collective efforts to heal the sick—all these behaviors are within each individual's power. So *if* I am an individual who is individually following the Bible (not to withhold good when it is in my power to do good), then what in the Bible condemns me from lending my resources to support some form of collective health care? Jesus did not limit or specify how we were to care for the sick. (Remember, those who knew him personally practiced wealth redistribution). He just told us to do it, and if we are disciples of Christ (dedicated pupils who truly follow and study versus mere believers who drag up the rear), then we must take individual responsibility for our modern gift of the power to heal all manner of disease. No, not everyone can be a doctor, nurse, or a health care worker, but we can lend what resources we have— our voice and our vote for the healing of all.

President Obama used his natural power as president to ensure that 20 more million people would get access to health care. Because of this, millions of these people will be saved from curable diseases, and many more will avoid going bankrupt trying to pay for life-saving treatments. Is it credible to believe that God is displeased with this type of action? If God approves of healing the sick, then what is His reaction to Obamacare? How will our Heavenly Father view President Obama's using his political capital (the resource in his hands) to try to save twenty million people as a sin? Will the Lord be angry with Obama for trying to bring relief—naturally and economically—to those with preexisting conditions? Will He merely shrug?

Yes, Jesus loves Obamacare!

And politicians need to start phrasing it this way. Changing the phrase to "Jesus Loves Obamacare" forces Republicans to argue that God is angry with President Obama for trying to save millions of lives and stop millions more from going bankrupt. Democrats need to demand that Republicans find scriptural support that demonstrates Jesus' displeasure with providing citizens with affordable health care. Republicans will find none, although perhaps some could do some stretching, distorting, and hacking of Scripture to cobble together a weak argument. Moreover, the phrase will cause evangelicals to question and reflect on this notion. The message reaches them on their turf, and if enough politicians know these scriptures, we can begin to change hearts and minds for the greater good.

Think about what Republicans are actually proposing by planning to repeal Obamacare without first preparing a better plan. Suppose America strips twenty million people of health care, and as a result, insurance companies can revert to refusing coverage to people with preexisting conditions. Suppose they reinstate lifetime limits or kick children off of their parents' plans. In all of these cases, people will die. And many more will go bankrupt trying to pay for expensive treatments. Will God look at the results of the Obamacare repeal and say to Republicans, "Well done, my good and faithful servants"? Democrats need to use this type of language in order to force Republicans to justify how taking away health care from twenty million people aligns with the teachings of the Bible.

Politicians Should Reform Obamacare, Not End It

Obamacare was our first major step forward in reforming our nation's broken health care industry. By no means is it perfect. It needs modification. It has gaps and contradictions. Yet all other social improvement programs, including Medicare, got off to a rocky start. The answer is to improve it not abolish it—unless you can propose something that covers more Americans more efficiently and effectively. If so, we applaud you, and you can take all the credit and even call it Trumpcare.

We can argue about how to build a society that heals all manner of sickness and disease. No one party has all the best solutions. But one political party has made healing the sick a priority, and the other party has not. Matthew 6:21 states, "For where your treasure is, there your heart will be also." The spending priorities of the two parties prove where their hearts, their treasures, truly lie. What legislators choose to endorse gives voters insights into the real "treasures of their hearts." Giving lip service to being pro-life reeks with hypocrisy when you are proposing policies that will let people die and their economic lives be destroyed by illness, and you oppose putting any treasure behind policies to improve the health of the nation.

Yes, this might require some sacrifice and giving from those who have more to give. That should not be heresy to evangelical Christians, for as this book demonstrates, it's God's law—even taxation on a national level. In particular, our nation has done a poor job of standing up to the health care insurance lobby. Part of the insane rise of health insurance premiums in the past two years our government's refusal to negotiate on behalf of its 330 million citizens for cheaper drug prices.

There is much work to be done in our nation to make Jesus' vision a reality, but surely all of us with biblical values can agree that everyone in a country as rich as America should have access to affordable health care. However we define God (whether as a supreme anthropomorphic being, as the spirit of love, or the greater good for all), we get that God doesn't magic up His work in the world. We have to be His arms and legs. We are the instruments of bringing about God's will on earth, and that's what President Obama did for health care.

Democrats Expended Great Political Capital to Help The Sick; Republicans Refused

Christians often bemoan the bad morals of Bill Clinton—although that is harder now given Trump's rise to office. By contrast, Obama has been a faithful, loving father and husband, and he did the most Christian thing any politician has done in over thirty years. On this issue, he used the power of his office to give health care coverage to millions who otherwise couldn't afford it.

Yet Obama was not the first Democrat to expend significant political capital in order to help the sick. We Baby Boomers remember when Hillary Clinton advocated in the 1990s for a single payer health care system, a position that Senator and presidential candidate Bernie Sanders resurrected for millennials in 2016. Hillary's early efforts were promptly rejected, partly because as First Lady, she was being uppity to presume to meddle in national policy. Yet in the early 1990s, Republicans promised that *if* Hillary had worked for reforms through private health insurance, they would have supported a national health care initiative—a promise they abandoned after 2008. In the 1990s seeing an opportunity to humiliate Democrats, Republicans couldn't resist vilifying the First Lady. They did it in large part to sabotage the morale of Democrats, who would be less inclined to vote in the 1994 congressional midterms. They put the good of their own party ahead of the health of the nation, and they were rewarded for their devious efforts: they won control of Congress.

Yet even after this early setback, both Hillary and Bill Clinton continued to prod Congress to do something on health care. As the economy of the 1990s was booming, Hillary played a leading role in pushing congressional Republicans to adopt the Children's Health Insurance Program (CHIP) for low-income families. Upon viewing how Massachusetts had created a similar program, Ted Kennedy persuaded Republican Senator Orrin Hatch to cosponsor similar legislation, but many Congressional Republicans criticized Hatch when he dared to say that Congress had a moral duty to provide coverage to at-risk low-income children. The optional program gives grants to states that also make their own contributions toward children's health care.[50] Although Hillary was not the public face of the effort, she used the resources of the White House to study the program and to advance the legislation through Congress.[51] And she made a huge difference for millions of children.

During her presidential bid in 2016, Hillary Clinton posted a story about how CHIP enabled two parents to get expensive hearing aids and cochlear implants for their deaf baby girl, which they could not have afforded on their own. The program extended health care coverage to uninsured children in families with incomes that are modest but too high to qualify for Medicaid. Today, thanks to CHIP, this family's daughter speaks normally and has far exceeded all predictions made when she was born. The reasons for her success were CHIP and the 1975 law that required public schools to accommodate disabled children,[52] for which Hillary also worked during the 1970s while she was on staff at the Children's Defense Fund.[53] One thing about such efforts is that we never know when that child we save may become the next Einstein or Marie Curie. And it is clear that the beautiful young lady Sara is on her way to being a great contribution to society. She will be better able as an adult to repay in taxes and in contributions to society the health care benefits she received as a child.

You can demonize Hillary all you want, and you don't have to like her, yet the verified facts are that this woman has advocated for health care and improved opportunities for children throughout much of her adult life. Imagine what would have happened if the deaf girl, Sara, could not have obtained the expensive therapy she needed. Would Jesus be pleased with us for advocating a system that would leave her isolated and consigned only to a deaf world? You can see this family's personal story on YouTube at https://youtu.be/kUD7swQkgGA. It's a must-see when it comes to putting a human face on the health care debate. It will make even the most stoic among us tear up.

Before Elizabeth Warren was a senator, she was a professor at Harvard Law School, and my son Stuart was fortunate to be in her contracts class. Her fascinating research showed that one of the top reasons American families go bankrupt is not financial mismanagement or trying to live beyond their means. Rather, they fall into financial ruin because their breadwinners, middle-income workers, lose their jobs and then lose their employer-provided health insurance, leaving them vulnerable to a medical emergency.[54]

Alternatively, in decades past, the reverse happened. People fell sick and then got fired, leaving them without employer-based insurance and with no income to pay their medical bills. That's why in 1993 Bill Clinton led the fight for the passage of the Family Medical Leave Act, which stopped the practice of firing people because of illness and required employers to maintain health insurance for employees for up to twelve weeks of medical leave. In case, you aren't old enough to have lived through this era, the plan had previous bipartisan support, but President Bush 41 vetoed it.[55] I'm not sure what biblical justification he had, if any, but it certainly looks as if he was putting more families at risk of going into bankruptcy due to medical emergency. And despite all the prophecies of doom to the economy, the new law requiring employers to carry the burden of health insurance for twelve weeks of unpaid medical leave did not drive our country into recession.

President Obama and Democrats in Congress followed a Christian calling to bring some semblance of a conscience and good Judeo-Christian ethics to the health care industry. They were working toward a fairer health insurance marketplace, regardless of whether they connected it to their faith. But remember, Jesus doesn't judge us by whether we cry, "Lord, Lord." He judges us by our conduct. Obama staked his entire career and legacy on health care reform, and that demonstrates his heart was in the right place. Can we say Jesus wouldn't love that? "By their fruits ye shall know them" (Matthew 7:20 KJV).

Republican Hypocrisy on Health Care Makes the Devil Rejoice

In the Bible, there are many words for evil: Satan, Beelzebub, Lucifer, and the devil are common. Evangelicals believe that the devil is a supernatural being who is not as powerful as God but is granted temporary power over mankind in this world. In the Greek, the word *devil* means tormentor, a false accuser, or a slanderer, and the concept is that evil (or the devil if we personify evil as a personal being) revels in human suffering and torment.

Republicans try to claim Obamacare has been a disaster, which is not true. Ask the millions of people who now have health care. Some are angry about the increases in premiums, but even so, these people need to be reminded of their own saying, WWJD, "What would Jesus do?" Would He want to dismantle a system that is saving potentially millions of lives[56] in order to give a cut in premiums for everyone else?

Wouldn't Jesus want us to come together and take a stand for our community? Republicans have created unholy alliances with faith leaders on this issue, and I find it shameful. Yes, the law has its flaws, but some of those flaws Republicans intentionally made worse. They voted dozens of times for repeal, but they got a real chance to enact sabotage once they gained control of the Senate in 2014.

Was Marco Rubio Following Jesus When He Sabotaged Obamacare?

Florida Senator Marco Rubio actively worked to undermine Obamacare, as he was preparing to mount a presidential campaign. Rather than working to reform Obamacare, he used his party's control of Congress to sabotage it—most likely in an attempt to curry favor with the Republican base to boost his presidential chances. He put his own ambitions for high office above the health care of millions, and that's immoral from my reading of the Bible.

Rubio enacted a drastic cut of subsidies to insurance companies precisely at a time when Republicans knew that the insurance companies would be forced to take on more sick clients. Though sounding a bit wonky, the term is *risk corridors*. Once the Affordable Care Act forced insurance companies to stop discriminating against people with preexisting conditions, sicker clients, who had been previously denied coverage, would immediately begin buying and using health insurance; this in turn increases the costs for the insurance companies. Customarily, insurance companies pass on those costs to all consumers by increasing the monthly premiums of everyone else. So to avoid spikes in premiums for all, Democrats originally allocated extra funding to the insurance companies' *risk corridors*, in order to smooth out the risks (i.e., lower the costs) that would come from the sudden influx of new clients with preexisting conditions in the first few years of Obamacare. But once Republicans took control of Congress in 2014, Rubio cut off these risk corridors and cut the funding to insurance companies, just at a time when millions of previously denied patients were gaining coverage. This forced insurance companies to pass along the costs of their new sicker clients to their other customers.[57]

Rubio's plan worked. With more sick people coming into the system and smaller government subsidies to smooth out the transition, people's premiums spiked—right before the 2016 election. The media was all too quick to report the spike, and Republicans capitalized on the chaos they themselves caused.[58] Will Jesus look at Marco Rubio's leadership and say, "Well done my good and faithful servant. You advocated for a tax break and worked to sabotage health care for millions. Welcome to my kingdom"? Again, none of us can judge the souls of other people, but if Republicans like Marco Rubio want to inject God into our national conversation or tout their personal devotion to their faith, then it's fair for the public to put these questions back to them.

In the Bible, God held the leaders of Israel accountable for the well-being of the nation. If God has allowed a man to become blessed enough to serve in Congress, then surely basic biblical principles apply: "From everyone who has been given much, much will be demanded; and from the one who has been entrusted with much, much more will be asked" (Luke 12:48). If God has allowed us to obtain great power and we use it to further our own ambitions or to give tax cuts to the wealthy (aka the donor class), how is that being a good and faithful servant of Jesus? Being pro-life on abortion does not absolve American senators, governors, and congressmen of their duties to care for "the least of these" in society.

We must also recall that when Republicans had control of the White House and the Congress from 2001 to 2006, they did nothing to help people with preexisting conditions. "Your heart is where your treasure is," remember. When they had free rein (and reign) for five years, they used their legislative capital to pass two massive tax cuts for the rich and start a war in Iraq—which ran up huge deficits, the very thing they pretend to hate. They did, to their credit, enact Medicare Part D, which expanded prescription drug coverage for low-income seniors, though thanks to drug lobbyists, they forbade any government negotiation with pharmaceuticals over drug prices, leaving Americans to pay higher prices for drugs than the rest of the world.[59] Yet the program is seen as successful, and Obamacare has been fixing the coverage gaps in Part D.[60] As of 2017, Republicans control the White House, the Congress, and the Supreme Court. What will they do with that power?

Conservatives Begot Obamacare

What makes Republican hatred of Obamacare so perplexing is that a mandate for all to buy private health insurance was the brainchild of the Heritage Foundation, a conservative think tank, long the pipeline for Republican ideas. Republicans touted a proposal similar to Obamacare when they opposed Hillary's health care reform in the 1990s.[61] But after they used that argument to defeat Hillary's plan, Republicans took no action on it for fifteen years. In fairness, we acknowledge that Republican Mitt Romney helped enact such a policy when he was governor of Massachusetts,[62] although he was pushed to do so by his state legislature.[63] His was an excellent example of bipartisan work to heal the people, and Romney deserves credit. Here, he walked his Christian talk.

If you are a financially conservative Christian, Obamacare is the best option for you. It requires everyone to get private insurance, so there are no freeloaders. Young people add to the insurance pool, making them better off in case of an emergency, and everyone comes together as a community to ensure that sick children with heart conditions aren't denied coverage because they've hit their lifetime limits.

President Obama was naïve to think that Republicans would back health care reform if he adopted their prototype. He didn't know that on the night of his inauguration, they had actually met and vowed to oppose everything he proposed in order to ensure he failed, no matter what he did. But it was obvious soon enough, and yet Obama took the moral high ground and continued to try to work with Republicans.

He tried to work with Republicans Susan Collins[64] and Olympia Snowe[65] of Maine, yet neither so-called "moderate" ended up supporting the Affordable Care Act. Snowe later admitted that she had eight meetings with President Obama and got twelve phone calls from him—laying to rest the notion that Obama was unwilling to woo politicians across the aisle. He told her she could be a political Joan of Arc by bucking politics and answering the call of history. But she held true to her party and voted against the law. She retired shortly thereafter. What a legacy to leave behind![66]

Obama also tried to work with Iowa Senator Chuck Grassley, who had advocated the similar Heritage plan back in the 1990s.

Grassley reportedly told Obama, "If you can't get ten Republicans to stand with me, I can't support this bill."[67]

So despite President Obama's invitation to "Come now, let us reason together," Republicans fought him tooth and nail. And they are now primed to take away health care from millions of people who need it, purely to score political points and foster their vision of small government. Are Republicans following the Old Testament prophets or are they acting like the wicked princes of Israel?

America's Christian leaders need to answer this: Have Republicans come together in the spirit of brotherhood to try to provide Americans with better health care? Does anyone believe that Paul Ryan and Mitch McConnell were working in the spirit of charity or mercy when they vowed to sabotage Obama on day one of his presidency in all that he did? Again, that's not to say that one party has a monopoly on morality, but great things could be achieved if America's evangelical community forced Republicans to work with Democrats and find practical solutions to our health care crisis.

And Republicans, like Mitt Romney and John Kasich, could unite to oppose a change that will harm millions of Americans who cannot afford health insurance. Democrats need to take this message directly to Republicans, whether by appearing on Fox News, speaking at interfaith gatherings, or speaking at evangelical churches. Democrats may not win a lot of votes from these interactions alone, but they can begin to create a dialog that pricks the consciences of evangelicals, just as the prophet Nathan did for King David and Martin Luther King Jr. did for America.

Obamacare Is Consistent with the Bible

Obamacare was a strong, good-faith attempt to "Christianize" the health care industry by not driving the sick out into the cold. The attempt is laudable. Several of the specific provisions of Obamacare would make Jesus smile, because they put the good of the country ahead of large corporate profits, just as Jesus commanded us to serve the four classes of downtrodden people and put His kingdom above the god of Mammon. Any Republican who claims to be "pro-life" and "pro-God" needs to demonstrate how a potential replacement of Obamacare would reflect God's laws. Otherwise, they prove themselves to stand on the side of the wicked princes of Israel.

Obamacare Includes Treatment for Mental Health Needs

The Bible recognizes that mental health is a legitimate issue, and Democrats shouldn't be afraid to explain this in public. It's not as if only Democrats suffer from depression and heartache. More and more science is showing a correlation between happiness and health or, inversely, between depression and physical illness. The Bible reflects this understanding.

> The Lord is **nigh unto them that are of a broken heart**; and saveth such as be of a contrite spirit. (Psalm 34:18 KJV)

> **A merry heart doeth good like a medicine:** but a broken spirit drieth the bones. (Proverbs 17:22 KJV)

> **The spirit of a man will sustain his infirmity**; but a wounded spirit who can bear? (Proverbs 18:14 KJV)

> Why art thou cast down, O my soul? and why art thou disquieted within me? hope thou in **God:** for I shall yet praise him, **who is the health of my countenance**, and my God. (Psalm 42:11 KJV)

> **For they** [God's words] **are life unto those that find them, and health to all their flesh.** Keep thy heart with all diligence; for out of it are the issues of life. (Proverbs 4:22–23)

> **Hope deferred maketh the heart sick**: but when the desire cometh, it is a tree of life. (Proverbs 13:12 KJV)

> The words of the reckless pierce like swords, but **the tongue of the wise brings healing**. (Proverbs 12:18 KJV)

> A merry heart maketh a cheerful countenance: but **by sorrow of the heart the spirit is broken.** (Proverbs 15:13 KJV)

These scriptures acknowledge that mental anguish can be harder to bear than physical infirmity. If your inner spirit is high, you can bear your physical pain, according to the Bible, but when your heart is crushed and you despair, there's nothing to sustain you through life's infirmities. Many studies demonstrate how a positive mental attitude affects recovery. Further, science is also showing that mental disorders are largely biochemical, as well as circumstantial. Some people suffer horrible losses that few can recover from without outside help. The way the brain manufactures certain mood stabilizing hormones varies from person to person, making some more fragile and less able to rebound from life's setbacks and tragedies than others. Someone must serve as a balm in Gilead for them.

Obamacare forced insurance companies to cover mental health and substance abuse treatment in nearly all new insurance plans.[68] Obama tackled mental illness and drug addiction, knowing that it wasn't the easiest of health disorders to sell politically (compared to breast cancer or heart disease). Mental health issues have long been stigmatized as a character failing on the part of the sufferer. Many assume that depression sufferers are just lazy and wallowing in self-pity. People should just "get over it," or "it's their own fault for doing drugs." But Obama took action in an unpopular area to help hardworking Americans when they are literally at their worst. We've seen from Scripture that governments are judged by how they treat their people, and the Bible recognizes depression as a serious cause for concern. So covering mental health under the ACA is consistent with the Bible.

Sadly, Republicans ignored opiate addiction until it became known that white, affluent Americans were dying in unusually high numbers due to addiction to both illegal drugs and prescription painkillers.[69] Regardless, we are glad that they are paying attention to this issue now. As Christians, we can hold leaders accountable on their pledges to help struggling Americans—white or black—who are battling addiction and depression. Taking their Obamacare away won't help, and I can't imagine Jesus would be pleased if we let millions of people suffer alone when we have curative medicines that enable them to take back control of their lives and be productive citizens.

Obamacare Cuts Down on Usury!

One critical piece of economics that the Bible forbids is usury:

"If you lend money to one of my people among you who is needy, **do not treat it like a business deal; charge no interest.**" (Exodus 22:25)

He lends at interest and takes a profit. Will such a man live? He will not! Because he has done all these detestable things, he is to be put to death; his blood will be on his own head. (Ezekiel 18:13)

These are just a few of the many Bible verses that condemn economic exploitation, the topic of a sequel to this book. How can these verses not apply to insurance companies that hit customers with ever skyrocketing premiums? From 1999 to 2009, the Kaiser Family Foundation found that health care premiums had jumped 131%, and the employees' contribution to that system increased by 128%.[70] If that's not usury, then what is? And during this time, insurance companies' profits soared to record levels, as they have even outperformed the entire S&P.[71] Yet many are blaming the Affordable Care Act while insurance companies are reaping massive profits.[72]

Usury is exploitation when you (the lender, the one with the power) take advantage of and exploit someone who's at your mercy. It doesn't just apply to exorbitant interest on loans. It applies to situations where a seller is taking advantage of his product or his monopoly of the market, and he charges unfair rates to "the least of these," who have no direct control over the product. We don't let electric power, gas, or water companies have unbridled rein over the public, because people cannot live without light, heat, and water. These companies can make a good profit, but it's regulated, and their profit is reasonable. Yet a few insurance companies have now gained a near monopoly over health care, without which we cannot live, and they are exploiting the public, as costs and profits rise. And there's no mechanism in place for the private sector to stop this spiral on its own.

The pharmaceutical companies are also engaging in a type of usury. Take the price increases in the Epipen (an epinephrine injector), without which allergic people die after being stung by a bee or accidentally ingesting peanuts. From 2007 to 2016, the cost of the Epipen rose by 461%, and the CEO's salary increased by 671%.[73] If anything, Obamacare did not go far enough, because it permits the individual drug companies to run amok and charge whatever they can get away with. If we don't let the utility companies do this, why do we tolerate it with health care companies, who likewise hold a monopoly on whether we live or die? And power companies are still good investments for stockholders, providing strong capital growth and stable dividends. A curb on their profits is not a communistic takeover of their industry; it's regulated to prevent greed from abusing the common good.

Obamacare sought to tackle only part of this insidious, unethical practice by trying to bring spiraling insurance premiums down. Its effect may have been imperfect, but it helped. If the president of the wealthiest country on earth sees millions of people suffering due to the usurious rates of one industry, would Jesus cast him out for trying to right this wrong? Alternatively, if other "princes of Israel" see this problem and do nothing, would they not get condemnation from Jeremiah and Ezekiel?

Obamacare Curbs Excess Profits

One of the provisions in Obamacare required that 80% of all premiums be spent on actual health care services. They can't go to salaries of bureaucrats or big compensation packages for executives. In 2013, 8.5 million Americans got rebates from their insurance providers, who hadn't been complying with this new rule.[74] In 2014, another 6.4 million people got rebates from the large insurance companies.[75] Anything that cuts down on excess greed is compatible with biblical teachings. "Whoever loves money never has enough; whoever loves wealth is never satisfied with their income" (Ecclesiastes 5:10).

Also, the Affordable Care Act stops insurance companies from revoking coverage for people if they made minor mistakes in their paperwork. Michael Moore's *Sicko* illustrated several instances where hardworking Americans had played by the rules, paid their monthly insurance premiums, but once someone became ill and needed their insurance, the insurance companies looked for details or minor mistakes in paperwork to deny health care coverage at the time where it was literally a matter of life or death.

Obamacare Expands Medicaid for Working People

Many may argue that the Bible teaches, "If you "don't work, you don't eat" as laid out in 2 Thessalonians 3:10. Personal responsibility is a strong principle in the Bible, and liberals are foolish not to incorporate this into their policies. But the sad truth is that many Americans work two and three jobs, 60–80 hours a week, just to get by. Yet often working two or three part-time jobs doesn't qualify them for health insurance because they are not full-time employees with any one employer. That's why the expansion of Medicaid was so critical. Many poor welfare recipients get health care through Medicaid, but if these poor people seek employment, they may earn just enough money to lose their health care coverage, yet they get no coverage through their work. That is a perverse incentive. But Obamacare fixed this by expanding Medicaid. Thus, the working poor who had been just above the federal poverty line were now eligible for health care subsidies. In fact, Obamacare increased Medicaid eligibility up to 138% of the poverty line, giving millions of working Americans the chance to get quality health insurance at a subsidized rate.[76]

So thanks to President Obama, working people can move from welfare to work without fear of losing their health care. Actually, the principal elements of Obamacare support future generations of entrepreneurs. If you had a great idea for a new product or service but you or a family member had a preexisting condition, you weren't going to leave an unhappy job because of your employer-provided coverage. Few would risk their own or their family's health to start a new business. But because of the Affordable Care Act, young entrepreneurs are freer to start their own businesses, knowing that lifesaving insurance will always be available.

Rather than celebrating this achievement, most Republican governors sought to sabotage Medicaid and refused to accept the federal funding, which required that states pay only 10% of the Medicaid expansion after getting the first few years for free. A few governors courageously followed the greater good, and they chose to accept the federal funding for increasing Medicaid under the Affordable Care Act.

One inspiring example was John Kasich, who is by no means a liberal or even a moderate. He is vigorously antiunion and anti-choice on abortion. But following biblical principles, he appealed to people's hearts and asked for Republican leaders to have compassion. "We cannot take health-care coverage from people just for a philosophical reason," Kasich explained.[77] Quite rightly, Kasich referred to his faith in order to prod Ohio's Republican legislature into action. "The most-important thing for this legislature to think about: Put yourself in somebody else's shoes. Put yourself in the shoes of a mother and a father of an adult child that is struggling. Walk in somebody else's moccasins. Understand that poverty is real."

Kasich continued:

I had a conversation with one of the members of the legislature the other day. I said, "I respect the fact that you believe in small government. I do, too. I also know that you're a person of faith. Now, when you die and get to the meeting with St. Peter, he's probably not going to ask you much about what you did about keeping government small. But he is going to ask you what you did for the poor. You better have a good answer."[78]

I may disagree with Kasich on many things, but on this point, he earned my respect. He advocated for compassion for other people, those who have less, and he directly invoked his faith as the justification. Of course, this made him a heretic to the Republican base. He would have been my preferred candidate from the GOP field in 2016 for president.

Kasich wasn't the only one, however, who saw the wisdom in expanding Medicaid. Consider Jan Brewer, likewise no progressive, a leader whom many Latinos view as hostile to their community. She was also famous for wagging her finger at President Obama when he visited Arizona. Yet she stood up to her party and won. In 2013, she told the Republican controlled Arizona legislature that she'd veto every single bill until the Medicaid expansion was approved.[79] Imagine that kind of courage: "I'll veto everything until you adopt a key piece of Obamacare."

Other Republican governors have followed suit, though certainly not the majority. But imagine if Democrats had the "chutzpah" of Jan Brewer or John Kasich. Imagine that they were willing to veto everything until their legislators did right by the working poor. Isn't Jesus smiling on these two governors—at least for this one act of charity and compassion? Jan Brewer could learn a lot from reading the next chapter (biblical commandments on treatment of immigrants), but she was righteous on health care, and she and Kasich demonstrate how Democrats can work with Republicans and evangelicals to advance the greater good.

More Republicans might be willing to do this if more Democrats laid down the biblical foundation to bring evangelicals onto the right side of this issue. If they lobbied the evangelicals the way pharmaceuticals lobby politicians, they could begin to build understanding.

Abolishing Preexisting Condition Denials and Lifetime Limits Is Pro-Life

I am shocked and dismayed that the pro-life movement has been silent on these issues. They have every right to advocate for the unborn and vote for politicians who reflect their beliefs. But they disregard the fact that the Affordable Care Act made it illegal for insurance companies to deny coverage to people with preexisting conditions. This is partly the fault of Democrats for not getting into churches and explaining that this is a vital part of the "pro-life" movement and partly due to the hypocrisy of many Republican elites.

What's pro-life about letting a mother or a father die of cancer because they can't afford treatment? What's pro-life about allowing children to be kicked off their parents' plan, because they have a rare illness and hit their "lifetime limit" at a young age?

This is immoral—outrageous. Yet we Democrats lack the indignation that the right-wingers have around abortion and gay marriage. Shame on us! The Bible says little directly about abortion and gay marriage, yet it says much about helping the poor and the sick. God's commandments in the Bible put laws in place to ensure that the poor and sick received aid. Democrats need to frame this issue in the context of the pro-life movement, not to win votes, but to educate pro-life Christians into supporting health care reform.

Recently in southern Indiana, a Republican businessman running for Congress assailed Obamacare throughout the campaign. But then he met a pastor, a plainspoken white evangelical minister, who had a simple question. This pastor named Kevin had served the Lord for many years—no easy feat, considering that pastors have a higher dropout rate than any other profession, even psychologists. But when Kevin retired, he and his wife lost their health care coverage, which had been provided by their church.

Kevin's wife had a serious heart issue, and before the implementation of the Affordable Care Act, she had been denied coverage due to her preexisting condition. At a town hall with the Republican candidate, Kevin recounted the terror he and his wife experienced after losing their coverage. Here is their dialog:[80]

> "I don't believe government mandates and government monopolies will deliver the best outcome over the long term," said the candidate.
>
> "Right, now my wife is insured," Kevin replied. "Before she wasn't."

"A single instance doesn't mean it's working," the candidate retorted, completely oblivious to the man's suffering or his standing
in the community.

"That's the instance I care about," Kevin retorted.

That shocked the would-be politician and the crowd. I don't
know whether Kevin rallied against universal health care before he
and his wife lost their own health care coverage, but all too often
Republican politicians try to brand the recipients of Obamacare as
"those people," the dreaded others who live "in the inner cities" or
came in "illegally." But that's simply not the case. Millions of
Americans—white, black, and brown—are benefiting from the Affordable Care Act, including white evangelical pastors like Kevin
and his wife.

Many people choose career paths of service that don't provide
stable health insurance and 401(k) retirement plans. Should Kevin
and his wife be punished because they followed God's call to serve,
rather than pursuing a more lucrative career? We need to ask ourselves, would Jesus be pleased if Kevin and his wife lost their health
insurance after years of Christian ministry? Whatever your view of
preachers, most pastors faithfully serve their congregations and
work long hours—often 24/7. Parishioners expect, even demand,
that their pastors always answer their calls, whether the pastor is
eating dinner, on a family outing, or sleeping. Pastors are the first
line of support for people in need—at times of sickness, disaster,
divorce, death, and personal crises.

No doubt many Republicans will wail that there are better
ways to do this. We agree. So please propose one. For six years,
we've been waiting for one concrete plan to improve or replace
Obamacare, but so far there's been not one. No, not one. And
when they were in control of the Congress and the White House,
they created no major health care overhauls. At what point will
Christians ask Republican leaders, "You found money for two giant
tax cuts and wars in Iraq and Afghanistan. Why can't you find
money to help the sick and follow Jesus' commandments?" Remember, Matthew 6:21: "Where your treasure is, there will your

heart be also." If Americans can't find ways to protect Pastor Kevin and his wife or sick children who reach their lifetime limits, then on some level we're accountable to God for not voting for politicians who will work for such a pro-life cause as health care.

Free Preventive Care is Pro-Life

All new insurance policies sold after September 23, 2010, must give free—that's right—FREE preventive services for clients, included in the cost of the monthly premium. That means no co-pays. And there's no deductible to meet before you get the free preventive services. So what is included?

Here are some of the numerous benefits provided for children.

- ✓ Free testing for autism in infants
- ✓ Free vision screenings
- ✓ Free hearing tests for newborns
- ✓ Free screenings for genetic disorders
- ✓ Free blood screenings for children that test for anemia or sickle-cell anemia
- ✓ Iron supplements for children with deficiencies
- ✓ Free lead screenings (to see whether children are suffering from lead poisoning)
- ✓ Free fluoride supplements (for children who need them)
- ✓ Free screening for tuberculosis (This one hits home for me personally, because my grandfather, whom I never met, died of tuberculosis at a young age.)[81]

And most important, the Affordable Care Act provides children with free vaccinations for:

- ✓ Measles, mumps and rubella
- ✓ Tetanus

✓ Flu

✓ Meningitis

✓ Pneumonia[82]

Jesus said, "Let the little children come to me, and do not hinder them, for the kingdom of heaven belongs to such as these" (Matthew 19:14). And Jesus said that if you did not take care of the sick among the least of these, the little children, who are small in stature and powerless to make their voices heard, then you were not of His kingdom.

The religious Right makes protecting the unborn their sole test for choosing a politician, but what about children that are born on this earth with health difficulties? Early childhood development is key to a child's ability to compete later in life as an adult. And how can we say that giving parents free tests to assess their children's special needs is a bad thing?

You can argue economically that we cannot afford it, but you can't argue that it doesn't have a foundation in the Bible. How we treat our children is how we treat Jesus. Just look at how Governor Rick Snyder of Michigan has treated the children of Flint by turning a blind eye, allowing poisonous amounts of lead to go into their drinking water then delaying any remedy for the poisoning his administration caused. He cannot in good conscious call himself a pro-life politician when he put pinching pennies above the lives of children.

A test for lead poisoning or autism may not seem like a big deal—until it's your child at risk, and then it's everything. But imagine if you were struggling to get by, and you couldn't afford these screenings for your child. You might wrongly perceive autism as bad behavior or believe that you had reared an unusually difficult or "bad child." For hearing or visually impaired children, early screenings make all the difference between growing up to have a healthy normal life where they contribute to society (and pay more in taxes) or one where their disability limits and isolates them, or worse—leaving them dependent on the state.

Coverage for Pregnant Women is Pro-Life

Protecting the unborn is a key tenet for Republicans, but what about protecting pregnant women who are carrying the unborn? Before the Affordable Care Act, only 12% of insurance plans covered maternity care, and those that did often had high deductibles, making them ineffective. As of 2012, *all* insurance plans must include maternity care, and it's estimated that nearly 9 million women got access to maternity care due to Obamacare![83] Does that not protect the life of the unborn?

Often preexisting conditions and lifetime limits hit women the hardest. Keep in mind that prior to Obamacare, pregnancy was a preexisting condition, so insurance companies were allowed to charge you more if they thought you might become pregnant soon. Some young women in their twenties (seen as more profitable to insurance companies because they are healthier) could be charged 150% more in premiums than men of the same age simply because they could become pregnant.[84] And new insurance plans allow pregnant women to see an OB-GYN without a referral from a general practitioner,[85] so they no longer need to pay the middleman before seeing the appropriate specialist. So if we want to foster a culture where women choose to have more children, rather than resorting to abortion, how is it inconsistent with Christian principles to ensure that pregnant women have access to good health care?

I wasn't aware of these facts until I began researching the ACA for this book. Insurance coverage policies, by the nature of the industry, are driven by profit and are not necessarily pro-life. Before the ACA, there were no free cancer screenings, no free pregnancy health checkups, no free vaccinations, and no free tests for newborn infants. Yes, some charities provided them for the poor, as well as Planned Parenthood, which Republicans are crusading to destroy. But such individual efforts were not universal and could not serve all. If we claim to protect the unborn, it's the height of hypocrisy not to work toward ensuring that pregnant women get high-quality, affordable health care during pregnancy.

Free Cancer Screenings Are Pro-Life

I have to declare an interest in this, as my mother and I have survived breast cancer. We were fortunate to have access to great care and to have caught it in time. But for many women by the time they notice the lump in their breast, it's too late. So I applaud President Obama and the congressional Democrats who ensured that mammograms and colonoscopies are included in all insurance plans sold after 2010.

One study by the New York Commonwealth Fund found that before the Affordable Care Act, 52% of women delayed preventive checkups due to the costs.[86] When you are busy working and rearing children, trying to make ends meet in between paychecks, setting aside a few hundred dollars for a mammogram doesn't seem like a priority, for your car needs repair, your children get sick, or some other setback strains your budget. Well, not until you find that lump. Until you get the "Big C" diagnosis, you have no idea how important those screenings are. And after you get past your initial reaction of "I'm dying," you do learn to treasure each day above ground. Colonoscopies are even more critical because symptoms do not manifest until it is too late, and at that point, the treatment costs are astronomical, whereas a colonoscopy easily removes precancerous polyps as part of the screening procedure.

Prior to the ACA, a whopping 38% of women who tried to purchase insurance on the individual marketplace were either denied coverage, charged more than men, or given insurance that excluded certain female sicknesses. In 2008, 21 million women and girls didn't have health insurance. Surviving cancer isn't a line item in a balance sheet: it's someone's mother, daughter, or sister. It was morally wrong to throw cancer survivors to the mercies of the for-profit insurance industry.

Additional Preventive Services for All Adults

The Affordable Care Act also includes provisions for all adults, including:

- ✓ Free screenings for colorectal cancer
- ✓ Free tests for blood pressure
- ✓ Free tests for cholesterol
- ✓ Free screenings for lung cancer and advice for smokers on quitting smoking
- ✓ Depression screening
- ✓ Diet counseling
- ✓ Free flu shots and vaccinations (which may not have been administered as a child)[87]

The top three cancers in men are prostate cancer, lung cancer, and bowel cancer.[88] Obamacare covers screenings for all of them. Benjamin Franklin popularized the phrase "an ounce of prevention is worth a pound of cure," and Obamacare takes affirmative steps to help people get insurance and treatment early, before these top health risks kill them or drain their pocketbooks. Treatment of any cancer in stage one or stage two is much cheaper than treatment at stage four.

Sadly, despite these awesome benefits, this is one of the least discussed aspects of the Affordable Care Act. As of 2014, only 43% of the population knew that these free preventive treatments were covered thanks to Obamacare.[89] Democrats and faith leaders need to do more to highlight this. It's good politics, and it's pro-life. Getting people screened early will inevitably save lives and costs for us all.

Christian Leaders around the World Endorse Universal Health Care

There are many issues in politics about which reasonable minds may differ. Yet any Christian who is committed to aligning politics with biblical values must favor some way of making health care affordable and accessible for all Americans, for that's what Jesus would want. If you are a Christian and want to get into God's kingdom, ensuring that your less fortunate compatriots get access to adequate, affordable health care is a commandment. In fact, one could argue that world leaders have a duty to ensure that all people everywhere gain access to medical treatment, since we are all God's children, and all are precious in His sight.

Oddly, it is mainly American white evangelicals who perpetrate the myth that Jesus opposes universal health care. Nearly every other major religious institution in the world endorses universal health care as a key way to mirror God's vision for the world, helping God's will to be done on earth as it is in heaven.

Pope Benedict, the far more conservative pope who preceded Pope Francis, said that health care is an "inalienable right." He asserted that it was the duty of nations to guarantee access to health care for all of their citizens.[90] Pope Francis, a hero to liberals, echoed this sentiment:

> Health is not a consumer good but a universal right, so access to health services cannot be a privilege.... Health care, especially at the most basic level, is indeed denied in many parts of the world and many regions of Africa.... Access to health care services, treatment and medicines remains a mirage. The poorest are unable to pay and are excluded from hospital services, even the most essential primary care."[91]

If health care is not a consumer good, then health care cannot be left to the private marketplace where people can be denied coverage. Whether it's the Catholic Pope of Rome, the Archbishop of Canterbury in England, the head of the Lutheran church in Germany, or the patriarch of the Greek Orthodox Church, major

Christian leaders across the world have embraced the notion of universal health care as an essential part of their faith. Evangelicals may reject their theology, but their commitment to their faith can't be questioned. Also, Jewish scholars believe that the Hebrew Bible mandates universal health care.[92] So Protestant ministers would do well to reexamine whether all of these faith leaders are wrong about such a critical issue, particularly when the health care outcomes are better in other countries. Is there really no merit in how these other religious leaders tie their faith to government policy? Should evangelical Protestant pastors question whether they have unknowingly abandoned the sick in favor of their personal freedom and profits for wealthy insurance companies? The Bible teaches us to bear one another's burdens in order to fulfill the law of Christ (Galatians 6:2). That definitely impinges on my personal freedom.

From my experience, Southern white evangelicals who decry "socialized medicine" are of the same ilk as those who denounced the civil rights movement and claimed that John F. Kennedy would be a puppet of Rome. Many evangelical leaders of the South loudly claimed that the Bible approved of slavery and Jim Crow. So on the whole, their record in America shows that they've often lagged behind the curve on major issues when it comes to respecting life. And as Dr. Martin Luther King demonstrated, the way to move them is to appeal to their religious hearts. One of my close friends notes that Dr. King "shamed them in the name of Jesus." And just as he did it with regards to segregation, so we too should call them out on health care.

Democrats shouldn't be afraid to quote the pope in their speeches and their messaging. Republicans have no qualms about noting the pope's pro-life stance on abortion, yet they ignore his stand on universal health care. It doesn't work like that, but they do it anyway. You don't get a pro-life pass by saying, "Since I support anti-abortion judges, I get to disregard all the explicit commands of Jesus." Let's find common ground on providing health care for all because that's what Jesus wants.

Some Republicans may say, "Well, I'm not Catholic, and the pope is wrong on this issue." Regardless of our denomination, we must admit that the pope is a man who has studied the Bible for decades and his opinion on religion and universal health care deserves careful consideration. Moreover, Democrats can use the pope's words to expose the hypocrisy of Catholic Republicans who run for office but refuse to accept the pope's vision of justice— Newt Gingrich, Rick Santorum, Marco Rubio, and Paul Ryan, to name a few.

Pastors and faith leaders among evangelicals have become politicized over abortion at the cost of the broader range of pro-life issues that are explicitly laid out in the Bible. After all, if the prophets in the Old Testament spoke up for the sick, the poor, the immigrant, and the oppressed, not to mention Jesus, should not modern Bible preachers do the same? As pastors go silent on other social issues, I hope this book will help more pastors muster enough courage to say, "*Jesus loves Obamacare; this I know: for the Bible tells me so!*" We've given you the scriptures to prove it, so let's urge our faith leaders to heed God's call and take a stand to preserve the key pro-life elements of Obamacare.

Regardless, Democrats and progressives who hail from religious upbringings need to harness our knowledge of the Bible and channel our collective passions toward just causes. As this book has already demonstrated, God put an affirmative duty on governments to take care of the poor and the sick. God didn't bless tax cuts for the rich in the hopes that they would trickle down. He commanded His prophets to take action to reform an unjust economic system. And all who want a compassionate society need to master the right Bible verses and stories to drive this narrative home with evangelical Christians.

4

Jesus Loves Illegal Aliens

I was a stranger, and ye took me not in. (Matthew 25:43)

I grew up exposed to people from different countries and assorted ethnic backgrounds—though all were Christians. As I mentioned earlier, a young lady from Mexico stayed at our home extensively from the time I was one till I was three or four. She even kept us on a few rare occasions when my parents went out of town. She was (and is) an extremely loving person and an amazing storyteller. Later, during summer breaks from school, my mom began doing missionary work in Mexico, and she took us with her. We loved the culture and the food, which we thought was terrific.

When I was in the second grade, my mom, who was "given to hospitality" as the Scripture commands, hosted a Christian bishop from India. He wore a big white turban, which looked like what Sikhs wear today. At one time the turban might have been a class symbol, but I never knew or don't recall the reason for our guest's turban. He may have been a converted Sikh and merely continued his tradition. (Sikhs, by the way, are often confused with Muslims, which they are not. The Sikh religion is inclusive and preaches love for all.) We just accepted his attire as part of his culture. The great thing for me was that he taught my mom how to make a tasty, spicy hot chicken curry, which became a favorite treat. Keep in mind, this was in the 1950s before Indian food was even known or as easy to find as it is today.

At another time, a man in Mexico, who was half Chinese and half Mexican, taught my mom how to make a delicious "Chinese fish"—a dish with spices, tomatoes, celery and rice, another family staple. Consequently, we grew up believing that other countries were amazing and had much to offer. One of my mother's greatest frustrations was that when she took American friends with her on mission trips, within three days they were whining to go find an American hamburger. We had little sympathy for such attitudes in the face of such tasty food available abroad, and we sensed that their complaining came from ethnic bias.

All of us are greatly influenced by our personal experiences. They become filters through which we see the world and categorize people. So if you think I'm too softhearted on immigrants, you can blame my missionary minded mother.

Most Americans know that we are a nation of immigrants. Every group of immigrants to this country—after our initial intrusion upon the "Indians"—has been met with hostility, resentment, and even persecution. The 19th-century rhetoric against Italians, Irish, Jews, and Poles sounds like what we heard during the 2016 campaign about the Mexicans and Muslims.[93] There were several movements by nativists, nationalists, and the "know-nothings" that fostered hateful rhetoric that lives on today. The Ku Klux Klan, which promoted itself as a "Christian" organization, hated all these groups—because they were non-Protestant and/or had darker skin.[94] The KKK's empowerment with Trump's election scares me.

When I first started investigating this subject, I had no idea that so many Bible passages emphasized protection for strangers (aka foreigners, immigrants) in the land. In the King James Version, the term *stranger* referred to people who originated in another country but who now lived in Israel—the native land that was the focal point of the people in their story, just as America is the focal point of our story. The Bible lays out quite clearly and convincingly how they should be treated. God loves them; Jesus loves them, and followers of Jesus are commanded to love them, as were the ancient Hebrews. Consequently, those who want to bring God back into our politics must square how Trump's rhetoric on building a wall and labeling immigrants as rapists and terrorists is consistent with Scripture.

Some may assume that KJV scriptures regarding strangers refer to people who are just visiting or are fellow citizens whom we have not yet met—for instance, the man two blocks away is a stranger to me. But this is not the case. The Hebrew word for *stranger* means a foreigner or an alien. In fact, whereas the King James Version repeatedly uses the word *stranger*, the New International Version consistently translates the term as *foreigner*, and you will see both versions in this book. They both refer to immigrants. The Bible often uses the term sojourner to describe foreign people who were merely passing through, like merchants traveling in a camel train. The Bible, of course, required the Israelites to be good to the sojourners as well. But from the Hebrew meaning of the word, the historical context, and the direct phrases in the Bible, the strangers were not fellow citizens that Hebrews had not yet met. They were foreigners, what we would term illegal aliens, undocumented workers, or immigrants.

So loving the stranger was far more than hosting one individual in need of a place to crash for a few nights or giving someone a hot meal. Strangers were different from the Israelites in their race, culture, and religion, but they had come to reside long term (permanently) in Israel. These strangers hadn't been invited to come to Israel; they didn't have passports, and they weren't necessarily sponsored by rich Israelites. They merely showed up and needed help, so by today's language they were "illegal aliens." I use the term "illegal aliens" in this chapter not to dehumanize or belittle undocumented immigrants, but to highlight the potential hypocrisy of those who would cry, "Lord, Lord," who claim to want our national policies to follow the Bible but have used cruel, unflattering language to describe another group of people, many of whom are our brothers and sisters in Christ—and all of whom are God's children.

The Bible doesn't discuss boundary lines, nor does it deal with regulations regarding who can move in or out of the country. In Bible days, people freely moved from place to place. Bible stories show how drought and famine forced people to migrate from one country to another, and it shows that countries with resources took in those who came seeking shelter:

> Abraham had moved to Egypt during a famine (Genesis 12).
>
> Isaac moved from Canaan to Gerar, where Abimelech, king of the Philistines, took him in (Genesis 26).
>
> Jacob and his family moved to Egypt where his son Joseph, Pharaoh's second in command, had stored up food (Genesis 42).
>
> And one of the most beautiful love stories in the Bible showed how Ruth, a Moabite, a foreigner, immigrated to Israel after her husband died. She was accepted and became part of the lineage of King David, which the Bible traces directly to Jesus. That alone makes a profound statement about immigrants.

Of course, when immigrant strangers entered the land, they had to abide by Jewish laws, but they were to be treated with dignity and compassion. The Torah, dictated to Moses by God Himself, required the ancient Hebrews to treat the stranger as one of their own. This was a law that applied to the entire nation—a government mandate, not a mere admonition that one could choose to ignore.

I myself am not sure how we apply these principles today given the realities of globalization, but my loyalty to biblical principles calls me to propose a way of including those who live among us. We cannot harass, vex, or drive them out, if we want to claim any connection with Bible principles. Many Christians have used their faith to advocate for comprehensive immigration reform, but prior to writing this book, I thought that was liberal overreach. The Old Testament, in particular, is clear about how immigrants should be treated.

Old Testament Commands

Most of my life, I shied away from some books of the Old Testament because some prohibitions are hard to fathom, and certain punishments are draconian to the modern mind. Scholars understand that the revelation of enlightenment evolves over time, and certain prohibitions may have been useful in ancient cultures living under primitive conditions and threatened with extinction. We are tempted to assume that primitive cultures were more violent and warlike, though nothing in Bible times rivals the sheer death and horror perpetrated in the last hundred-plus years with two world wars and other acts of genocide, given our modern weapons of mass destruction. So I was determined to give the Old Testament a second look with an open mind.[95]

Certain prohibitions arose for health reasons, like not eating pork and shellfish. Today, we understand that ancient people had few options for preservation, and carnivorous animals were more likely to be infected with parasitic diseases, such as trichinosis. The same with shellfish, which are bottom-feeding scavengers. But few Christians today, if any, would advocate closing all Red Lobster restaurants. So even evangelicals don't really believe the Bible literally, as they reinterpret hard passages and then cherry-pick certain verses to take literally.

Yet when I finished my review of the subject of how to treat immigrants, I was grateful for my Bible-believing heritage. Throughout the Old Testament, and in the midst of some extremely strict laws, was a recurring admonition to accept immigrants into one's country and to treat them with respect, fairness, and dignity. The Bible also gave a strong prohibition against vexing and oppressing immigrants. Now, try selling that to the Trump camp.

Even as a Democrat, I find myself resisting the Lord's commandments on how we treat the stranger because God required us to love them all. It's hard to welcome people who don't look and act like us or share our culture. Personally, I think we need reasonable border controls to stop would-be terrorists from attacking this country, and we also need to take action to discourage the influx of undocumented workers, which actually slowed to a near stop under President Obama—despite the terrifying fake "news" that millions are sneaking across our borders. And of course, any savvy would-be terrorist would know to enter through Canada, not Mexico. But that's me speaking as a reasonable attorney, not as a Christian ethicist. The Bible's policies on dealing with immigrants and refugees make me squirm. If I didn't know these rules came from the Bible, I'd swear they were radical left-wing rubbish. But maybe having divine Word challenge my comfort zones is a good thing. Our highest moral standards should cause us to question our selfish motives. The Bible calls me to examine my own moral development, and it forces me to consider how we can make our immigration system more humane, for I freely admit that I don't know how to square up perfectly the Bible's commands with the realities of modern life.

> But the stranger that dwelleth with you shall be unto you as one born among you, and thou shalt love him as thyself; for ye were strangers in the land of Egypt: I am the LORD your God. (Leviticus 19:34 KJV)[96]

Ouch! How can we not analogize that to America today? All Americans in this country (or their ancestors) were first strangers here—except for the Native Americans. It is ironic that we are so anti-immigrant after we ourselves were immigrants who pushed out and decimated the indigenous peoples of this land. Maybe that's why we fear Mexicans' doing that to us, for we subconsciously know that what goes around comes around.

Direct Taxation to Benefit Immigrants

Although we covered the following passages in detail in Chapter Two, Debunking the Myth That the Bible Only Endorses Small Government, it bears repeating that the Bible required ancient Hebrews to pay a percentage of their crops towards the poor and the immigrant.

Deuteronomy 14:28-29 and 26: 8-13 outline a special tithe taken every three years that was collected and stored in towns for the immigrant and the poor

Leviticus 19:9-10 and 23:22 forbade farmers from harvesting the corners of their fields, which were left for the poor and immigrant to harvest.

Deuteronomy 24: 19-21 prohibited landowners from passing through their fields a second or third time to glean crops that hadn't yet ripened. These too were left for the poor and the immigrant.

Nevertheless, as this book shows, the Bible is 100% crystal clear on this point. God commanded the Jews to remember how they had been aliens in another country and not to mistreat the aliens who now stood in a similarly precarious position. So they were commanded to forego a percentage of their wealth for the poor and the foreigner and to remember how they had been persecuted in times gone by. Remember, this part of the Torah was national law.

Not to Oppress the Stranger

The Jews were commanded *not* to vex or oppress the stranger. It wasn't enough to leave crops for them each year as we saw in Chapter Two regarding government; you had to be nice to them. Please bear with me as I repeat these verses both in the KJV and the NIV—lest anyone think I'm changing principles by switching versions.

Thou shalt neither vex a stranger, nor oppress him: for ye were strangers in the land of Egypt. (Exodus 22:21 KJV)

Do not mistreat or oppress a foreigner, for you were foreigners in Egypt. (Exodus 22:21 NIV)

The word *vex* in the Hebrew means to rage or be violent, to suppress, to maltreat, to destroy, or **to thrust out by oppression**. There's no danger of one-verse theology here.

Also **thou shalt not oppress a stranger**: for ye know the heart of a stranger, seeing ye were strangers in the land of Egypt. (Exodus 23:9 KJV)

Do not oppress a foreigner; you yourselves know how it feels to be foreigners, because you were foreigners in Egypt. (Exodus 23:9 NIV)

Thou shalt not oppress an hired servant that is poor and needy, whether he be of thy brethren, or **of thy strangers** that are in thy land within thy gates. (Deuteronomy 24:14 KJV)

Do not take advantage of a hired worker who is poor and needy, whether that worker is a fellow Israelite or **a foreigner** residing in one of your towns. (Deuteronomy 24:14 NIV)

Since the message is clear—you could not thrust out the stranger from your midst—this surely indicts our national call to drive 11 million strangers from America, strangers who have picked our fruit, tended our children, and done jobs that we American don't want to perform or that we refuse to perform at the low wages we pay them. Even if evangelical Christians don't take the Bible literally, the Bible verses commanding God's people to be good to immigrants are so numerous that we should feel ashamed when our politicians stoke racial resentment and bigotry for political gain. Progressives have strong biblical authority to call out politicians who claim to revere their faith yet demonize immigrants. Both Republicans and Democrats have done this over the decades. And even if we need to tighten our immigration laws to protect our nation, our leaders must do so in a way that does not vex immigrants or encourage citizens to act violently toward them.

God's Commands to Love the Stranger

Alas, it wasn't enough just to be fair, to feed them, to pay tithes for them, and not to mistreat them; you had to love those pesky intruders.

For the LORD your God is God of gods, and Lord of lords, a great God, a mighty, and a terrible, which regardeth not persons, nor taketh reward: He doth execute the judgment of the fatherless and widow, **and loveth the stranger, in giving him food and raiment. Love ye therefore the stranger:** for ye were strangers in the land of Egypt. (Deuteronomy 10:17–19 KJV)

And if **a stranger** sojourn with thee in your land, ye **shall not vex him**. But the stranger that dwelleth with you shall be unto you as one born among you, and **thou shalt love him as thyself**; for ye were strangers in the land of Egypt: I am the Lord your God. (Leviticus 19:33–34 KJV)

Loving someone in your heart is a very different thing from paying taxes grudgingly. You can pay your taxes (or your tithes of harvested crops) but still resent the stranger in your heart. But the Old Testament, usually known for its harsher "eye for an eye" positions, commands God's people to love immigrants. How can we claim to be followers of Jesus if we allow our politicians to get away with demonizing those whom God commands us to love? Even if we don't support immigration reform as it's laid out presently, we must urge our leaders to remain openhearted.

Who would dare argue that calling all or most immigrants rapists, criminals, and drug smugglers represents Judeo-Christian compassion—not to mention that such words are vicious slander? What do we say to Trump supporters who vex foreigners and citizens of a different race or faith? The Southern Poverty Law Center recorded 867 hate incidents in the ten days after Trump was elected.[97] Where is the voice of the evangelical Right, calling on their fellow Trump supporters to stop violating God's laws?

This vile hatred became painfully evident in 2016 in Louisville at Christmas time when an older white lady at the J.C. Penney store in the Jefferson Mall viciously accosted a younger Latina customer already in line ahead of her. When the Latina's friend brought her an additional product (not holding up the line, not cutting in line but adding to her items), the older white lady started cursing her, accusing her of being on welfare and buying her goods with taxpayer dollars, and she ordered her to go back to where she belonged.[98] The Latina patiently turned the other cheek, as she did not address the hateful woman. I felt sad that no other customers spoke up to make the older woman stop her invectives, not even the clerk. Most likely, everyone was so stunned that they were frozen in shock. At least, another customer captured the incident on her cell phone. As I look for a silver lining, I keep hoping that Trump's election will help us cure a hidden cyst in our national consciousness by bringing the poisonous boil to the surface so it can be seen, lanced, and drained.

Adopting Strangers into the Faith – A Precursor to Immigration Reform?

> The Lord said to Moses and Aaron, "These are the regulations for the Passover meal: No foreigner may eat it. Any slave you have bought may eat it after you have circumcised him, but a temporary resident or a hired worker may not eat it. It must be eaten inside the house; take none of the meat outside the house. Do not break any of the bones. The whole community of Israel must celebrate it. **A foreigner residing among you who wants to celebrate the Lord's Passover must have all the males in his household circumcised; then he may take part like one born in the land.** No uncircumcised male may eat it." (Exodus 12:43–48)

Strangers who resided with the Israelites could keep the Passover if they were circumcised, which signified their acceptance of God's covenant with Israel. So the nation of Israel did in fact have an early form of a pathway to citizenship, if you please. We can argue about whether it should be adopted in present-day America, but it is in the Bible, and we cannot pretend that it is not.

When the prophets envisioned Israel's restoration after their captivity in Babylon, they included the stranger who would be welcomed and become their friends.

> For the Lord will have mercy on Jacob, and will yet choose Israel, and set them in their own land: and **the strangers shall be joined with them, and they shall cleave to the house of Jacob.** (Isaiah 14:1 KJV)

The NIV's poetic phrasing is worth repeating:

> The Lord will have compassion on Jacob; once again he will choose Israel and will settle them in their own land. **Foreigners will join them and unite with the descendants of Jacob.** (Isaiah 14:1)

We can't be united if one group is second-class in legal rights to another. Isaiah continues his vision of a more perfect age when the stranger who believes in God is to receive an inheritance with the native-born Israelite. This is a profound passage that shows God's vision to include all the outcasts of the nation. Since from the outset land was distributed only to eleven of the twelve tribes of Israel and could never be permanently alienated, only leased for forty-nine years, this prophecy is all the more radical.

> Thus saith the Lord, Keep ye judgment, and do justice: for my salvation is near to come, and my righteousness to be revealed. Blessed is the man that doeth this, and the son of man that layeth hold on it; that keepeth the sabbath from polluting it, and keepeth his hand from doing any evil. **Neither let the son of the stranger, that hath joined himself to the Lord**, speak, saying, The Lord hath utterly separated me from his people: ... **Also the sons of the stranger, that join themselves to the Lord, to serve him, and to love the name of the Lord, to be his servants**, every one that keepeth the sabbath from polluting it, and taketh hold of my covenant; **Even them will I bring to my holy mountain, and make them joyful in my house of prayer:** their burnt offerings and their sacrifices shall be accepted upon mine altar; **for mine house shall be called an house of prayer for all people.** The Lord God, which gathereth the outcasts of Israel saith, Yet will I gather others to him, beside those that are gathered unto him. (Isaiah 56:3,6–8 KJV)

Like Isaiah, the prophet Ezekiel prophesied that God showed him a vision where in a more perfect age, the strangers would be treated equally with the Israelites, and when the Messiah returned, the strangers would also get an inheritance in God's kingdom. This is remarkable because the original Judaic law limited land ownership to those born to the tribes of Israel. Some commentators see this as a prophecy of the Gentiles' receiving the gospel of Jesus centuries later, and the passage is susceptible to that interpretation. The interesting thing is that in the stories of the prophets, we see godly people expanding their vision of God, redemption, salvation, and blessings outside their own tribal limits.

> "You are to allot it as an inheritance for yourselves and for the foreigners residing among you and who have children. You are to

consider them as native-born Israelites; along with you they are to be allotted an inheritance among the tribes of Israel. In whatever tribe a foreigner resides, there you are to give them their inheritance," declares the Sovereign Lord. (Ezekiel 47:22–23)

In fairness, many evangelical Christians do interpret this passage as a call for immigration reform and giving undocumented workers the chance to emerge from the shadows to gain legal status, especially Hispanics. When you walk with people through their difficulties, your view of the world changes. Ezekiel's vision promotes the notion of a more perfect earthly kingdom, and he sets forth an ideal. Although it is a vision, its express purpose was to cause the leaders of his day to reflect on their behavior and change their ways. The message is clear: in a vision of a godly society, the stranger (i.e., "illegal aliens") are accepted and blessed. One can reasonably analogize the American dream to the inheritance that Ezekiel envisioned.

Regardless, there is biblical support that our own undocumented immigrants, who have been here, working and paying taxes and otherwise obeying the law, deserve a chance. The law always balances good and bad in proportion to each other. Yes, the undocumented worker broke the law by overstaying his visa, but his history of good behavior and contribution to the country must be weighed when we decide what penalty is appropriate for his original violation. Justice always requires us to look at the totality of circumstances.

One System of Justice for Natives and Strangers

Hebraic law required one system of justice both for the native-born and for the stranger. The standards of justice and the laws applied to both groups equally.

"The same law applies both to the native-born and to the foreigner residing among you." All the Israelites did just what the Lord had commanded Moses and Aaron. And on that very day the Lord brought the Israelites out of Egypt by their divisions. (Exodus 12:49–51)

Ye shall have one manner of law, as well for the stranger, as for one of your own country, for I am the LORD your God. (Leviticus 24:22 KJV)

A foreigner residing among you is also to celebrate the Lord's Passover in accordance with its rules and regulations. **You must have the same regulations for both the foreigner and the native-born.** (Numbers 9:14)

One must ponder why the scriptures kept repeating the command to treat the stranger fairly and to prohibit his persecution. It must have been because the leaders knew that people resist it. Human nature is wired to be tribal. We not only prefer those who agree with our faith, values, and customs—and those who look like us, but we also hold those outsiders to a different standard from our insiders. We always want to treat those in our group better than those "other people." This is human nature, but God calls us to do better than what seems easy in the moment.

Despite its harshness in some areas, Old Testament law made exceptions and created avenues for mercy. The law established six cities of refuge where those guilty of manslaughter (accidentally or unintentionally killing someone) could claim asylum and be protected against blood vengeance (an eye for an eye), which was permissible under Old Testament law. The perpetrator of the accidental killing was then assured of a fair trial, and if he were found innocent, i.e., to have unintentionally killed, he could live out his days in the city of refuge.

These six cities shall be a refuge, **both for the children of Israel, and for the stranger,** and for the sojourner among them: that every one that killeth any person unawares may flee thither. (Numbers 35:15 KJV)

The cities of refuge had to give asylum to both the stranger and the native-born, and there was due process for the individual to present his cause. These refuge cities could be compared to sanctuary cities. Again, there was no enforceable immigration law at the time, so the metaphor isn't as solid as the others in this chapter, but Christians could certainly argue that the spirit of the law suggests that God is fine with sanctuary cities.[99]

So the Bible included some protections for undocumented workers. The law of the Sabbath year of rest applied both to the native-born and to the immigrant.

> And **the sabbath of the land** shall be meat for you; for thee, and for thy servant, and for thy maid, and for thy hired servant, and **for thy stranger** that sojourneth with thee. (Leviticus 25:6 KJV)

Likewise, the Day of Atonement included the stranger.

> And this shall be a statute for ever unto you: that in the seventh month, on the tenth day of the month, ye shall afflict your souls, and **do no work at all, whether it be one of your own country, or a stranger** that sojourneth among you: For on that day shall the priest make an atonement for you, to cleanse you, that ye may be clean from all your sins before the Lord. (Leviticus 16:29–30 KJV)

The Bible went out of its way to make sure that everyone understood that one system of law applied equally to both groups. So shouldn't laws regarding the minimum wage and safe working conditions also apply to immigrants? Often, we turn our backs on the suffering of these people who are exploited by unscrupulous business owners. "They chose to be here, so they can tough it out." That may be the easy way to size up the situation, but it is not the Christian way.

Inherent in the above scriptures is the requirement that strangers obey Israel's laws. The Bible commands the strangers to obey the law, just as the Hebrews did, and prohibitions against conduct considered abominable applied to both groups.

> But **you must keep my decrees** and my laws. **The native-born and the foreigners residing among you** must not do any of these detestable things, for all these things were done by the people who lived in the land before you, and the land became defiled. (Leviticus 18:26–27)

In Leviticus 24:16 the stranger got the same punishment (hence the same administration of justice) that was given to those born in the land—in this case, death for blasphemy of the name of the Lord. Remember, Old Testament government was a theocracy. There were other provisions that required foreigners to conform to Hebraic law, but they don't change the propositions here. We would be doing the progressive cause a disservice if we said that all immigrants could come to our country illegally with no consequence. Strangers were required to obey the law, just as the Hebrews were. And the Bible condemned strangers who came into Israel to harm it.

> Your country is desolate, your cities are burned with fire: your land, strangers devour it in your presence, and it is desolate, as overthrown by strangers. (Isaiah 1:7 KJV)

That's not to say that the Bible never posed any restrictions on immigrants. A stranger could not be a king of Israel (Deuteronomy 17:14–20), just as today the US Constitution does not allow foreign-born citizens to be president but rather required one to be native-born. Yet Hebraic law required people to treat immigrants fairly and prohibited oppression.

The God of the Old Testament promised to look out for the stranger, the foreign immigrant.

> **The LORD preserveth the strangers**; he relieveth the fatherless and widow: but the way of the wicked he turneth upside down. (Psalm 146:9 KJV)

Even if we as a nation do nothing on immigration reform, we should hold our own "princes of Israel" to account for rhetoric that demonizes immigrants and prompts other people to oppress and vex them. We cannot claim to be followers of Jesus and look the other way when this hate emanates so blatantly.

We can both advocate for immigration reform and strongly protect the nation's security. President Obama once said that if Republicans doubted his commitment to punishing terrorists, they should "ask Osama bin Laden." We all can and should remain vigilant to prevent and overcome terrorism, but we can't be heartless toward immigrants if we authentically follow the Bible. Politicians can achieve a balance and stay true to the spirit of God's law while protecting the American people.

New Testament Affirmations for Loving and Providing for the Immigrant

The previous Old Testament scriptures give context to Jesus' words. It is undisputed that much of the New Testament repeats ideas from the Old, and Jesus said that He came to fulfill the law, not to do away with it. In Matthew 25 when He commanded His followers to provide for the immigrant, as well as the poor, the sick, and the prisoner, Jesus was reiterating Mosaic Law. Jesus, of course, went further and showed how the stranger could be more righteous in deed and in spirit than the native-born.

Jesus' Healing a Stranger and Nine Native-Born Lepers

As he was going into a village, ten men who had leprosy met him. They stood at a distance and called out in a loud voice, "Jesus, Master, have pity on us!" When he saw them, he said, "Go, show yourselves to the priests." And as they went, they were cleansed. One of them, when he saw he was healed, came back, praising God in a loud voice. He threw himself at Jesus' feet and thanked him—**and he was a Samaritan**. Jesus asked, "Were not all ten cleansed? Where are the other nine? **Has no one returned to give praise to God except this foreigner?**" Then he said to him, "Rise and go; your faith has made you well."(Luke 17:12–19)

Notice how the foreigner, the *stranger* as the term is consistently used in the KJV, was the only one of the ten healed lepers who returned to say thank you. Again, in ancient societies, people reacted to lepers as they first did in the 1980s with AIDS victims. There was so much fear of contagion that these people were quarantined and forbidden access to normal social commerce. Today, however, we know that 95 percent of those with leprosy, now called Hansen's disease, are not actually contagious. Nevertheless, in this story we see Jesus taking up for the social pariahs and by example encouraging us to do the same.

It was no coincidence that the gospel writer pointed out that only the stranger (the foreign Samaritan) returned to express gratitude for his healing. It would appear that the native-born who received the same blessing didn't bother to say thank you for such a monumental transformation. Jesus places a mirror up to our own national psyche and asks us to examine whether or not we've been grateful for the blessings we've received.

The Good Samaritan—a Stranger Helping a Stranger

Luke 10 tells the story of the Good Samaritan, which is now synonymous with a good person helping others. Jesus told this story in response to the question of what one must do to inherit eternal life. Jesus said, "Thou shalt love the Lord thy God with all thy heart, and with all thy soul, and with all thy strength, and with all thy mind; and thy neighbour as thyself" (Luke 10:27 KJV).

The next question was, "Well, who is our neighbor?" Jesus' answer in Luke 10:30-37 asserts that the stranger (the foreigner) is our neighbor. Most readers know the basics of how the Good Samaritan passed by an injured man on the road, a man who was the victim of a brutal robbery. But we may not know that at the time of Jesus' parable, the Samaritans were despised and labeled as foreigners. To call someone a Samaritan was an insult. For instance, "The Jews said to Jesus, 'Do we not say rightly that you are a Samaritan and have a demon?'" (John 8:48 NKJV). Samaritans, like our immigrants of today, were associated with disgusting evil.

Those who doubted Jesus cast aspersions on his birthplace, bloodline, and theology. The "birthers" were alive and well back then. The Samaritans lived in the northern kingdom of Israel (after the nation of Israel split in two following the death of Solomon). They were a racially mixed society with Jewish and pagan ancestry. Although they worshipped Yahweh (Jehovah), their religion was considered heretical because they veered from mainstream Judaism and accepted only the first five books of the Bible (the Torah). Because of their mongrel bloodline and their doctrinal differences, they were so despised that the Jews would travel far out of their way not to step foot in their territory. Hence, Jesus' visit to Samaria and granting salvation to a Samaritan woman were all the more radical—and His story here, all the more unsettling to the national psyche.[100]

What did the Good Samaritan in Jesus' parable do? He clothed the injured man. He ministered to his wounds. He gave him transportation, food, and lodging until he could stand on his own. Jesus pointed out that the highly esteemed religious leaders, a Levite and a priest, passed by the injured stranger, being too busy or too high and mighty to dirty their hands in the matter. And they were following their religious rules that forbade leaders from defiling themselves before going to the temple. Yet the man who loved his neighbor as himself was the despised foreigner. Yes, Jesus commanded individuals to open their hearts to engage in specific instances of charity, but He said nothing about repealing the laws of the Old Testament that enshrined charity to the strangers in the nation's statutes. And He was making a subversive statement that love trumps even divinely ordained religious laws, since He made a subtle criticism of the revered clergy of His day, who were obeying the legal prohibitions not to defile themselves by touching blood or dead beings before going to worship God in the temple. Caring for the injured was more important than going to church and keeping pure and holy.

Jesus showed the pious Pharisees how a "mulatto foreign heretic" can engage in charity to fulfill the great commandment: to show your love of God by loving your neighbor as yourself, and He showed that your neighbor included anyone you passed—not just the neighbor who lives next door. And He gave this example to answer the question of how we attain eternal life. When we know the history of the Samaritans, we can unmask Republican attacks on Obama—and the racist, "birther" invectives hurled at his heritage or his lead to improve health care. It's just a repeat of the hypocrites of Jesus' day.

Christians Commanded Not to Discriminate against Other Christians as Foreigners

Christians are to treat themselves as one and all humans as God's children. We are not to make citizenship distinctions. The story of the apostles shows the gradual expansion of the good news of the gospel to groups previously disdained. Their outreach ministry began with the Samaritans—those despised foreigners. In Acts 8, Philip traveled to a city of Samaria to preach the gospel. Later, Peter and John joined him there, and many villages throughout Samaria heard and believed the gospel. After that, the gospel spread to Gentiles in other lands. The apostle Paul was jailed and beaten because he dared assert that Jesus' love included the foreigners as well as the native-born (see Acts 22:21–24). Alas, the idea of recognizing all humans as part of God's family is as radical today as it was two thousand years ago.

Early on, even the original followers of Jesus who were Jews resented letting these strangers into their fold on equal footing with the native-born, for these Gentiles were uncircumcised and did not follow the observances of the Torah. Acts 11 tells how the Jewish Christians "contended" with Peter over allowing the uncircumcised Gentiles to receive the Word of God. After Peter testified to them of God's vision for all, "they held their peace, and glorified God, saying, Then hath God also to the Gentiles granted repentance unto life" (Acts 11:18 KJV).

The battle to include the strangers, the foreigners, was not won overnight. It continued throughout Peter's and Paul's ministries:

> After much discussion, Peter got up and addressed them: "Brothers, you know that some time ago **God made a choice among you that the Gentiles might hear from my lips the message of the gospel** and believe. **God**, who knows the heart, showed that he **accepted them** by giving the Holy Spirit to them, just as he did to us. **He did not discriminate between us and them, for he purified their hearts by faith.** (Acts 15:7–9)

Is this beautiful or what! When our hearts are purified by faith, we do not "discriminate between us and them."

The apostle Paul addressed these doctrinal differences extensively in Galatians 3. He concluded that by faith in Jesus Christ, one achieves the same status as being physically of the seed of Abraham (hence achieve the same status as those who were native-born).

> So in Christ Jesus you are all children of God through faith, for all of you who were baptized into Christ have clothed yourselves with Christ. **There is neither Jew nor Gentile, neither slave nor free, nor is there male and female, for you are all one in Christ Jesus. If you belong to Christ, then you are Abraham's seed**, and heirs according to the promise. (Galatians 3:26-29)

The admonition to give up national distinctions continues:

> Do not lie to each other, since you have taken off your old self with its practices and have put on the new self, which is being renewed in knowledge in the image of its Creator. **Here there is no Gentile or Jew, circumcised or uncircumcised, barbarian, Scythian, slave or free, but Christ is all**, and is in all. Therefore, **as God's chosen people, holy and dearly loved, clothe yourselves with compassion, kindness, humility, gentleness and patience.** (Colossians 3:9-12)

In order to put on Christ's mercy and kindness, we have to stop lying to each other and stop denying that we all are made in the image of our Creator. Among the reasons for the spread of Christianity were its universal acceptance of everyone; its transcendence of national and ethnic boundaries; its vision of love for all human beings, regardless of racial, ethnic, or national heritage; and its extensive caring for the sick, performed at great risk and personal sacrifice—all compassionate behaviors atypical of the culture of the Roman empire.

Hence, the admonition to love and accept others—those who were previously despised, those who were different—was a lot more radical than on its face it may appear to a modern reader. Yet applying these moral imperatives is still revolutionary in today's world. Witness the previously mentioned assault in my own town at Christmas on the Latina woman who was doing what we all do: when we have forgotten something, we send our companion to run and pick up our item while we hold our place in line.

Therefore, remember that formerly you who are Gentiles by birth and called "uncircumcised" by those who call themselves "the circumcision" (which is done in the body by human hands)—remember that at that time you were separate from Christ, **excluded from citizenship in Israel and foreigners to the covenants of the promise,** without hope and without God in the world. But **now in Christ Jesus you who once were far away have been brought near by the blood of Christ.** For he himself is our peace, who has made the two groups one and has destroyed the barrier, the dividing wall of hostility, by setting aside in his flesh the law with its commands and regulations. His purpose was to create in himself one new humanity out of the two, thus making peace, **and in one body to reconcile both of them to God through the cross, by which he put to death their hostility.** He came and preached peace to you who were far away and peace to those who were near. For through him we both have access to the Father by one Spirit. **Consequently, you are no longer foreigners and strangers, but fellow citizens with God's people** and also members of his household, built on the foundation of the apostles and prophets, with Christ Jesus himself as the chief cornerstone. (Ephesians 2:11–20)

Here the scripture outlines the doctrine that faith in Christ unites us all as one and eradicates national identities. This is also the promise of communion—that we all become one as part of the body of Christ as we are reconciled to God. For those who limit this passage only to professing Christians (versus extending it to mean the universal Christ consciousness of love), I remind you that most Latinos in America are Christians, much more so than white Americans.[101] Over three-quarters are your brothers and sisters in Christ.

Now, when this passage is brought before some right-wing Republicans, they will likely agree but say that this applies to our hearts (our personal piety) or to our churches, not to our social or legal philosophy. That kind of thinking is boxing in our truths to prevent their application to all segments of our lives. Integrity requires that we live consistently with our values across the board. That's like saying, "I must be kind in my personal family relationships, but it's okay if I am cruel in my business dealings." It's a self-deluding rationalization that if I follow the Bible in one sphere, I can disregard applying it to other spheres.

Progressives must also highlight that in the context of ancient Israel, these commandments translated into real political consequences and legal rights. Immigrants received tithes; they were to be treated with respect and loved. God endowed immigrants with certain rights, so who are earthly politicians to take them away?

Even if such scriptures are not mandates for government, it cannot be wrong to make government align with the principles of the Bible.

> **Keep on loving one another as brothers and sisters. Do not forget to show hospitality to strangers,** for by so doing some people have shown hospitality to angels without knowing it. (Hebrews 13:1-2)

This New Testament passage highlights what the Bible has demonstrated repeatedly: performing an act of charity for a foreigner (not just a friend of a friend or a distant cousin) is akin to communing with the divine. The word *angel* here means messenger of God—so it could be a supernatural angel or a special envoy doing God's work in the world. You know that your crazy cousin or angry uncle ain't no angel. But nevertheless, the Bible commands us to reach out and to love not only our obnoxious relatives, but also those who are truly in a strange land and have no one to turn to, for that is how we connect with God's representatives on earth.

If we have any remnant of Christian conscience, we must realize that God is judging us based on how we treat "the least of these." Whether we like it or not, the Bible commands that those who follow in the footsteps of Jesus love immigrants on all levels—legally, socially, and personally. Democrats can't convert all evangelical Christians into liberal voters, but it is possible that we can use Scripture to urge evangelicals to hold "pro-life" politicians to a higher standard, a biblical standard that blesses and respects the dignity of all human beings throughout each stage of life.

The Bible rips the mask of pretense from us all. We cannot use our personal rights to inflict harm and injustice on others. We must love the strangers, the foreign immigrants. The strangers are our neighbors, whom we must love as ourselves—but only *if* we care about following God's command and getting into His Kingdom.

It is disgraceful that those now in charge of our nation label all poor undocumented workers in this country criminals, terrorists, rapists, and welfare vampires. These are lying words, for statistics show that the vast majority are hardworking and law-abiding people who pay taxes with no hope of receiving welfare or Social Security benefits. "Illegal aliens" cannot get welfare or food stamps. This has been proven again and again, yet people would rather believe the lying words from their leaders to the contrary.[102] Most undocumented aliens try hard to stay under the radar, for any minor infraction or application for benefits would expose their undocumented status and cause them to be deported. They even suffer criminal abuse without reporting it to police, for fear of being noticed and then deported.

There are problems with gangs and criminals in poor neighborhoods among citizens as well as "strangers." And yes, we need to do more to stop crime. Undocumented immigrants who commit crimes can and should be deported or jailed. Although the objective data don't match the hateful rhetoric,[103] those in power know that if they keep the underclass obsessed with fighting someone lower down on the socioeconomic ladder, they won't notice how those at the top are ripping them off.

One issue where many progressives and conservatives may feel torn is refugee status for Syrians, who are trying to flee a bloody civil war. We are turning our backs on the thousands of Christian refugees in Syria who need our help—all because hypothetically, an ISIS militant could masquerade as a war refugee.

The same rationale was used in World War II to bar German Jews from sanctuary in this country. When over 900 Jews showed up on a steamship, the *SS St. Louis*, and asked for asylum, the slanderous lie was put out that among them were possible German spies intent on destroying America from within. That lie followed these Jews, as other countries caught the virus of paranoia. These Jews

were returned to Germany—and to their deaths in the concentra-
tion camps and gas chambers.[104] We must ponder: does that not
make us complicit with the Nazis? The American public also refused to grant 10,000 German Jewish children temporary asylum.
Our paranoia and fear caused great cruelty and injustice—thousands
of times worse than any damage one or two spies could have done
to us. The arguments of Trump and Chris Christie today use rhetoric nearly identical to the reasoning back then.[105] This contradicts
biblical commands as well as international law.

We progressive Christians must keep reminding people that
God's way is not to give in to a spirit of fear, but to stand firm with
love, peace, and a sound mind (2 Timothy 1:7). What a disgraceful
legacy we are leaving to future generations for our cowardice. And
we talk about the blood of innocents on terrorist hands! Sending
war refugees to their deaths is hardly different from blowing them
up. We just get the luxury of not witnessing their slaughter. We
should all feel ashamed that other western European countries have
responded more compassionately, even at the risk of suffering acts
of terror by choosing to minister aid to these refugees.

It's ironic that in our country some who most loudly proclaim
to be Bible believers are the most vociferous in promoting fear of
outsiders and reliance on our military might. Not much trust in the
Lord there. As a rational attorney, I accept that we must put our
nation's security first. But as a Christian, I'm forced to insist that
we balance this with mercy and international law and treaties,
which require countries to take in war refugees.[106] It's possible to
accept people and vet them—though it costs more. Most acts of terrorism in this country have come from the native-born, not recently admitted refugees.[107] Shouldn't we focus some of our counterter-
rorism efforts into counteracting the propaganda of hate fostered by
radicals who are brainwashing disaffected American youth? We
need to be building alliances with Muslim leaders to overcome ex-
tremist thinking.

In the long run a legacy of hate and cruelty will reap more resentment and retaliation against the US from radicals in third world

countries, for we will have behaved cruelly and proven that we are indeed the monsters they have portrayed us to be. So on one level our fear will ensnare us, just as the Bible proclaims, "The fear of man lays a snare, but whoever trusts in the Lord is safe" (Proverbs 25:29). Hey, I get it: trust in the Lord and keep one eye open.

5

Jesus Loves Reformed Welfare For the Poor

let none of you imagine evil against his brother in your heart.
(Zechariah 7:10 KJV)

By this point, the reader has no doubt read numerous scriptures, in which the Bible condemns people who vex and oppress the poor, the immigrant, and the downtrodden. In Chapter Two: Debunking the Myth That the Bible Only Endorses Small Government, we proved that in the Bible:

- Programs for feeding the poor were required by national law

- The wealthy were required to contribute the most toward social welfare

- The "tithe burden" was well above 10% (potentially around 22%) and every third year, property owners paid a special tithe for the immigrant and the poor

- Farm owners had to set aside a section of their planted lands for the poor and the immigrant to harvest, which likely caused them to lose more than 20% of their profits

- Early Christians practiced redistribution of wealth.

So if you are reading this book out of order, be sure to read that chapter to inform your view of the role of government in programs protecting the poor. These were legal mandates, not optional suggestions that the rich were free to disregard. In this chapter, we build on the Bible verses previously presented. Here, we are asking readers to examine their hearts, to acknowledge their feelings toward the poor and to be mindful of their inner biases and beliefs when electing leaders.

On one level, it's easy to think that because we are not physically or verbally attacking poor people, we are not falling afoul of God's law. What concerns me about our modern debate over welfare is that many have developed a callous attitude. Tones become hateful and dismissive; people refuse to examine solid evidence; they scapegoat others in order to feel superior, and they find elaborate excuses to justify why they deserve government benefits more than others do.

Jean-Paul Sartre, a famous French philosopher and playwright, poignantly addressed how we imagine evil against others in a brilliant essay, "Portrait of An Anti-Semite," which I believe ought to be in the curriculum of every high school senior or college freshman. In ten pages, Sartre gives us a crash course in critical thinking skills and understanding why we rely on ethnic or racial prejudice. We need instant certitude; we can't bear to admit that truth is a searching process, a journey, not a fixed object (a philosophy that scriptures support: cf. 2 Timothy 2:15 ["study to show yourself approved of God"] and Isaiah 28:9-10 ["Whom shall he teach knowledge? and whom shall he make to understand doctrine? them that are weaned from the milk, and drawn from the breasts. For precept must be upon precept, precept upon precept; line upon line, line upon line; here a little, and there a little..."]). Prejudice is a passion that makes us feel good about ourselves, projects our own inner evil outward onto others, and deludes us with a false sense of control over a scary, uncertain universe.[108] Wow! How piercingly Sartre looked into the human heart. Although Sartre was discussing religious and ethnic intolerance toward the Jews, whom the Germans demonized as foreign immigrants taking over their land, his analysis demonstrates how mainstream societies often demonize groups that they find undesirable, such as the poor or today's Mexican immigrants or Syrian refugees. Remember, Jesus called us to examine the hateful, evil thoughts and motives in our hearts and in our speaking, for He shows us that our hostile thoughts are linked to the same sinful deeds that we all condemn.

In protest against Obamacare, one Tea Party activist notoriously paraded around with a placard that read, "Get the Government Out of My Medicare." Now, this was a stupid sign worthy of Bill Engvall's humor. Aside from the obvious contradiction, since Medicare is a government program, the protester was saying, "I deserve government health care, but 'those other people' don't." It appears that between 800 BC and 2016, humans have learned little, for the Bible addresses this very problem.

The Bible continually warned people not to demonize or oppress the poor. As the next scripture shows, lying words can be as destructive as violent acts. Indeed, lying words often lead to violence and oppression.

> The instruments also of the churl are evil: he deviseth **wicked devices to destroy the poor with lying words**, even when the needy speaketh right. But the liberal deviseth liberal things; and by liberal things shall he stand.... (Isaiah 32:7–8 KJV)

In the above passage, it is ironic that the prophet praises "the liberal." Here, the word *liberal* means inclined, willing, noble, or generous. It comes from a root word that means to incite, impel, make willing; to volunteer; and to make freewill offerings. It implies going above and beyond the minimum required by law. Wonder how being a liberal got to be such a dirty word!

I recall that in the 1970s, '80s, and '90s the enemy of our country was "all these lazy bums on welfare who are skimming in big bucks from us hardworking folks. They're riding around in Cadillacs, and eating filet mignon while we struggling middle class taxpayers can barely afford a Chevy and a hamburger." Even a popular country song, "Welfare Cadillac," derided the integrity of welfare recipients and belittled aid to the poor as a big rip-off. This song became a favorite of Richard Nixon.[109] To his credit Johnny Cash

refused to sing "Welfare Cadillac" for the then president when he
visited the White House, for he understood firsthand how hurtful it
was. Instead, he sang songs that contradicted Nixon's harsh politics,
songs that showed his solidarity with the oppressed, the sick, the
lonely, and the soldiers.[110] Johnny Cash also wrote a counter protest song about working on an assembly line and not being able to
afford the Cadillacs he was making.[111] Johnny Cash's entire musical
career, which also included songs of compassion for prisoners,
showed that he followed Matthew 25.

Stereotyping poor people and their meager welfare as providing
them Cadillacs demonstrated the lying words that our modern false
prophets spewed, for the data were indisputable. The vast majority
of people on welfare were single mothers with young children.
Welfare payments are designed to provide only 80% of what the
state calculates that you actually need to sustain yourself.[112] Yes,
there is always a small percentage of abuse that people jump on to
generalize and then hastily slander the entire group, but the vast
majority of welfare recipients are in dire straits.

There's nothing new under the sun, says the writer of Ecclesiastes. Slandering the poor is not new, and the lying words of oppression often blame them for their plight. If human beings were not
prejudiced against the poor and downtrodden, the prophets would
not have bothered to mention it. As Sartre pointed out, and as the
prophets demonstrated, the first step toward oppressing groups of
people is to dehumanize them and blame them for the evils of our
society and our own failings. Then it's easier to persecute and finally exterminate them. It is one slippery slope, which history has
proven to have occurred all too frequently.

If we see the poor as merely "those in the inner cities" and not
our brothers and sisters in Christ, it's easier to feel okay with allowing Congress to pass laws that cut food stamps and other social service programs, all the while making those cuts under a pretense of
piety. Congressman Paul Ryan tried to pass a massive cut of $3.3
trillion (with a T), claiming that he was inspired to do so because of

his Catholic faith.[113] Gimme a break! I wasn't buying it, and neither were the many Catholic scholars who rose up to challenge him. One scholar said, "Your budget appears to reflect the values of your favorite philosopher, Ayn Rand, rather than the Gospel of Jesus Christ."[114] Amen to that. You're free to propose laissez-faire capitalism, but you can't do it in the name of Jesus.

The Old Testament prophets decried a systemic problem in society that rulers had a duty to address. Notice in the long quotation below that there is no reference to individual charity.

> The word of the Lord came to me: "Son of man, will you judge her? Will you judge this city of bloodshed? Then confront her with all her detestable practices and say: 'This is what the Sovereign Lord says: You city that brings on herself doom by shedding blood in her midst and defiles herself by making idols, **you have become guilty because of the blood you have shed** and have become defiled by the idols you have made. You have brought your days to a close, and the end of your years has come. Therefore I will make you an object of scorn to the nations and a laughingstock to all the countries. Those who are near and those who are far away will mock you, you infamous city, full of turmoil. **See how each of the princes of Israel** who are **in you** uses his power to shed blood. **In you** they have treated father and mother **with contempt; in you they have oppressed the foreigner and mistreated the fatherless and the widow. You have despised my holy things and desecrated my Sabbaths.'"** (Ezekiel 22:1-8)

At first glance, this passage appears as one more nail in the coffin of the false argument that taking care of the poor is not a matter for government, for this passage indicts the princes of Israel (the rulers of Ezekiel's day). And this is true. But when we slow down and carefully parse the grammar, we see something even more profound. The rulers are doing their wickedness through the people. Notice that the phrase "in you" is repeated three times: *in you* they exercise their power to shed blood; *in you* they show contempt for father and mother (the elderly); *in you* they have oppressed the foreigner, the fatherless, and the widow. Rulers propagandize their people for good or evil. They get their people riled up against the poor or against the undocumented worker. They don't have to go out and directly oppress the poor. They get their citizens to do it for them. Sound like anyone we know?

Let's consider in more detail the passage from Zechariah that opened this chapter.

> Thus speaketh the Lord of hosts, saying, Execute true judgment, and shew mercy and compassions every man to his brother: **And oppress not the widow, nor the fatherless, the stranger, nor the poor; and let none of you imagine evil against his brother in your heart. But they refused to hearken, and pulled away the shoulder, and stopped their ears, that they should not hear. Yea, they made their hearts as an adamant stone, lest they should hear the law,** and the words which the Lord of hosts hath sent in his spirit by the former prophets: therefore came a great wrath from the Lord of hosts. (Zechariah 7: 9–12 KJV)

In this passage the prohibition against oppression is followed by the admonition not to think up evil against your brother. The KJV uses the word *imagine* ("do not imagine evil against your brother"), whereas the NIV uses the word *plot*—both showing a thought, an intention to do harm. In order to oppress people, we must first imagine evil against them in our hearts, for the thought, the intent, precedes the action. Once we demonize or dehumanize people, we can easily mistreat them because we make them less worthy than ourselves. And notice that rejecting these words against oppression was a rejection of the law. This is essentially what Sartre expressed in more modern terms.

In Zechariah's day, the Jews were beginning to return to Israel from their exile in Babylon. Zechariah was a man of privilege. As a high priest, he was intimately familiar with the rituals and traditions of Israel's elites. And even when Israel was in crisis, trying to rebuild her conquered nation, Zechariah criticized the rich for mistreating the poor. He went on to pronounce vengeance—divine payback as evil rulers would take charge and wreak more havoc.

> Then the Lord said to me, "Take again the equipment of a foolish shepherd. For I am going to raise up a shepherd over the land who will not care for the lost, or seek the young, or heal the in-

jured, or feed the healthy, but will eat the meat of the choice sheep, tearing off their hooves. Woe to the worthless shepherd, who deserts the flock! May the sword strike his arm and his right eye! May his arm be completely withered, his right eye totally blinded!" (Zechariah 11:15-17)

In the last book of the Old Testament, the prophet Malachi echoes this same theme. He lists adultery, false swearers (lying under oath), and then oppression against laborers, widows, fatherless, and foreigners—all as behaviors that will bring down God's wrath.

> "So I will come to put you on trial. I will be quick to testify against sorcerers, adulterers and perjurers, against those who defraud laborers of their wages, who oppress the widows and the fatherless, and deprive the foreigners among you of justice, but do not fear me," says the Lord Almighty. "I the Lord do not change. So you, the descendants of Jacob, are not destroyed." (Malachi 3:5-6)

Malachi called out his countrymen for acting immorally. He did prophesy about the Messiah, who would come ultimately to heal the world, but he admonished his fellow citizens to mend their wicked ways in the here and now. We all envision that the world could be better. We need a vision of hope to drive us forward, whether that's a future utopia here on earth or in the hereafter, but the prophets leave no doubt: our duty is to work for righteousness now on earth.

Moreover, the Old Testament prophets never said that being good to the poor was optional or that it should be left for private individuals to decide. They decried an entire economic system that oppressed the poor, as they reminded people of national law and the duties of their rulers to care for "the least of these."

Wickedness = Oppressing the Poor

Throughout the Bible, afflicting or oppressing the poor is a sign of wickedness. The Psalms describe how wicked people ensnare the poor:

The **wicked in his pride doth persecute the poor**: let them be taken in the devices that they have imagined. For **the wicked boasteth of his heart's desire**, and blesseth the covetous, whom the Lord abhorreth…. He hath said in his heart, I shall not be moved: for I shall never be in adversity. His mouth is full of cursing and deceit and fraud: under his tongue is mischief and vanity. He sitteth in the lurking places of the villages: in the secret places doth he murder the innocent: **his eyes are privily set against the poor.** He lieth in wait secretly as a lion in his den: **he lieth in wait to catch the poor: he doth catch the poor, when he draweth him into his net. He croucheth, and humbleth himself, that the poor may fall by his strong ones.** He hath said in his heart, God hath forgotten: he hideth his face; he will never see it. Arise, O Lord; O God, lift up thine hand: forget not the humble. (Psalm 10:2-3, 6-12 KJV)

[Speaking of the wicked] For he never thought of doing a kindness, but **hounded to death the poor and the needy and the brokenhearted.** (Psalm 109:16)

Throughout the Bible, how you treated the stranger, the poor, the fatherless, and the widow was a big deal. Violation of this moral and legal imperative incurred the wrath of God.

The wicked shall be turned into hell, and all the nations that forget God. **For the needy shall not always be forgotten: the expectation of the poor shall not perish** for ever. (Psalm 9:17-18 KJV)

The evangelical community often quotes verse 17 in the above passage—to defend the concept of hell, which in this instance means *Sheol*, the realm of the dead (which is how the NIV translates the word). But they omit verse 18, which tells why the wicked will be turned into hell. The punishment is a vindication of the poor and needy. When we put the two phrases together, we gain new insight into this scripture.

According to one source, the words *poor* and *poverty* appear 446 times in 384 separate places in the Bible. This site also states that the concept of justice, which repeatedly emphasizes not respecting the rich over the poor, is mentioned twice as many times as the words *love* or *heaven*, and *seven* times more often than the word *hell*.[115] I ran a quick search through Biblegateway.com on the KJV's terms for the poor and found comparable counts. Since the same concepts are expressed with different words, our numbers may vary slightly.

Word	Count
Poor	199
Poverty	5
Needy	37
Oppressed	38
Hungry	29
Fatherless	43
Widows	82
Total	443

The word *adultery* appears in the Bible 33 times. Obviously, emphasis on the poor is ten times greater than emphasis on sexual fidelity.[116] The word *wicked* appears 453 times, and wickedness is often defined as oppressing the poor, including the fatherless, widows, and aliens.

> The **wicked** draw the sword and bend the bow to **bring down the poor and needy**, to slay those whose ways are upright. (Psalm 37:14)

> **How long**, Lord, will the wicked, how long **will the wicked** be jubilant? They pour out arrogant words; **all the evildoers are full of boasting**. They crush your people, Lord; they oppress your inheritance. **They slay the widow and the foreigner; they murder the fatherless**. They say, "The Lord does not see; the God of Jacob takes no notice." Take notice, you senseless ones among the people; **you fools, when will you become wise?** (Psalm 94:3-8)

> **Whoever oppresses the poor shows contempt for their Maker**, but whoever is kind to the needy honors God. (Proverbs 14: 31)

The above scriptures link boastful words with oppression of the poor, and we see such arrogant disdain permeating our leaders and culture today. "I got ahead and pulled myself up by my own bootstraps, so anyone who does not do likewise is just lazy." Such statements are rarely true, as nearly all successful people have stood on someone else's shoulders and received special breaks or opportunities that most people don't get. To oppress the poor shows contempt for God. The KJV renders the word *contempt* as reproach—a stain, a dishonor. If we want to honor our Maker (the spirit of life that created us all—however we define "God"), we must have mercy on the poor. Surely this means not only following the principles of aid and kindness (and the moral laws of feeding and clothing them) but also having mercy in our thoughts and attitudes.

Three more scriptures from Proverbs will drill thumbscrews into our conscience if we give any credence to learning from the Bible: failure to regard the plight of the poor is just as evil as if we personally oppress them. We don't get a free pass for ignorance.

> **Whoever shuts their ears to the cry of the poor will also cry out and not be answered.** (Proverbs 21:13)

> Those who give to the poor will lack nothing, but **those who close their eyes to them receive many curses.** (Proverbs 28:27)

> **The righteous considereth the cause of the poor: but the wicked regardeth not to know it.** (Proverbs 29:7 KJV)

The NIV translates the words *considereth* and *regardeth* in the above scripture as caring: "The righteous care about justice for the poor, but the wicked have no such concern." The *Strong's Concordance* gives these words the connotation of knowing and making the cause known, and it explains *regarding* as to know in the sense of distinguishing, to mark, to perceive. Both translations clarify that it is wicked to ignore or disregard the plight of the poor.

Ouch. This is a big indictment of us all. If we are being "biblical," then we must acknowledge that the poor have a cause, that they have a right, and that through national law we must provide them with opportunities for upliftment. It is wicked to turn a blind eye to the plight of the poor or a deaf ear to their cries. When we ignore the facts and refuse knowledge of the poor, we align with wickedness. Today, too many people disregard fact-checkers and national statistics that belie their common myths about the poor and the stranger (the immigrant). They would rather believe the lie that makes them feel superior than investigate the true facts.

During World War II, a famous Lutheran pastor and philosopher, who became a martyr for his faith as he opposed the Nazis, eloquently explained how willful stupidity is worse than malice.

> **Stupidity is a more dangerous enemy of the good than malice.** One may protest against evil; it can be exposed and, if need be, prevented by use of force. Evil always carries within itself the germ of its own subversion in that it leaves behind in human beings at least a sense of unease. **Against stupidity we are defenseless.** Neither protests nor the use of force accomplish anything here; reasons fall on deaf ears; facts that contradict one's prejudgment simply need not be believed—in such moments the stupid person even becomes critical—and **when facts are irrefutable they are just pushed aside as inconsequential, as incidental.**[117]

Pastor Bonhoeffer's words align with the Bible. Both he and the above scriptures are criticizing the willfully stupid, those who refuse to investigate the truth, not those whose IQs limit their comprehension.

The Bible Excoriates the Rich Who Pretend to Be Pious but Oppress the Poor

Unfortunately, the words of the Old Testament prophets are as relevant today as they were in ancient times. Isaiah confronts all of Israel for its phony religiosity. They attended religious services and practiced fasting rituals designed to incur favor with God, all the while doing wickedness to the poor. Isaiah tells the true purpose of fasting: going without food so we can give bread to the hungry and clothe the naked. And he asserts that health and healing will come from doing justice and giving to the poor. Loosing the bands of wickedness meant giving relief to the poor. All kinds of blessings result from doing justice for the poor and feeding the hungry.

> **Is not this the kind of fasting I have chosen: to loose the chains of injustice and untie the cords of the yoke, to set the oppressed free and break every yoke? Is it not to share your food with the hungry and to provide the poor wanderer with shelter—when you see the naked, to clothe them, and not to turn away from your own flesh and blood? Then your light**

will break forth like the dawn, and your healing will quickly appear; then your righteousness will go before you, and the glory of the Lord will be your rear guard. Then you will call, and the Lord will answer; you will cry for help, and he will say: Here am I. If you do away with the yoke of oppression, with the pointing finger and malicious talk, and if you spend yourselves in behalf of the hungry and satisfy the needs of the oppressed, then your light will rise in the darkness, and your night will become like the noonday. The Lord will guide you always; he will satisfy your needs in a sun-scorched land and will strengthen your frame. You will be like a well-watered garden, like a spring whose waters never fail. (Isaiah 58:6–11)

Isaiah was not the only prophet to repeat the same admonition to his country and its rulers. The wicked have grown rich by ignoring the poor. This next passage doesn't accuse the wicked directly of stealing from the poor. Their crime is one of omission: failing to advocate for the poor while they themselves prosper. Ignoring the cause of the poor is wicked.

Among my people are **the wicked** who lie in wait like men who snare birds and like those who set traps to catch people. Like cages full of birds, their houses are full of deceit; **they have become rich and powerful and have grown fat and sleek. Their evil deeds have no limit; they do not seek justice. They do not promote the case of the fatherless; they do not defend the just cause of the poor.** (Jeremiah 5:26–28)

Like Isaiah, Jeremiah goes on to link national prosperity with stopping oppression of the downtrodden.

This is what the Lord Almighty, the God of Israel, says: **Reform your ways and your actions, and I will let you live in this place.** Do not trust in deceptive words and say, "This is the temple of the Lord, the temple of the Lord, the temple of the Lord!" If you really change your ways and your actions and deal with each other justly, **if you do not oppress the foreigner, the fatherless or the widow and do not shed innocent blood in this place,** and if you do not follow other gods to your own harm, then I will let you live in this place, in the land I gave your ancestors for ever and ever. (Jeremiah 7:3–7)

Notice that Jeremiah once again explained that lip service to church and God doesn't matter: evil people talk much about "the temple of the Lord," but the test of true allegiance to God is how we treat the poor and whether we shed innocent blood. The prophets were talking about national policy, not mere personal morality. The above passage addresses the condition for Israel to keep her country together and to keep the land she claimed as her own. Remember, the Jews were periodically carried off into captivity and had lost the integrity of their government and self-autonomy. So when the prophets called for freedom from oppression, they weren't calling for a supernatural reward in heaven. They wanted their people to take action immediately to remedy their wrongs on earth.

Here, the Hebrew word *oppress* means to defraud, violate, overflow, deceive, or do violence or wrong to, or to exploit. And while cheating was condemned on an individual basis, the Bible makes clear that this should be a top priority of government (see Chapter Two).

All the concerns about government in the Old Testament addressed whether the earthly rulers were following these commands for social welfare and whether they were acting justly, not taking bribes, not favoring one group over another, and not using their positions for personal gain. What would happen if our analysis today pivoted on the same criteria? Is our government just? Is it serving the poor, the immigrant, and the greater good? The Bible holds that failing to follow God's provisions for the poor and the oppressed is a form of robbery and wickedness. God gave poor people rights, and it was the law for the rich to follow.

The Poor Widows and Fatherless

Many scriptures about the poor use the terms *fatherless* and *widows*. To appreciate this more fully, we need to recall history. In ancient days and even into modern times, men were the providers and the breadwinners, and men inherited their fathers' lands. Think of the law of primogeniture, which favored the firstborn son. Men held nearly all the power in society. Women could not independently own wealth, make contracts, or control their own property, for wives and children were considered the property of men. In biblical times, the raping of a woman was seen as an affront to her father or husband, rather than a violation of the woman's own body.

Treating women as inferior and as property that belonged to men continued from Bible days into the late 19th century. The US only began to pass Married Women's Property Laws in the 1800s. Even by 1877, one-third of US states gave married women no property rights outside of what they received from their husbands. When a woman married, if she had an inheritance, her husband got control over *her* wealth. For most of America's history and the history of the world, women could not obtain their own wealth, control their family's wealth, make contracts in their own name, and buy and sell property—apart from the consent of their fathers, husbands, or other male relatives left in charge. So in Bible times, losing a father or a husband usually meant becoming destitute and homeless.

One is hardly spinning the scriptures to infer that the term *fatherless* includes orphans and children in single female-headed households. Unpaid child support is still a great cause of women's and children's poverty in America. Consider this verse:

> **Anyone who does not provide for their relatives**, and especially for their own household, **has denied the faith** and is worse than an unbeliever. (1 Timothy 5:8)

Many men today have skipped out on their child support to the mothers of their children, yet pretend that they are upstanding citizens, even Christians. I've even known fundamentalist preachers who have done this. And women too sometimes evade their support obligations when fathers have full custody.

Regardless, in the Bible, being widowed or fatherless meant you were poor and needy. Old Testament law prohibited afflicting and oppressing the poor and promised severe retribution for doing so.

Ye shall not afflict any widow, or fatherless child. If thou afflict them in any wise, and they cry at all unto me, I will surely hear their cry; And my wrath shall wax hot, and **I will kill you with the sword;** and your wives shall be widows, and your children fatherless. (Exodus 22:22-24 KJV)

Strong language. Afflicting the poor was a capital offense? The word *afflict* in Hebrew includes the idea of browbeating or looking down to depress, abuse, defile, deal hardly with, or exercise force against them. The NIV translates the phrase as "do not take advantage of," an all-inclusive term from mild to violent oppression. But here, the KJV seems to reflect the stronger implication of the Hebrew text. Mistreating the foreigner and the poor ranked up there among the greatest abominations in the Bible. It was on par with murder and profaning God. Later, we shall cover in more detail how King David pronounced death on a rich man who stole his neighbor's one sheep. He well knew the principle that his duty as king was to protect the poor and punish the oppressor (see 2 Samuel 12:1-7).

Many of our economic policies and cultural practices today afflict the poor—not just pay-check advance stores and loan sharks, but also food deserts where the poor pay more for inferior food, ghettos we put them in because we don't want subsidized or low-income housing in our neighborhoods (a form of oppression we achieve through our zoning laws), and our evil stereotypes that pronounce doom on their future.

Throughout the Bible, all forms of oppression are wrong.

Ye shall not therefore oppress one another; but thou shalt fear thy God: for I am the LORD your God. (Leviticus 25:17 KJV)

Most Christians well know that the word *fear* in the Old Testament meant reverential respect and awe, not merely to cower under anticipation of harsh punishment. And respecting God meant that you would treat your neighbor (and the four special classes of downtrodden people) right. Remember, all these commands were national laws, not just personal exhortations.

For the Lord your God will bless you as he has promised, and **you will lend to many nations** but will borrow from none. You will rule over many nations but none will rule over you. **If anyone is poor among your fellow Israelites in any of the towns of the land the Lord your God is giving you, do not be hardhearted or tightfisted toward them. Rather, be openhanded and freely lend them whatever they need.** Be careful not to harbor this wicked thought: "The seventh year, the year for canceling debts, is near," so that you do not show ill will toward the needy among your fellow Israelites and give them nothing. They may then appeal to the Lord against you, and you will be found guilty of sin. Give generously to them and do so without a grudging heart; then because of this the Lord your God will bless you in all your work and in everything you put your hand to. There will always be poor people in the land. Therefore I command you to **be openhanded toward your fellow Israelites who are poor and needy in your land.** (Deuteronomy 15:6–11)[118]

The above passage required you to lend to the poor sufficient for their needs. You couldn't refuse.

Old Testament Food Stamps

In addition to the aforementioned laws regarding tithing, corners, and gleanings, the Israelites had even more food laws, so that no one would go hungry. The Bible allowed anyone who was poor and hungry to walk onto anyone else's vineyard or farm and eat his or her fill. However, hungry people could not use a container to carry anything away from the farm. They could go and pluck by hand someone's corn, but they could not use a sickle to cut down the harvest. Now, that sounds like an invitation to mayhem. But it was their national law, and evangelicals purport to view this as divinely inspired law.

If you enter your neighbor's vineyard, you may eat all the grapes you want, but do not put any in your basket. If you enter your neighbor's grainfield, you may pick kernels with your hands, but you must not put a sickle to their standing grain. (Deuteronomy 23:24–25)

Remember, this was in addition to tithing (taxation) laws. The KJV translates the NIV's term *grainfield* as "standing corn," and *Strong's Concordance* explains the Hebrew word as a mature stalk of grain. The Bible effectively decriminalized stealing if you were immediately hungry and picking the raw produce. You couldn't steal your neighbor's bread after he ground the flour and baked it. Imagine what we would say if anyone advocated such a practice today.

In 2016, Republicans proposed cutting food stamps by a whopping $23 billion.[119] But there was no mention of including a provision that would allow those left hungry a free pass to go to a grocery store and eat fresh produce. To apply this law literally couldn't work, but the point is that the Bible had national laws that provided for you when you were immediately hungry. So there is nothing immoral about having a Food Stamp program that does the same thing. If God wanted His people not to starve, then we need to have a debate on what amount is reasonable for food stamps to allow people access to nutritious food.

This passage raises one other point. The Bible gave the hungry access to fresh produce—not processed junk. In 2013 Congresswoman Barbara Lee of California led a protest where she and twenty-five other congressional Democrats lived off the daily food-stamp allowance, a mere $4.50 a day, to protest massive cuts that the Republicans proposed.[120] Then an aide to Republican Congressman Steve Stockman tried to counter the Democrats' food stamps challenge by claiming that the Dems were buying overpriced food. The aide seemed to be doing okay for a few days; however, he was unable to purchase any vegetables. Later, he was forced to admit that he couldn't complete the challenge.[121] How immoral is that—to propose and advocate cuts when you know for a fact that you yourself cannot live on what you are imposing on others? Sister Simone Campbell from the "Nuns on the Bus" tour gave GOP leaders an earful and decried the food stamp cuts.[122] GOP leaders would tell their voters that churches and charities can pick up the slack from the cuts, but this is simply not true.

Unfortunately, despite the efforts of "Nuns on the Bus" and Congresswoman Lee, Republicans in Congress forced through a cut of $8.7 billion to the food stamp program in 2014.[123] At the time Fox News spread stories that the fraud associated with food stamps was rampant and at an "all time high." But this was false. In 2011 only 1.3% of the program was spent fraudulently. This was down from 3.8% in 1993.[124] The US Department of Agriculture called on Fox News to print a retraction. A spokesperson equivocated: "We are not quite sure where this came from. We saw that there was a story on Breitbart. We have not issued a report on this recently. There is no new rate that we've published. So we're not quite sure why they're so interested in stirring this up."[125] Under pressure Fox News then issued the retraction.[126] An allotment of $4.50 a day is hardly lavish. It would barely include any meat, let alone the pricy steaks that Republicans tell the electorate about when debating such matters. We need to look at this issue with compassion, not using lies from the racist alt right to kick people when they are down. Basic standards of journalism require the media to report the true facts. They shouldn't need to be pressured to tell the truth and revise mistaken reports. The Bible goes further, however. By scriptural standards, it's an abomination to use lies to convince people to oppress the poor.

> The instruments also of the churl are evil: **he deviseth wicked devices to destroy the poor with lying words**, even when the needy speaketh right. (Isaiah 32:7 KJV)

New Testament Commands

Since the three major religions in America—Christians, Jews and Muslims—all accept the Old Testament as part of their faith heritage, we ought to reach consensus on the underlying goals for our social policy if we make any pretense of adhering to our faith. If our political policies are in integrity with our professed religious principles, then we must account for how our society as a whole treats the stranger, the poor, the fatherless (i.e., orphans), and the widow (today, we would include all spouses left destitute because of death).

For those tempted to disregard Old Testament statutes, we repeat 2 Timothy 3:16, "all scripture is profitable..." and the admonition from 1 Timothy 5:8, which mirrored this Old Testament law (not providing for your relatives and household made you worse than an infidel). Jesus was clear that He came to complete the Levitical law of rules, procedures, and rituals, to fulfill them so that we would no longer be bound by rigid rules, for the hateful hypocritical Pharisees were neglecting the spirit of the Old Testament law, even as they strictly observed certain rituals. They were so bound to looking pious that they paid no attention to their fellow man. Jesus never said, "Now that I've fulfilled the law, it's every man for himself!"

Jesus made adherence to the morality underlying the Old Testament laws actually harder, because he claimed that God would examine our hearts and our motives. We lawyers call this *mens rea*, which is a central foundation block of modern criminal law: assessing whether the criminal had wrongdoing in his mind (i.e., heart). That's why we distinguish penalties (both criminally and civilly) between intentional wrongs and accidental wrongs.

Jesus wasn't asking people to forget the Old Testament law whereby the government required giving to the poor. He merely sought to take this further by getting people to acknowledge and take responsibility for their own wickedness within. It wasn't enough to abstain from the physical act of adultery; you had to examine the lust in your heart. But while asking people to cleanse their hearts, Jesus wasn't giving them permission to flout the law and commit adultery. Jesus and the early church did not undo the Old Testament commands for considering the poor. Rather, they demonstrated an even higher level of generosity—a level that few of us today would ever attain.

Matthew 25 was not the only place where Jesus advocated generosity to the poor. On several occasions, He told his disciples and would-be followers to sell everything they had and give to the poor.

> Jesus answered, **"If you want to be perfect, go, sell your possessions and give to the poor,** and you will have treasure in heaven. Then come, follow me." When the young man heard this, he went away sad, because he had great wealth. (Matthew 19:21–22)

The same story and admonition is found in Mark 10:20–22 and Luke 18:18–23. (See also Luke 12:33.)

It's funny how so many evangelicals want to take the Bible literally when it comes to the earth being a few thousand years old or every species of animals throughout the world fitting into Noah's ark (as if such a belief makes much difference in how we behave today). Yet few fundamentalist Christians advocate taking these sayings of Jesus literally—not even seriously. They knot their theology into a pretzel, trying to transmute Christ's admonition into a plea for us to give privately, so we can avoid a mere 3% tax increase on the wealthy.

And don't forget Matthew 19:24: "Again I tell you, it is easier for a camel to go through the eye of a needle than for someone who is rich to enter the kingdom of God." This verse is repeated near verbatim in Mark 10:25 and Luke 18:25. Listen to the circumlocutions fundamentalists go through to get around that verse. Their literalism vanishes. "Oh, this was not speaking of a sewing needle but a smaller gate in Jerusalem where the camels had to bend down and crawl through"—a proposition for which there appears little evidence, as if that undermines the essential proposition that great wealth is a great obstacle to the kingdom of God.[127] The more we have, the more we are attached, and the more we fear losing our possessions. "Maybe Jesus just said that because certain rich people were too in love with their possessions, but for the rest of us, we do not need to give so much," we comfort ourselves. Jesus' words are outrageous and unreasonable to the modern mind, even to progressives.

Here is where most of us part ways with Jesus, if we're being honest with ourselves. It's just too radical to be practical. Plus, we can't square this commandment with our own hatred of the poor, whom we view as undeserving, lazy bums. At least, those are the lying words we tell ourselves, so we can feel good about being good Christians while driving our SUVs to the black Friday sale, so we can buy the latest TVs, video games, and smart watches as we hoard even more clutter in our cushy homes—all in honor of baby Jesus.

Since Jesus told specific followers to sell all their goods and give to the poor (which would be nearly impossible for most of us to do), then why is it wrong or unchristian for citizens of this country, who live like kings compared to many developing countries, to pay a small extra portion in taxes to help the poor? I invite you to find one Bible verse that makes such a proposal immoral by God's law.

I can understand being selfish. To a certain extent, society works better when we acknowledge and promote our instinct for self-preservation. Communism didn't work. And I'm not signing up to give away all my worldly goods as the early Christians did. So I honestly confess that I am a hypocrite in this regard. But I don't object to paying a bit more in taxes so that we create a safety net for the poor, for safe housing, food, health care, educational opportunities, and a livable minimum wage.

The following passage condemns us all. How many of us at our private or public celebrations bring in the poor, the homeless, the disabled, or the despised? It makes me feel ashamed that my life revolves around fellowshipping near exclusively with my friends, whom I dearly love as extended family and who are in my own affluent, well-educated world. When charities do fund-raisers, they invite only the rich, and that's practical. If you want rich people to donate money, you have to wine and dine them, give them special treatment, and promote their access to dignitaries. That's a rule of life. Far fewer would attend such events if they had to mingle with the homeless and poor their money goes to aid—let alone the disabled.

Then Jesus said to his host, "When you give a luncheon or dinner, do not invite your friends, your brothers or sisters, your relatives, or your rich neighbors; if you do, they may invite you
back and so you will be repaid. **But when you give a banquet,
invite the poor, the crippled, the lame, the blind, and you will
be blessed.** Although they cannot repay you, you will be repaid
at the resurrection of the righteous."(Luke 14:12–14)

Jesus may have been referencing the second year festival tithe—
another tithe that mandated inclusion of the stranger and the poor
(Deuteronomy 14:22–27). All, both the poor and the wealthy, were
to come together for those events, and the poor and the stranger
were entitled to enjoy the feasts along with everyone else. Notice
that this scripture addresses the disabled as well as the poor. This
book cannot begin to address the suffering that disabled people en-
dure just trying to live from day to day.

Other New Testament writers well understood Jesus' words.

Religion that God our Father accepts as pure and faultless is this:
to look after orphans and widows in their distress and to keep
oneself from being polluted by the world. (James 1:26–27)

Now why would the Bible keep talking about those people?
The KJV uses the word *visit* instead of "look after," and *Strong's
Concordance* explains it as meaning to inspect and to relieve. This
goes far beyond gracious greetings or social calls; it requires us to
render aid. Loving in word and in deed is a strong principle of the
New Testament. Faith without works is dead. If we have faith, we
must couple that faith with good works. In the above scripture,
looking after the poor came before keeping yourself unpolluted
from the world. That doesn't change the command that Christians
are to live consecrated lives. It just emphasizes the priority of caring
for others.

Consider the second chapter of James, which strongly rebukes
Christians for favoring rich people over poor people, and which
exposes the hypocrisy in seeing our brother or sister naked and destitute, wishing them well yet doing little to relieve their suffering.

Suppose a brother or a sister is without clothes and daily food.
If one of you says to them, "Go in peace; keep warm and well

fed," but does nothing about their physical needs, what good is it? In the same way, faith by itself, if it is not accompanied by action, is dead.... As the body without the spirit is dead, so **faith without deeds is dead**. (James 2:15–17, 26)

The book of James points out the irony of how we love the rich, even though they oppress us and keep us in line by threatening to sue us. Consider the popularity of TV shows like *Lifestyles of the Rich and Famous*, *Entertainment Tonight*, or the *Real Housewives* series—not to mention the national obsession with *Keeping Up With The Kardashians* or the appeal of Donald Trump. We enjoy their wealth vicariously and identify with them because we want to be just like them, and we fantasize that one day we will be one of them. We love rich people, even if they cheat their workers and contractors by not paying their bills and import steel for their hotels from China, all the while promising to protect American workers. And we rarely get justice through lawsuits because they can wear us out and exhaust our resources with their teams of smart lawyers, who prolong expensive litigation for years on end.

> Listen, my dear brothers and sisters: Has not God chosen those who are poor in the eyes of the world to be rich in faith and to inherit the kingdom he promised those who love him? **But you have dishonored the poor. Is it not the rich who are exploiting you? Are they not the ones who are dragging you into court?** Are they not the ones who are blaspheming the noble name of him to whom you belong? (James 2:5–7)

Other New Testament scriptures mirror the same theme.

> **...not looking to your own interests but each of you to the interests of the others**. (Philippians 2:4)

> **Give, and it will be given to you.** A good measure, pressed down, shaken together and running over, will be poured into your lap. For with the measure you use, it will be measured to you. (Luke 6:38)

> **Carry each other's burdens**, and in this way you will fulfill the law of Christ. (Galatians 6:2)

> **If anyone has material possessions and sees a brother or sister in need but has no pity on them, how can the love of God be in that person?** (1 John 3:17)

The KJV renders the latter Scripture as, "But whoso hath this world's good, and seeth his brother have need, and shutteth up his bowels of compassion from him, how dwelleth the love of God in him?" *Strong's Concordance* tells us that the Hebrews regarded the bowels as the seat of tenderer affections, such as kindness, benevolence, and compassion. I like the expression because it makes me think of gut-wrenching empathy, not just cerebral sympathy. How can we see so many needy in our country and shut our bowels of compassion toward them? Because the love of God is not in us or in the people we elect. Do we get a pass because we occasionally give a few dollars to charities while ignoring our national policies that oppress the poor, the disabled, and the stranger, as we fail to use our individual resources (our power to vote and our voice) on their behalf?

The Christian Right does advocate charity on an individual level, and many of their churches do admirable work, but they oppose charity on a national policy level. To me this approach is schizophrenic: they want our national policies to reflect personal piety and personal righteousness (no fornication among same-sex people, no abortion, no premarital sex), but they viciously oppose our government being charitable toward the poor and the stranger. These people are kindhearted. Many will put themselves out individually if a fellow church member's home is burned or if another suffers a tragedy. They have just swallowed uncritically the lying words from the gods of Mammon, so they are blind to the huge gaps in their integrity.

Of course, some changed their tune when President George W. Bush announced faith-based initiative grants for churches. Democrats would be wise to embrace such policies if they are accompanied by real reforms that help the poor. The reality is that our churches, working as hard as possible, cannot create a safety net as well as the government can. They may each help a few, even a few hundred, and they can seriously impact a few neighborhoods here and there, but many other needy people will necessarily fall through the cracks. This is like making our bridges, highways, and railroads a matter of private businesses and personal charity. Having a well-paved road to travel is a great blessing. Our whole economic system would collapse without government support for these underpinnings of commerce.

We all should give the Catholic Church credit for one thing. It has been consistent on issues of justice. The denomination as a whole has been pro-life from the womb to the grave. They oppose abortion and the death penalty, and they have long stood for civil rights, programs that help the poor, and education for the disenfranchised. They sponsor refugee ministries when other evangelicals are crying to keep those "dangerous people" out.

I get that it's not fun to be taxed to do these things. But it is biblical. So why do we give carte blanch to military spending, but not to social programs? The vast majority, if not all, of Americans favor efficiencies and elimination of waste. We all want our tax dollars spent wisely and not wastefully. We don't want welfare payments going to the rich or disability payments going to the able-bodied. We don't oppose reasonable requirements that poor people do some form of work or community service—whether it's volunteer work or enrolling in school—so they are contributing or bettering themselves for the long run. And for mothers with young children, we must provide them with day care and transportation as we impose such burdens. The sad reality is that many in our country are already working two and three jobs, yet they still need food stamps because we don't have the courage to pass fair minimum wage laws.

Regardless, there is no scriptural basis for opposing tax dollars to do the very things that the Bible commands us to do—both by ancient law and by personal exhortation. Even if the Bible is not taken as a legal mandate, surely any reasonable effort to promote humane biblical policies must be good. But by labeling any restraint on greed and profit as "communistic" or "socialist," conservatives join the side of evil by reframing and then distorting Jesus' commands into lying words. Democrats of faith need to stand up and own our true Bible heritage.

The power to define is the power to determine. We need to stand up and define what it means to be a Christian nation. According to Jesus, such a nation would be one that takes care of the sick, the stranger, and the prisoner, and feeds the hungry, gives drink to the thirsty, and clothes the naked. It takes great leaps of logic to make capitalism the way of Jesus, especially since the early church practiced pure communal pooling and sharing of resources so that everyone had their needs met.

Except for the homeless and hungry in our country, a number that is way too high,[128] most of us in America are wealthy compared to past peoples and those in third world countries. And we are charged with doing good.

> **Command those who are rich in this present world** not to be arrogant nor to put their hope in wealth, which is so uncertain, but to put their hope in God, who richly provides us with everything for our enjoyment. Command them **to do good, to be rich in good deeds, and to be generous and willing to share**. In this way they will lay up treasure for themselves as a firm foundation for the coming age, so that they may take hold of the life that is truly life. (1 Timothy 6:17–19)

This is totally consistent with all the passages we reviewed in the Old Testament.

> Do not withhold good from those to whom it is due, when it is in your power to act. (Proverbs 3:27)

Welfare for the Rich Vs. Welfare for the Poor

Many politicians will demonize a single mom on welfare, calling her lazy and a "taker." Yet if progressives point out the inequities in the tax code that favor the rich and large corporations, then they are accused of engaging in "class warfare"—an argument that deflects the point and promotes ignorance. Progressive rhetoric is not nearly as caustic as the prophets' words. And we all need to know the true facts in this regard. The reality is that most successful business owners get more corporate welfare in one month—with all their tax write-offs—than a welfare recipient gets in an entire year, and the big corporate giants get hundreds times more. As an attorney, I know whereof I speak. Yet if you don't believe this, I recommend two books: *Rich Dad, Poor Dad* by Robert Kyosaki, and *Perfectly Legal: the Covert Campaign to Rig Our Tax System to Benefit the Super Rich—And Cheat Everybody Else* by David Cay Johnston.

Much of a business owner's entertainment "expense," equipment (like personal computers, mobile phones, nice cars), sports tickets, and dinners out are free of income tax, i.e., they are paid with pretax dollars, whereas the average Joe acquires such benefits with his after-tax dollars. Here's how it works: if you are a business owner, earning $75,000, but you get to deduct your car expense, phones, computers, electronic equipment, rent for an office in your home, vacation "business" trips—all as legitimate business expenses under the tax code, then you pay taxes only on say $50,000. But if you are just an employee earning $75,000 and you want these same items, you pay your taxes first on the full $75,000, and then you have to buy these perks out of what's left over. I'm not saying that entrepreneurs and small businesses don't deserve expense write-offs and tax incentives; I'm merely showing that our tax code favors business owners over regular employees. And the inequity is more easily observed when we look at large corporations and the tax breaks they get.

As long as you stay angry with the lazy mom across town who gets a monthly check and food stamps, you don't notice the corporate fat cat who's raking in far more in free giveaways off the backs of middle income workers. It's no different from any other form of welfare, yet the Bible gives us no moral imperative to help the rich. It does enjoin us to be fair to all. Most of us good entrepreneurs like our corporate welfare. That's why we are likely never to support a flat tax. We like it that the system is rigged in our favor, though we whine if anyone suggests even a modest tax increase.

Consider the sweet deal that General Electric, a company in which I own stock, and other large companies finagle in order to pocket the state income taxes from their workers. First exposing it in his 2003 book *Perfectly Legal*, David Cay Johnston gives further data in 2012. The workers don't get relief from their state payroll taxes. They faithfully pay them, but the company gets to pocket those taxes (yes, the employees' state tax payments) to offset its investment in equipment and facilities. That right. The company deducts the state payroll taxes from workers' paychecks and then keeps the money—allegedly to offset their investment in building a company that created jobs. That could be fair *if* it were merely an advance or loan, but it's a permanent gift. The company gets to keep the profits created from those taxpayers' subsidies. There's no recapture as there is with depreciation.[129] It makes sense to give incentives for companies to invest by advancing them a loan, but when our government gives them a break on the front end, once the investment produces profits, shouldn't the government share more in the profits on the back end? Why should the company keep those payroll taxes permanently as a gift?

Our corporate tax laws and incentives amount to big government welfare that makes services to the poor and immigrants pale by comparison. It's corporate socialism on steroids, and it works by stealth because common workers are oblivious to these subsidies, while they sing about welfare Cadillacs or "illegals getting free food stamps"—another set of lying words they have swallowed since undocumented immigrants cannot get welfare or food stamps.

Democrats Must Embrace Welfare Reform

If we progressives request that people pay more in tax to help the poor, we have a moral duty to ensure that people are doing their best to improve their lot. We acknowledge 2 Thessalonians 3:10, which says essentially, "If you don't work, you don't eat." The Bible endorses hard work and condemns laziness. The Old Testament legal welfare provisions required the poor to put forth some effort to get the free food and grain: they had to go into the fields and harvest it themselves and then bake their own bread.[130] Democrats shouldn't be afraid to incorporate this principle into their policies. There are fair ways to require work or community service in order to receive food stamps.

Republican-controlled state legislatures are taking on reforms,[131] but while state Republicans are adding work requirements, federal Republicans are advocating brutal cuts, and that's not right. Something is wrong when breadwinners work two and three twenty-hour jobs, but because of low minimum wages, they are still eligible for food stamps. They, of course, cannot do any more, and low-income working parents deserve food stamps and health insurance. But requiring fair work incentives for welfare benefits makes sense.

Maine offers a case in point. Its Governor Paul LePage is repugnant to me in many ways. His rhetoric is divisive, often borderline racist. He verbally abuses journalists and political opponents and seems to be a thoroughly unpleasant person.[132] But progressives must give Republicans credit where they get things right if we are to maintain credibility when criticizing them for getting things wrong. Regardless of my disgust for this individual, he deserves acknowledgment for getting this one right, and Democrats should take note.

In October 2014 LePage instituted a policy that required Maine's able-bodied adults with no children to work, train, or volunteer at least on a part-time basis in order to receive food stamps. Those who refused to comply with the new requirements were cut off after three months. The number of people on food stamps dropped from 16,000 to 4,500 in under five months.[133] So if adding work and volunteer requirements is effective, then why don't Democrats advocate passing part of those savings back to the truly needy by advocating an increase in benefits for those who are working and still cannot feed their families on their low wages?

Democrats should be just as vigilant in cracking down on fraud as Republicans are. In fact, we have a duty to be more vigilant. Republicans say, "People are cheating, so dismantle the whole thing." Democrats, who might advocate keeping the programs or expanding them, need to be open to sound facts and reasoning from right-leaning think tanks or conservative journalists who find that welfare dollars are being misused. We all need to learn and grow. The Bible repeatedly condemns lying, cheating, and laziness, so we need to be consistent. We want to preserve our compassionate hearts but also be wise stewards for the resources and money God has entrusted to us.

My academic career has allowed me to witness that welfare reform can work well—if it's done properly. We can't hamstring people with rules that they cannot reasonably fulfill. When I finished my master's degree in English, I took a job teaching in an adult education program for the Louisville public schools, where former dropouts were studying to pass their GED exams and get their high school diplomas. My daytime classes were comprised primarily of mothers on welfare. I then learned that under Republican President Nixon, Congress had recently passed a welfare-to-work program (aka the WIN program, which may have been our local term), as well as Basic Educational Opportunity Grants that helped low-income students pay for college tuition (this was the precursor of today's Pell grants).

Many of my students, impoverished single mothers, shared their dream of going on to college. I was eager to see how they fared because they were so grateful for the opportunity to get an education, and they did not want to spend their lives on welfare. I learned that local social workers had cobbled together provisions from both the WIN and the BEOG so they could have day care, transportation, and money for tuition and books in order to obtain a college education and prepare for meaningful careers rather than taking short-term training programs that locked them into low-wage dead-end jobs. We want parents to work, but if they don't have day care and transportation, they cannot. Minimum wage jobs barely cover these costs, let alone provide anything left over to sustain one's family.

Two years later a position opened up for me at Jefferson Community College, and I simultaneously enrolled in a doctoral program at Indiana University Bloomington in higher education administration. For my dissertation, I decided to study the success rates of about 250 welfare mothers who had enrolled in the college under the WIN program. I compiled their transcripts and demographic data, and then I surveyed a large segment of them individually. Because I needed to get the project done, I limited my timeframe to a four-year period, which gave all the students in my study enough time to finish at least one year of college, which was my definition of success. I found that at the time of my follow-up, over 70% had completed 24 credit hours of college with a C or better average and were either still in college or working.

I discovered that higher education significantly changed their thinking processes and improved their employment prospects. The study bolstered my belief in the importance of a basic liberal arts education, for learning to think critically and rationally has a big impact on how we function in society and rear our children. Repeatedly, during in-depth interviews, these mothers emphasized how college had transformed their lives. They noted that whereas previously they would have smacked their children, they now more often reasoned with them to help them understand why they needed to follow the rules. Whereas previously they yelled at their children to go do their homework, now they sat with them at the kitchen table, ensuring that the work was done correctly. They were not the same people they were when they entered school. Vocational training gives people useful moneymaking skills (like being a plumber or a machine operator), yet we need liberal arts programs to equip people to think critically and rationally.[134]

As an administrator of federally funded grants through the US Department of Education, I led several initiatives to improve academic success rates of low-income first generation college students, and I witnessed firsthand the measurable difference we made, while our academic standards remained in integrity. And yes, I'm aware of all the challenges, brick walls, and setbacks inherent in working with individuals who didn't get the same kind of home training and life skills that middle class students receive. Yet I am evangelical about education's power to transform lives. As a teacher of low-income disadvantaged students, I learned that you don't lower standards; you set standards, but you give the poorly prepared multiple opportunities, additional tutoring, and support services so they can meet those standards. These experiences shaped my view of government programs to aid the poor. We can find common ground with Republicans to ensure that a social safety net doesn't become a hammock. But we must also do so in a spirit of compassion as laid out in the Bible.

Blessings and Promises

Numerous studies show that taking care of the sick and the poor benefits us all. There is objective evidence that supports the old adage that we are only as strong as our weakest link.[135] If diseases ravage the poor, the rest of us may well get infected. When people are disaffected and without hope, they are more prone to evil philosophies, violence, and terrorism. When inner city youth have no jobs and no after school sports activities, they vandalize, steal, and do drugs. "An idle mind is the devil's workshop." My purpose here is not to collect sociological studies or to argue these things from enlightened rationalism, but to show the biblical bases that support compassionate social policies for our nation. It's in our best self-interest to take care of the sick and the poor.

The Bible repeatedly explains that the poor, the stranger, the widow, and the fatherless are special classes of people whom God loves, and it promises blessings for those who aid the poor.

> **Blessed is he that considereth the poor:** the Lord will deliver him in time of trouble. The Lord will preserve him, and keep him alive; and he shall be blessed upon the earth: and thou wilt not deliver him unto the will of his enemies. **The Lord will strengthen him upon the bed of languishing:** thou wilt make all his bed in his sickness. (Psalm 41:1-3 KJV)

If this passage reflects divinely inspired wisdom, then what kinds of blessings would we have as a nation to consider the poor? Throughout the Bible, health and healing go hand in hand with caring for the poor, just as we saw Jesus insisting that we care for all four classes of people together. The word *consider* in the above passage doesn't mean just to think about them. It does include wise understanding and insight, but it also means to cause to prosper.

Various scriptures promise that God will protect the poor and lift them up. Sincere worshippers of the Almighty (be they Christian, Jew, or Muslim) understand that we humans are God's legs and arms on earth. We work to fulfill God's promises. And visions of a more perfect age, an age of justice and righteousness, include remedying the oppression of the poor.

> **"Because the poor are plundered and the needy groan, I will now arise,"** says the Lord. "I will protect them from those who malign them." (Psalm 12:5)

> Then my soul will rejoice in the Lord and delight in his salvation... **You rescue** the poor from those too strong for them, **the poor and needy from those who rob them.** (Psalm 35:9–10)

> [speaking of God] **He raises the poor from the dust and lifts the needy from the ash heap;** he seats them with princes, with the princes of his people. (Psalm 113:7–8)

> **The Lord will maintain the cause of the afflicted, and the right of the poor.** (Psalm 140:12 KJV)

In this latter scripture, the Hebrew word *right* refers to a legal ordinance, a judgment from a court or place of authority. God's law gave rights to the poor. If you want to be on the side of God's blessings (or universal goodness), you must assist the poor—not just by giving at church, but also by demanding that your politicians take action.

> It is a sin to despise one's neighbor, but **blessed is the one who is kind to the needy.** (Proverbs 14:21)

> **Whoever is kind to the poor lends to the Lord,** and he will reward them for what they have done. (Proverbs 19:17)

> **The generous will themselves be blessed, for they share their food with the poor.** (Proverbs 22:9)

It is a universally accepted truth that we reap what we sow: what goes around comes around—good karma and all that. So by biblical logic, if we want our nation to prosper, our leaders should use their power to help the poor and "the least of these."

> **Defend the weak and the fatherless; uphold the cause of the poor and the oppressed**. Rescue the weak and the needy; deliver them from the hand of the wicked. (Psalm 82:3–4)

6

Jesus Loves Prison Reform

I was ... in prison, and ye visited me not. (Matthew 25:43 KJV)

This book was inspired by Matthew 25, where Jesus commanded His followers to care for the prisoner. We've already established
that the word *visit* in the Greek means to inspect in order to help or
to benefit, to have care for, to provide for. In fact, the New International Version renders the text this way: "I was sick and in prison
and you did not look after me." Jesus is not commanding a mere
social visit, though for those in lockup, personal visits do much to
lift morale and inspire hope. Throughout history, prisoners have
been among "the least of these" in society.

Bear in mind that this was Jesus' only test to get into the kingdom of heaven. Those who failed to do these things went to eternal
punishment. Here, the sin of omission is deemed as wicked as affirmative acts of harm. That's not my pronouncement; it's there in
black and white, regardless of which translation you use. Conservatives could argue that having empathy for prisoners or ministering
to them is for individuals or for churches, not for the state, though
they don't argue that the churches should maintain the prisons and
physically care for the prisoners. But the Bible commands us that
whenever we have the resources to help others, we are to use them.
Unlike the people of the Bible who lived under foreign oppression
and fear of execution, we have a resource to use—our democratic
government, which we can sway. And this book has already shown

that the Bible does not condemn government programs designed to help the downtrodden.

Writing this chapter has forced me to own up to my own selfish biases. By ordinary logic, there is no political gain for politicians to follow Jesus' command and advocate improving care of prisoners. Most of us feel little empathy for scumbags who committed terrible crimes and blew their opportunities at freedom. Some prisoners are sociopaths who pose grave danger to the rest of us. As one circuit court judge once told me privately, "Let's face it; there's a whole segment of society that is no damn good." I acknowledge that such a callous attitude is unchristlike. And watching a movie like *Dead Man Walking*, which dramatizes the work of Sister Helen Prejean among death-row inmates, will convict us all of our assumption that we should throw away even the most depraved of criminals.[136] We need to remember also that a former slave ship captain, who had been instrumental in human genocide and the heinous institution of slavery, wrote the most famous and perhaps most beautiful Christian hymn in the world, "Amazing Grace."[137]

In researching these verses, I was reminded that Jesus spent most of his time with the poor, the despised, the tax collectors, prostitutes, and sinners. When the disciples asked Him why He spent so much time with these lowly people, He stated, "It is not the healthy who need a doctor, but the sick. I have not come to call the righteous, but sinners" (Mark 2:17). Jesus saw value in everyone, even those who had made terrible mistakes. He promised paradise to one of the thieves who were crucified alongside Him, and we are led to believe that those two thieves were justly convicted of their crimes.

So the Bible prods me to examine whether our prison system as a whole embodies empathy and compassion as the Bible commands. Do we as Americans—Democrats or Republicans—believe that our prison system embodies any of the teachings of Jesus? If I am both compassionate and fiscally responsible, can I not advocate some way to reform our criminal justice system?

Jesus made more than one statement about prisoners. Previously, we covered how Jesus stood up in the synagogue and read aloud a famous passage from Isaiah, which declared, **"The Spirit of the Lord is on me,** because he has anointed me to proclaim good news to the poor. **He has sent me to proclaim freedom for the prisoners ..."** (see Luke 4:16–19). However we interpret this, we see that God's vision for the world is good news for the poor, healing for the sick, and freedom for the prisoner.

Other New Testament writers continued Jesus' admonition.

Continue to remember those in prison as if you were together with them in prison, and those who are mistreated as if you yourselves were suffering. (Hebrews 13:3)

The author of Hebrews is not expressly stated, though many assume it was St. Paul. The book of Hebrews was written to explain how Jesus had given the Jews a more perfect law to follow. The author calls for empathy for prisoners: to actively imagine that you yourself were in prison. Of course, Paul and other Christians were jailed, persecuted, and imprisoned for their faith. Yet the passage doesn't differentiate between those falsely and those justly imprisoned.

In the abstract, I feel empathy for many in prison, but in real life I want to be as far away from these fallen souls as possible. If I go and work with such people, some wacko may stalk or rob me. Yet the Scripture is clear. As we saw in prior chapters, Jesus did not say visit the good prisoners and ignore the bad ones. He did not distinguish between those who were justly and unjustly imprisoned. He said only, "Take care of the prisoners." And Jesus was upholding Old Testament morality.

For the LORD heareth the poor, and despiseth not his prisoners. Let the heaven and earth praise him, the seas, and every thing that moveth therein. (Psalm 69:33–34 KJV)

It is counterintuitive that the concept of everything praising God comes on the heels of helping the poor and the prisoner, and yet there it is in black and white. God does not despise people who are in prison, and the Bible commands us to love them.

The Lord looked down from his sanctuary on high, from heaven he viewed the earth, **to hear the groans of the prisoners and release those condemned to death.** (Psalm 102:19–20)

Wow, here is God caring for those on death row. The Bible goes on to say:

He is the Maker of heaven and earth, the sea, and everything in them—he remains faithful forever. **He upholds the cause of the oppressed** and gives food to the hungry. **The Lord sets prisoners free**, the Lord gives sight to the blind, **the Lord lifts up those who are bowed down**, the Lord loves the righteous. (Psalm 146:6–8)

Discussions of the "Day of the Lord," when people are restored to God (hence a vision of the ideal state), include setting the prisoners free. In the following scriptures, righteousness is associated with freedom for prisoners.

There the wicked cease from troubling; and there the weary be at rest. **There the prisoners rest together; they hear not the voice of the oppressor.** The small and great are there; and the servant is free from his master. (Job 3:17–19 KJV)

I, the Lord, have called you in righteousness; I will take hold of your hand. I will keep you and will make you to be a covenant for the people and a light for the Gentiles, to open eyes that are blind, **to free captives from prison and to release from the dungeon those who sit in darkness.** I am the Lord; that is my name! I will not yield my glory to another or my praise to idols. (Isaiah 42:6–8)

Of course, we rejoice when prisoners of war or hostages are released, or when the wrongly convicted are exonerated, but it's hard to see this vision for freeing those who actually did crimes. But the Bible doesn't make a distinction. It advocates empathy for all who are bound.

Fortunately, prison reform is beginning to receive bipartisan attention. For one thing, it costs more to keep someone in prison than to reeducate him and train him so he can live a better life. When you come out of jail as a convicted felon, no one will hire you, and you have few options except to return to a life of crime. It's a vicious circle.

Solid data and clear evidence show that higher education pays off for prisoners. Even conservative economists recognize that higher education reduces recidivism by 40%.[138] Comprehensive law reviews over long-term trends bolster the point.

In 1965 Title IV of the Higher Education Act was passed to help finance college for those who could show need. The act created the precursor to the Pell grant for financial aid. This legislation permitted prison inmates enrolled in college courses to apply for federal financial aid.

I personally witnessed some history in this regard. In the 1980s and early '90s, prisoners could get federal financial aid to take college courses, and several instructors at my local community college faithfully taught classes at the nearby men's and women's state prisons. But then the tide changed as politicians started looking for areas to get tough on crime. They rallied the electorate to block our tax dollars from going to help criminals, and the law was changed to forbid prisoners from getting federal subsidies or loans. Then courts held that prisoners have no liberty interest in obtaining an education while incarcerated.[139]

In 1994 bipartisan support prompted the Omnibus Violent Crime Control Act, which denied federal financial aid to citizens in prison.[140] And President Bill Clinton, a Democrat, signed it into law. The decision had a superficial rational basis: supposedly prisoners were eating up available funds so that non-offenders who had been law-abiding citizens could not get aid for their college, and one senator proclaimed that 100,000 law-abiding students were denied college aid because offenders were taking their funds.

If this were true, it would be reasonable for people to be upset. Government resources are scarce, and why should thousands of law-abiding students lose out to criminals? But the General Accounting Office totally debunked this lie and verified that less than 0.001% of the Pell Grant budget was going to prisoners—a miniscule amount by any measure—and that no qualified low-income citizen had been denied federal aid due to prisoner benefits.

But everyone believed the slanderous lying words that would oppress the poor rather than fact-checking to establish the truth, so
they jumped on the bandwagon that financial aid for prisoners was
a taxpayer rip-off.

It is hard to anticipate the future consequences of choices, as
this crime bill not only increased a trend toward mass incarceration
but also dismantled the one program that best prevents recidivism
among the prison population.[141] The movement to prevent prisoners from benefiting from this educational opportunity was part of
the knee-jerk reaction to get tough on crime and stop mollycod-
dling criminals. Of course, time has shown that making legal policy
based on revenge and quick-fix solutions creates more problems in
the long run. It has proven terribly myopic. We were merely cutting off our noses to spite our faces, because one extra year in prison
is five to ten times more costly than a full year's tuition at most
community colleges.[142]

As humans, we are innately drawn to the "eye for an eye" doctrine. Revenge is hard-wired into human emotions. Our criminal
justice system is based on punishment, partly so that citizens won't
take revenge into their own hands, leaving us with anarchy from
roving vigilantes. Most of us favor fair consequences that will let
offenders experience firsthand that it's better to do right than to do
wrong. So I'm not advocating that we let dangerous criminals go
free or that we fail to impose consequences that fit the crime. We all
admit, however, that our prisons are burgeoning with nonviolent
criminals who happened to have an ounce too much of a banned
substance, and we the taxpayers are paying the tab for our excessive
"war on drugs" and "tough on crime" mandatory sentencing from
the 1970s through the 1990s.

While we have people incarcerated, however, it seems foolish
not to try to influence their thinking and improve their ability to
function. Does the Bible favor a prison system that can be used to
correct and teach people?

For you, God, tested us; you refined us like silver. **You brought us into prison and laid burdens on our backs.** You let people ride over our heads; we went through fire and water, **but you brought us to a place of abundance.** (Psalm 66:10–12)

We can quibble over the extent to which this is to be interpreted literally, but the Bible squarely lays out that God can use a prison experience to correct and refine people and to bring them to a better place. This verse combined with so many others establishes a moral imperative to use prison as an opportunity to instruct the incarcerated. I support faith-based prison ministries to help teach prisoners religious and moral values, which can help teach self-discipline and impulse control, but do we not also have a duty to educate them, so they can follow in the path of righteousness when they are released? If the Bible gives prisoners new ways to look at themselves, should not the government also give them new skills and education while they are locked up?

Anyone who has been stealing must steal no longer, but must work, doing something useful with their own hands, that they may have something to share with those in need. (Ephesians 4:28)

How can people who stole work if no one will hire them and they lack employable skills? The above scripture shows that the purpose of rehabilitating thieves is to enable them to work so they can contribute to someone else who is needy. Hurrah for the company, Dave's Killer Bread! It was formed to give employment to ex-convicts who have a hard time reentering society. Not only does its purpose follow the Bible, but also it manufactures delicious whole-grain organic bread.

Nothing in the Bible contradicts the notion of using incarceration to improve people. In fact, the Bible clarifies that affliction and punishment should be instruments for the people's long-term good. God brings grief, but His unfailing love brings people to redemption. He does not desire to crush prisoners underfoot.

For **no one is cast off by the Lord forever.** Though he brings grief, he will show compassion, so great is his unfailing love. **For he does not willingly bring affliction** or grief to anyone. **To**

crush underfoot all prisoners in the land, to deny people their rights before the Most High, to deprive them of justice—would not the Lord see such things? (Lamentations 3:31–36)

The story of the Bible is a story of hope for redemption and affirmation that no one is cast off forever. Educating the prisoners is so far one of the best-proven plans for bringing about any biblical version of redemption. While some Christian ministries focus only on getting prisoners to adopt a theology, most prison ministries look to provide support when inmates are released. Any effort that gets them closer to replacing hatred with love and destructive behavior with positive conduct is bringing them closer to God, who still loves us all in spite of our many failures and wrongs.

As a progressive lawyer, it's easy for me to champion the Innocence Project. Founded in 1992 by Peter Neufeld and Barry Scheck at the Cardozo School of Law, this program exonerates the wrongly convicted through DNA testing and advocates reforms to the criminal justice system that will prevent future injustice. So far, nearly 350 people have been exonerated with the help of DNA. And the project has been picked up by many state attorneys, who are also working to undo past mistakes.[143]

As to prisoners, the basic facts are irrefutable, and most studies agree (even if the specifics of the percentages vary):

- The majority of men in prison read poorly and lack a solid educational foundation.

- It costs five times more to keep a man in prison than to give him a year of college. Some studies show that jail is 10 times more expensive than college. Obviously, costs vary by each state.

- Prisoners who complete higher education programs have lower recidivism rates than those who do not.

- The United States incarcerates a larger percentage of its population than do oppressive regimes like North Korea.[144]

Research by the RAND Corporation concludes: "Educating prisoners, even at taxpayer expense, results in a major financial savings to taxpayers to as much as $95,000,000 for every 1,000 inmates who complete a college education program."[145] You'd think the mere economics of it would bring about reform. Everyone purports to want to cut waste and trim the budget.

Numerous other studies reinforce the RAND Corporation's findings. Below are a few.

The Results of a Comprehensive Evaluation by Lois M. Davis, Jennifer L. Steele, Robert Bozick, Malcolm Williams, Susan Turner, Jeremy N. V. Miles, Jessica Saunders, Paul S. Steinberg found that "Inmates who participate in correctional education programs had a 43 percent lower chance of recidivating than those who did not—a reduction in the risk of recidivating of 13 percentage points."

In "Measuring The Power Of A Prison Education," Eric Westervelt states:

[F]or every dollar invested in a prison education program it will ultimately save taxpayers between $4 and $5 in reincarceration costs. That's an enormous savings.

Just to break even, you'd only have to reduce the risk of reincarceration by one to two percentage points. But, the fact that there is a 13-point reduction in risk means you really are achieving substantial cost savings. And this is a conservative estimate of savings because we are not taking into account the indirect costs both to crime victims and the criminal justice system.[146]

See also Eric Blumenson and Eva S. Nilsen, "How To Construct An Underclass, Or How The War On Drugs Became A War On Education" *The Journal of Gender, Race & Justice*, Vol. 62.6 (2002) [147]

In 2010, the average cost of incarceration was about $31,000 per inmate across all states.[148] An article in the *New York Times* notes that in New York it now costs $60,000 a year to keep someone incarcerated.[149] Correlations by all measures show that the cost of educating a child is far less than the cost of keeping an adult in prison.[150] A simple Google search reinforces this with large amounts of irrefutable data.

A few more reports are worth noting.[151] One writer sums up much research:

> The link between a poor education and incarceration is borne out in data. Dropouts are 3.5 times more likely to be arrested than high school graduates. Nationally, 68 percent of all males in prison do not have a high school diploma. Only 20 percent of California inmates demonstrate a basic level of literacy, and the average offender reads at an eighth grade level.
>
> Many so-called dropouts who end up in jail are actually pushouts. Under the guise of zero tolerance, initiated after Columbine, students are often asked to leave school as a first response rather than a last resort. Discriminatory practices are common.
>
> In 2011–2012, black youth represented 16 percent of the juvenile population, but 34 percent of the students expelled from U.S. schools. Black students are three times more likely than whites to be suspended. The majority of teens in the juvenile justice system engaged in non-violent crimes such as truancy or disruptive behavior.[152]

Studies also show that caring for animals and growing crops have a therapeutic effect on the incarcerated.[153] As an avid gardener, I can testify to the inspiration that comes from watching a tiny seed turn into a plant that produces over 20 pounds of tomatoes. The act of planting, nurturing, waiting, and then harvesting teaches people to think long term, to anticipate the future consequences of choices today.

A comprehensive listing of studies that objectively measure the benefit of prison rehabilitation and education programs can be found at: http://static.nicic.gov/Library/026917.pdf.

This downloadable file of an annotated bibliography, "Evidence-Based Practices in the Criminal Justice System," also lets you link to most of the studies listed there. Or you can find the studies through Google.

Prison reform is in everyone's best interest. If prisoners cannot honestly earn a decent living when they are released, and if their thinking and impulse control mechanisms have not improved, then they have few options but to return to a life of crime or drugs. Even ancient wisdom recognized that when people lack means, they are more prone to steal.

> Two things I ask of you, Lord; do not refuse me before I die: Keep falsehood and lies far from me; **give me neither poverty nor riches**, but give me only my daily bread. **Otherwise**, I may have too much and disown you and say, "Who is the Lord?" Or **I may become poor and steal**, and so dishonor the name of my God. (Proverbs 30:7–9)

This may be why the Hebrews had so many rules and reminders to give opportunities to the poor. When people are desperate and destitute, they are more prone to commit crime. Conservatives are now recognizing the moral and legal imperatives of criminal justice reform.

> Reducing recidivism should be a central focus of conservative efforts to reform criminal justice. Conservatives understand that reforming offenders is both a moral imperative and a requirement for public safety. Breaking the cycle of crime and turning lawbreakers into law-abiding citizens is a conservative priority because it advances public safety, the rule of law, and minimizes the number of future victims.[154]

A 2015 article by Rachel Lu in the online conservative magazine, the *Federalist.com*, lists seven reasons why conservatives are supporting prison reform:

1. Prisons Are Expensive

2. Conservatives Love Freedom

3. Conservatives Are Serious about Personal Responsibility

4. Conservatives Know Justice Should Be Colorblind

5. Conservatives Value Family and Community

6. Conservatives Are Eager to See Victims Compensated through Just Restitution

7. Conservatives Care Whether Policies Actually Work[155]

This is something around which we all should rally. It's biblical. It's cost-effective. It makes us safer. It fulfills the Bible's perspective of redemption and accountability. And this is one area where
we all want big government programs to shrink: the more people in
prison, the more tax dollars it takes to build facilities, house, feed,
and guard them—and the more human lives are wasted and the
more families are devastated. It's time we all push this through.

The Bible and Medicinal Marijuana

The topic of prison reform begs us to address the debate regarding marijuana legalization. The ACLU found that in 2010, 52% of
all drug-related arrests were marijuana offenses. And out of the 8.2
million marijuana arrests between 2001 and 2010, 88% were for
mere possession of marijuana—not selling or distributing it.[156] As an
attorney, I understand that not all marijuana arrests will lead to
criminal convictions that include prison time, but this imposes a
heavy administrative burden on the police and the criminal justice
system. I'd much rather have the police looking for murderers and
investigating other serious crimes than booking stoned kids. Of
course, drug addiction does lead to much theft.

Even if young people don't go to jail, having an arrest record
can harm their career prospects later, and should they ever be on
the wrong side of the law again, the marijuana offense can be used
against them in sentencing. Whether marijuana legalization is the
"Christian thing to do," I cannot say. I know, however, that my
sense of compassion for prisoners and desire for criminal justice reform must include some reform to ensure that low-level pot offenses don't ruin a young person's life. If young men are locked up in
prison for nonviolent, low-level marijuana and other minor drug
offenses, they're not contributing to their families or the wider
communities. (I have no personal ax to grind here, as none of my
children or grandchildren has ever been arrested for such offenses
or even had issues with pot.)

Luckily, there is some bipartisan movement in this area. To his credit, Rand Paul has pushed for reforming the criminal justice system to keep nonviolent drug offenders out of prison and young men out of the criminal justice system.[157] Senator Paul also supports getting the federal government out of drug policy and leaving it to the states to decide when it comes to marijuana and other drugs.[158] I disagree with his stance on health care, but I acknowledge him for attempting to be consistent in the area of small government. He deserves praise for moving his party on this issue.

Twenty-eight states have now legalized marijuana use in some form: most for medicinal purposes only, although eight states have legalized recreational use. Many conservatives might decry this as a sign of social deterioration. In 1 Corinthians 6:19 Christians are admonished to respect their bodies as a temple for the Holy Spirit. But from what we know, marijuana is often helpful and no worse than alcohol and tobacco. The Bible permits drinking wine; it only condemns drunkenness—and gluttony (Proverbs 23:21; Ephesians 5:18). One of Jesus' miracles was turning water into wine at a wedding party (John 2:1–11). Yet it's harder to assess marijuana use for purely recreational purposes. I doubt many conservative Christians would be convinced that people could smoke marijuana recreationally without becoming "too high."

Some advocates for recreational marijuana use assert that the Bible justifies their position. Their argument seems tongue-in-cheek to me, but I'll throw it out anyway:

> And **God said**, Behold, **I have given you every herb bearing seed**, which is upon the face of all the earth, and every tree, in the which is the fruit of a tree yielding seed; to you it shall be for meat. And to every beast of the earth, and to every fowl of the air, and to every thing that creepeth upon the earth, wherein there is life, **I have given every green herb for meat**: and it was so. (Genesis 1:29 KJV)

The affirmation is repeated in Genesis 9:3 (KJV): "Every moving thing that liveth shall be meat for you; even as **the green herb have I given you all things**." This is not the strongest argument in this book, but I find it interesting, and it's also not the biggest stretch in modern interpretations of Scripture. If conservative Christians can perpetrate the belief that God only condones small government, then marijuana advocates have a right to point out that the Bible allows them to use herbs, and marijuana is definitely a green herb.

This shows how both sides like to cherry-pick Bible verses that support their position. Many Christians take much of the first chapter of Genesis literally, in that they believe the earth is no more than 7,000 years old. So if Genesis is to be taken literally, why not allow people to use marijuana—at least for medicinal purposes? They argue that the first 28 verses of Genesis are literally "true," but suddenly the 29th verse is a metaphor. Long ago my son joked, "If conservatives want to stop teaching evolution in schools, they should legalize pot; let's keep our interpretation of Genesis consistent!" Perhaps both sides can meet in the middle and agree on legalizing medicinal marijuana use.

> And by the river upon the bank thereof, on this side and on that side, shall grow all trees for meat, whose leaf shall not fade, neither shall the fruit thereof be consumed: it shall bring forth new fruit according to his months, because their waters they issued out of the sanctuary: and the fruit thereof shall be for meat, and **the leaf thereof for medicine.** (Ezekiel 47:12)

In 2 Kings 2:19–22, the prophet Elisha used an herb mixed with a plaster to heal an ailing king. So the Bible does have evidence that herbs can be used as healing.

Most heartrending are reports of people who suffer from seizures, including rare forms of epilepsy. They assert that marijuana treats them more effectively than other pharmaceuticals. Many parents like Matt and Paige Figi find that cannabis extract (oil derived from marijuana leaves) is the only effective treatment for children suffering from seizures. I can't imagine their pain, not only for their precious child who doesn't understand why her body convulses, but also for their agony in being powerless to relieve their suffering child.

Matt and Paige found that their second child, Charlotte, began suffering seizures at three months of age. The doctors could not find the cause, and conventional treatments didn't work. At first, doctors hoped Charlotte would outgrow her condition, but her seizures became more frequent and more painful. They saw specialists all over the country; they even got an experimental drug from France. Nothing worked. The seizures became so bad that their daughter lost the ability to walk, talk, and eat. In desperation, they began exploring medical marijuana.

While we don't know whether medical marijuana is safe for children, for the Figis, who watched their daughter deteriorate and nearly die, the potential rewards outweighed the risks. And to their amazement, after just a few drops of cannabis oil, the seizures stopped. Charlotte began walking and talking again. Matt was so excited that he wanted to scream about the benefits of medical marijuana from the rooftops. It saved his child's life. The concoction developed for the child had low levels of THC (the "high" producing factor). With compassion maybe we as a nation can come together to make medicinal marijuana available for people who need it.[159] I'm not endorsing recreational marijuana in all circumstances, but I can't imagine how stopping the Figis and others from obtaining this lifesaving drug is compassionate or Christian.

7

Good Government in the Age of Trump

Although democracy was largely unknown to ancient Hebrew writers, the Bible specifies clear standards for just rulers. These are rational standards on which we all can agree. We all want a government that is free from bribery, falsehoods, and favoritism; that upholds fairness, honesty, and decency; and that promotes our collective good. And for us Americans, we want a government that upholds our individual rights and our Constitution. Of course, we often dispute how far those individual rights extend. Although we may disagree on how to apply our fundamental rules, the biblical principles of honest, humble service for leaders are irrefutable. We can and should integrate such principles into our own standards for our democratically elected leaders.

Given the dramatic presidential election of 2016, it's fair to assess the behavior of Donald Trump and his cohorts up and down the administration. We would have done the same for his opponent, Hillary Clinton, had she won. Growing up, I was always taught to measure my own and others' behavior against the standards set forth in the Bible. So this book would not complete my own scriptural journey without holding up the mirror of God's Word to our next president and to all leaders—political, economic, and religious.

Many evangelical leaders used their positions in the ministry to condemn both Bill Clinton and Barack Obama. They castigated Bill

Clinton's extramarital affairs, as well they should have, though they ignored all the good he did. But with Obama, they attacked him in the most unchristian manner I have ever seen—and without a scintilla of evidence. Some Bible-believing Christians said that Obama was the Antichrist.[160] This is unthinkable—all because he obeyed Jesus by offering provisions for the working poor and the sick. And when they weren't making that apocalyptic pronouncement, they said he was a Muslim, a terrorist, and an atheist who wasn't even born in America.

Politicians are human beings. They all make mistakes. Even biblical heroes and prophets made egregious mistakes. We should be careful in condemning any leader who doesn't think the way we do. There are always multiple ways to achieve similar ends. But we can judge leaders based on their actions and words to see if their works comply with biblical standards.

Donald Trump is unlike any politician who's ever run for president before. In some ways he seems like the antithesis of a godly man. His business behavior is questionable—if not flat-out illegal, immoral, and unethical. He objectifies and demeans women in obeisance to the gods of glamour and lookism. He not only committed adultery, as did Bill Clinton, but he openly bragged about his celebrity privilege to grab women "by the p***y." At best, he tolerates racists in his inner circle; at worst he stokes racial divisiveness, which violates the Bible. Trump doesn't seem to hold a high regard for religion or religious people. His frequent statements ("I'm very, very rich") strongly suggest that his god is Mammon, and perhaps that is his biggest appeal. We believe that a moneymaker can bring our country prosperity—a belief not inherently wrong. So granted, I have a negative view of Trump, and many Christians are entitled to hold a positive view. But if we are going to put the Bible in the center of our politics, we must assess Trump's words and conduct against biblical standards.

Rulers Must Be Fair and Impartial

The Old Testament forbade rulers from showing favoritism for any one group.

> Do not pervert justice; **do not show partiality to the poor or favoritism to the great**, but judge your neighbor fairly. (Leviticus 19:15)

> And I charged your judges at that time, "Hear the disputes between your people **and judge fairly**, whether the case is between two Israelites or between an Israelite and a foreigner residing among you. **Do not show partiality in judging; hear both small and great alike.** Do not be afraid of anyone, for judgment belongs to God. Bring me [Moses] any case too hard for you, and I will hear it." (Deuteronomy 1:16–17)

Here's a test for our representatives today: Do they hear the small as well as the great? Not likely. They hear the donors to their campaigns. These commands are repeated several more times.

> He [the good king, Jehoshaphat] appointed judges in the land, in each of the fortified cities of Judah. He told them, **"Consider carefully what you do, because you are not judging for mere mortals but for the Lord,** who is with you whenever you give a verdict. Now let the fear of the Lord be on you. Judge carefully, **for with the Lord our God there is no injustice or partiality or bribery."** (2 Chronicles 19:5–7)

> These also are sayings of the wise: **To show partiality in judging is not good....** (Proverbs 24:23)

No modern writer could say it more eloquently than the Bible. Gifts, regardless of whether they are technically bribes, blind our perception and pervert the words of the righteous. Campaign donations certainly blind the perception of our leaders. History shows that Thomas Jefferson, a great yet flawed man, opposed slavery in his youth. But after he married and inherited 11,000 acres of land and 135 slaves, he changed his tune. The gifts from his wife perverted his words and blinded his eyes. He could not keep his land without his slaves, so his love of wealth and prominence overcame his conscience.[161]

Donald Trump garnered much respect among many working class people because he opposed the Republican establishment and expressed what many felt, although it was "politically incorrect," even for conservatives. He promised the giant Detroit automakers that if he were elected, he'd impose a tariff on Mexican built cars and auto parts, enacting a penalty on them for taking jobs out of America.[162] He opposed the Trans-Pacific Partnership Agreement (TPP), as did Bernie Sanders, because he believed it hurt American workers.

Trump also garnered respect from all because he self-funded his campaign. Therefore, he proclaimed that he would be beholden to none. His personal wealth gave him independence. He would not be at the mercy of large donors who could later call in favors. This was very appealing. He used his own jet, his offices, and his resorts for campaign functions, for which he did reimburse himself about 11 million, yet he wrote off significant loans he made to his campaign. Because of his history in television, he knew how to garner much publicity for free (about $5 billion worth), and he ended up spending over a third less than his opponent.[163] He defied all traditional ways of fund-raising and campaigning, and he won. So he deserves credit for that.

This rosy surface picture, however, has a dirty underbelly: super PACs. Although candidates are not supposed to know who their super PAC funders are, they do know. Linda McMahon donated over 7 million to a super PAC to help elect Trump, and she is now his pick to head the Small Business Administration. So far, Trump has tapped six big donors from his super PACs to serve in his administration. While past presidents have given choice diplomatic positions overseas to their big donors, it appears that Trump is staffing more of his Cabinet with them.[164] His top donor class is not only filling his Cabinet but also helping him pick the top leaders for his administration.[165]

Rulers Must Avoid Emoluments

In his vision of the ideal government, Moses recognized that people would someday want a king like other nations had. Throughout history, even today, people are drawn to strong leaders who promise prosperity and comfort them with a feeling of instant certainty about the world (even if such leaders are narcissistic and advocate tough repressive policies in other areas). But Hebrew law forbade such a leader from using his position to amass great personal wealth.

> When you enter the land the Lord your God is giving you and have taken possession of it and settled in it, and you say, "Let us set a king over us like all the nations around us," be sure to appoint over you a king the Lord your God chooses. He must be from among your fellow Israelites. Do not place a foreigner over you, one who is not an Israelite. **The king, moreover, must not acquire great numbers of horses for himself** or make the people return to Egypt to get more of them, for the Lord has told you, "You are not to go back that way again." **He must not take many wives, or his heart will be led astray. He must not accumulate large amounts of silver and gold.** When he takes the throne of his kingdom, he is to write for himself on a scroll a copy of this law, taken from that of the Levitical priests. It is to be with him, **and he is to read it all the days of his life** so that he may learn to revere the Lord his God and follow carefully all the words of this law and these decrees and **not consider himself better than his fellow Israelites and turn from the law to the right or to the left.** Then he and his descendants will reign a long time over his kingdom in Israel. (Deuteronomy 17:14–20)

God didn't want national rulers to use their positions to get rich for themselves or to think that they were better than their fellow citizens. Greed and lust in a ruler are a dangerous combination, according to Moses. And you can also see that God wanted His rulers to be knowledgeable of the law. The king was commanded to read God's law "all the days of his life." Granted, in those days the secular law and the religious law were combined. But certainly a godly, just president would be knowledgeable of the laws of the US and its Constitution.

Before Donald Trump was elected, I must confess that as a lawyer, I had almost forgotten about the emoluments clause in our US Constitution. Just in case you haven't studied this, here is Article 1, Section 9, Clause 8:

> No Title of nobility shall be granted by the United States: And no person holding any office of profit or trust under them, shall, without the consent of the Congress, accept of any present, emolument, office, or title, of any kind whatever, from any King, Prince, or foreign State.

The word *emolument* means profit, salary, fees, recompense, or compensation. In short, this means that federal office holders cannot accept gifts, profits, fees, or perks from foreign leaders or their governments. In the immediate aftermath of the Revolutionary War, the British and the French were trying to use the US in a proxy war for influence in the world. The US was relatively poor and didn't have the vast infrastructure we take for granted today. In their wisdom the founding fathers saw that foreign entities, having failed to conquer the US on the battlefield, might try to sway American policy by bribing government officials. While we all easily understand the idea of a present (a gift), the term *emoluments* broadens the concept considerably in order to encompass other kinds of personal favors, profits, or perks that may not be a "gift" in a technical sense but are still recompense.

Trump's international business dealings create a potential constitutional crisis if he and his family members don't divest themselves of their holdings, which is hard to do, considering the nature of his assets. Trump has ostensibly turned his businesses over to his children in a blind trust to create a barrier between his holdings and him personally, but then he has these same children sitting in on meetings with foreign dignitaries, thus erasing any concept of distance between those who run his business and those who will help run his administration. Stocks are easy to hold in a blind trust because your trustee can sell and trade them without your knowledge. But real estate, by its nature, is public. It would be hard not to know what was happening with it.

The bank of China has significant holdings in two of Trump's towers. Legal scholars were quick to point out that this could be a serious breach of the Constitution. George W. Bush's own legal ethics attorney, Richard Painter, warned:

> [Congress] should send a clear message to him that he should divest his assets, and that they will regard dealings with his companies that he owns abroad and any entities owned by foreign governments as a potential violation of the Emoluments Clause unless he can prove it was an arm's-length transaction.

In fact, Painter said running afoul of the emoluments clause would be grounds for impeachment.[166] Yes, impeachment! This isn't Clinton's lawyer or Obama's lawyer. This is Republican George W. Bush's top ethics attorney.

A consensus seems to be emerging that should foreign governments give Trump's businesses a favorable deal, paying anything above fair market value, then there is an instant violation of the emoluments clause. Painter went on to speculate that as Trump's name may increase in value, because he's the president, there may be a violation of the emoluments clause, even if there is no direct proof that Trump was purposefully trying to extort higher prices from foreign visitors.[167] But whether or not Trump has technically violated the Constitution, he seems perfectly okay with the obvious appearance of impropriety.

The *Washington Post* reported that hundreds of diplomats are already flocking to the new Trump hotel in Washington DC, and when the diplomats were off the record, they were happy to admit, "Why wouldn't I stay at his hotel blocks from the White House, so I can tell the new president, 'I love your new hotel!'"[168] Already, national security is implicated if foreign businesses and governments can use the Trump brand to curry favor with the president. But all Christians on the left and the right should ask, "Is this moral?" Is using the presidency to promote your hotel, vodka, steaks, condominiums, or golf resorts complying with the spirit of the law or the Bible?

When President Obama was campaigning for the presidency, he sought legal counsel and liquidated all of his investments. Ronald Reagan, Bill Clinton and both Bush presidents put their assets into blind trusts.[169] That wasn't partisanship; it was ethical. But they didn't hold hotels all over the world that needed cooperation and favors from foreign governments.

There is ancient wisdom in the Bible, regardless of our beliefs about its inspiration. When people in power are tempted with bribes, favors, or special gifts, bad things happen. The Bible brings this up repeatedly.

> Judges and officers shalt thou make thee in all thy gates, which the Lord thy God giveth thee, throughout thy tribes: and they shall judge the people with just judgment. Thou shalt not wrest judgment; **thou shalt not respect persons, neither take a gift: for a gift doth blind the eyes of the wise, and pervert the words of the righteous.** (Deuteronomy 16:18–19 KJV)

> Do not accept a bribe, for **a bribe blinds those who see** and twists the words of the innocent. (Exodus 23:8)

> When the righteous thrive, the people rejoice; when the wicked rule, the people groan. A man who loves wisdom brings joy to his father, but a companion of prostitutes squanders his wealth. **By justice a king gives a country stability, but those who are greedy for bribes tear it down.** (Proverbs 29:2–4)

> The greedy bring ruin to their households, but the one who hates bribes will live. (Proverbs 15:27)

These scriptures establish a pattern. God doesn't like rulers, kings, judges, or princes—even individuals—who take bribes and use their positions to amass wealth for themselves and pursue selfish ambition. Bribes and gifts will blind a good ruler and cause him to do bad things. This seems obvious in theory, so why are the American people giving Donald Trump a pass on this issue?

There is plenty of scorn to pour on both parties. Both Democrats and Republicans have been far too cozy with special interests and big money. Regardless, so far, Donald Trump has resisted calls to divest his business interests so that he can govern in a fair, impartial manner. Having your two children and a third party manage your real estate is not blind. Given some of his campaign rhetoric, people are right to question his ethics. He seems all too keen to let foreign governments and businesses curry favor with him by patronizing his businesses. And that looks like a bribe to me. Even if it's not a technical bribe under the US law, it certainly runs afoul of the spirit of US law and the Bible. Remember, the Bible says to avoid the *appearance* of evil (1 Thessalonians 5:22). One reason why is that the appearance of evil undermines faith and trust.

As we were finalizing this book, *Newsweek* ran an exclusive report that Donald Trump had in fact tried to use his position as president-elect to help persuade another country to help one of his businesses. Turkish President Recep Tayyip Erdogan called Trump to congratulate him on his election. Trump then took the call as an opportunity to hype up his business associate, Mehmet Ali Yalcindag, who runs the Trump towers in Istanbul. Trump showered compliments on Yalcindag.[170] The implication was obvious: "If you want to ingratiate yourself with the new Trump administration, you should be good to my business associates" (wink, wink).

But the Turkish president didn't do as Trump expected. President Erdogan has wanted a Turkish imam living in Pennsylvania to be extradited back to Turkey on suspicion of plotting a coup against him. Rather than rolling out the red carpet for Trump's business associate, Erdogan arrested him on spurious charges. Rather than using the carrot, the Turkish president was happy to use the stick. Erdogan was eager to move against Trump's business interest in order to influence US policy toward Turkey.[171] That's a dangerous precedent, and Trump is barely in office. If Turkey, a US ally, is willing to play hardball like this so soon, what will China or Russia do?

> Extortion turns a wise person into a fool, and **a bribe corrupts the heart**. (Ecclesiastes 7:7)

I first took the above scripture to mean that leaders must not use their position to extort the less powerful. Foolish leaders try to bully others; wise leaders don't. But this verse also focuses on the victim of extortion—meaning a wise ruler can be turned into a fool if someone is able to extort him. We've all seen TV shows where rich and powerful families of kidnapped children cave into outrageous demands and do foolish things because they fear losing their loved ones. When someone has great leverage over you (a family member or your wealth), it is difficult to be objective and effective, and Trump certainly loves his business empire. If Trump's financial interests make him susceptible to extortion by foreign interests, then it's a grave threat to national security.

Just Rulers Must Not Oppress or Defraud the Poor, the Laborer, or the Immigrant

Defending the poor is one of the Bible's leading commandments for rulers. The Bible mentions this issue more times than any other just quality in a ruler except for truthfulness and wisdom. One could reasonably conclude that this is because it is so easy to despise and oppress the poor. Greed, corruption, bribes, and favoritism all seem to follow from mistreatment of the poor. Earlier we saw that laws to provide for the poor were contained in the original legal system of the Hebrews. Righteous rule goes hand in hand with caring for the poor, the widow, the fatherless, the stranger—those who are the most defenseless in our society.

> God presides in the great assembly; **he renders judgment** among the "gods": "How long will you defend the unjust and show partiality to the wicked? **Defend the weak and the fatherless; uphold the cause of the poor and the oppressed**. Rescue the weak and the needy; deliver them from the hand of the wicked." (Psalm 82:1-4)

The following passage reinforces the point that advocating the cause of the poor is the responsibility of a leader.

> Endow the king with your justice, O God, the royal son with your righteousness. May he judge your people in righteousness, your afflicted ones with justice.... **May he defend the afflicted among the people and save the children of the needy; may he crush the oppressor.** (Psalm 72:1-2, 4)

A ruler who oppresses the poor is like a driving rain that leaves no crops. (Proverbs 28:3)

Kings and rulers are commanded to advocate for the poor and those who have no voice. We've already covered the instructions for a king stated by King Lemuel:

Speak up for those who cannot speak for themselves, for the rights of all who are destitute. Speak up and judge fairly; defend the rights of the poor and needy. (Proverbs 31:8–9)

How does all this apply to Donald Trump? Well, he's only begun governance, so we cannot say for sure what he will do. He has promised to improve opportunities for all. Yet my dad always told me that if I want to know how a man will behave in the future, I must look at what he's done in the past.

Rulers and Business Owners Must Pay Their Workers

Do not defraud or rob your neighbor. **Do not hold back the wages of a hired worker overnight**. (Leviticus 19:13)

Do not take advantage of a hired worker who is poor and needy, whether that worker is a fellow Israelite or a foreigner residing in one of your towns. **Pay them their wages each day** before sunset, because they are poor and are counting on it. Otherwise they may cry to the Lord against you, and you will be guilty of sin. (Deuteronomy 24:14–15)

A tyrannical ruler practices extortion, but one who hates ill-gotten gain will enjoy a long reign. (Proverbs 28:16)

God's Word is clear: employers should pay their workers and not try to cheat them out of their wages. This was the law, divinely dictated to Moses. Donald Trump made his business experience, particularly in the realm of construction and real estate, his prime selling point. But the numerous reports of Trump's not paying his employees and contractors is particularly troubling, as it gives us insight into his character.

In theory, a selling point for business leaders is that they will be fiscally responsible, and they'll treat the nation's finances as carefully as they'd treat their own. But conversely, a businessman who got rich by cheating people demonstrates that he's not above cheating the voters. Trump suggested the same by just analogizing the national debt crisis to his own bankruptcies.[172] In bankruptcy you force your creditors to accept pennies on the dollar, which gives those hopelessly in debt a fresh start—a provision that has blessed Trump multiple times throughout his career. But Trump suggested that our government should just write off our national debt as he did—forget all who get screwed in the process or the damage to the full faith and credit of the United States or the stock market.

Not paying your bills is the same as stealing, and it's wicked. **"The wicked borrow and do not repay**, but the righteous give generously" (Psalm 37:21). See also Ecclesiastes 5:4: "When you make a vow to God, do not delay to fulfill it. He has no pleasure in fools; fulfill your vow;" and see the exhortation from Romans 13:8: **"Let no debt remain outstanding**, except the continuing debt to love one another, for whoever loves others has fulfilled the law."

USA Today, no left-wing tabloid, did a comprehensive exposé on Trump's business dealings and found that thousands of businesses and employees have accused him of not paying them as he promised. Trump was involved in over 3,500 lawsuits.[173] Three thousand five hundred! Almost all these lawsuits were filed *before* Trump announced his candidacy. Can we honestly say that all of these people are lying? Yes, in the business world, both sides can play fast and loose with the truth. Each side has an incentive to cut its own costs and raise prices. But 3,500 complaints for nonpayment are a huge number.

And it wasn't just other big investors who were suing Trump. It was the little guys—average employees and small business owners, who filed suit because they believed that Trump didn't play fair.

> A glass company in New Jersey. A carpet company. A plumber. Painters. Forty-eight waiters. Dozens of bartenders and other hourly workers at his resorts and clubs, coast to coast. Real estate brokers who sold his properties. And, ironically, several law firms that once represented him in these suits and others.[174]

Also, since 2005 Trump's businesses have been cited twenty-four times for violating the law by failing to pay the minimum wage or overtime. Released documents show that on Trump's Taj Mahal casino in Atlantic City alone, approximately 253 subcontractors weren't paid in full or on time, including workers who installed walls, chandeliers, and plumbing. *USA Today* summarizes:

> The actions in total paint a portrait of Trump's sprawling organization frequently failing to pay small businesses and individuals, then sometimes tying them up in court and other negotiations for years. In some cases, the Trump teams financially overpower and outlast much smaller opponents, draining their resources. Some just give up the fight, or settle for less; some have ended up in bankruptcy or out of business altogether.[175]

Even the conservative *Wall Street Journal* noted that Trump's tactics were particularly aggressive for an industry where business owners often get into disputes with contractors. They went on to report that it wasn't just disputes with builders, but Trump regularly stiffed the workers and suppliers of his casinos once they were operating. Trump's own words are a bit scary:

> "If they do a good job, I won't cut them at all," Mr. Trump said of businesses he contracts with, saying "**it's probably 1,000 to one where I pay.**" He said he occasionally won't pay fully when work is simply satisfactory or "an OK to bad job.... If it's OK, then I'll sometimes cut them." In dealing with public projects such as bridge-building, he said, "that should be the attitude of the country."[176]

According to law, if parties want a certain quality, they must specify it in their contract. If it's an okay job, that means the person fulfilled his legal requirements, and you are required to pay according to your contractual agreement. It's fine to specify higher standards for a job, but Trump's admission that an okay job gets a unilateral price reduction is an admission of cheating—or at a minimum, breach of contract.

There is a human cost to this. Edward Friel was a small business owner who was working in Atlantic City. When Trump refused to pay Friel's company for the cabinets he had installed, Friel was shocked and protested the unfair treatment. But rather than pay up, Trump blackballed Friel's company, telling his colleagues in the area never to hire him. Friel's company went bankrupt several years later. Numerous people have come forward to claim that Trump used similarly unfair tactics.[177]

When aggrieved parties take Trump to court, Trump then uses his wealth and power to drag out the legal proceedings in the hopes that plaintiffs will give up or run out of money for lawyers. *USA Today* noted that Trump's "Goliath versus David" tactics help him avoid paying in court. And when courts or tribunals ruled against him, Trump still refused to pay.[178]

Many don't understand that a court judgment is merely a piece of paper saying someone owes you money or property. You then have to pay a second time for an attorney to enforce a judgment before you collect one dime. Collection attorneys often take 33–40% of the moneys collected, and that's not unfair because many steps may be required before you can garnishee a bank account or place judgment liens on real estate. The result is that the little guy—*if* he succeeds at trial and *after* he's already paid lawyers to litigate the matter—ends up with 60–70% of what he is owed. This is one reason why parties will settle for less. They come out no better if they litigate and win. Ruthless businesspeople know this, so they game the system to get out of paying their just debts.

Although we don't hear much about this coming from Republicans, the Bible recognized this very type of behavior.

> But you have dishonored the poor. Is it not the rich who are exploiting you? **Are they not the ones who are dragging you into court?** (James 2:6)

> Now listen, you rich people, weep and wail because of the misery that is coming on you.... **Look! The wages you failed to pay the workers who mowed your fields are crying out against you.** The cries of the harvesters have reached the ears of the Lord Almighty. You have lived on earth in luxury and self-indulgence. You have fattened yourselves in the day of slaughter. (James 5:1, 4–5)

Wow. Some progressives dismiss the Bible as no longer relevant, yet this New Testament scripture sounds like it was written yesterday as it takes aim at rich people who exploit the less wealthy and take them to court. And the Old Testament is just as strong.

> "**Woe to him who builds his palace by unrighteousness,** his upper rooms by injustice, **making his own people work for nothing, not paying them for their labor.** He says, 'I will build myself a great palace with spacious upper rooms.' So he makes large windows in it, panels it with cedar and decorates it in red. (Jeremiah 22:13–14)

Eerie. It's almost as if the prophet Jeremiah is speaking to Donald Trump directly. But there's more.

> The Lord enters into **judgment against the elders and leaders of his people: "It is you who have ruined my vineyard; the plunder from the poor is in your houses. What do you mean by crushing my people and grinding the faces of the poor?"** declares the Lord, the Lord Almighty. (Isaiah 3:14–15)

> See how each of the princes of Israel who are in you uses his power to shed blood...In you are people who accept bribes to shed blood; **you take interest and make a profit from the poor. You extort unjust gain from your neighbors. And you have forgotten me**, declares the Sovereign Lord. (Ezekiel 22:6, 12)

> "So I will come to put you on trial. I will be quick to testify against sorcerers, **adulterers and perjurers, against those who defraud laborers of their wages,** who oppress the widows and the fatherless, and deprive the foreigners among you of justice, but do not fear me," says the Lord Almighty. (Malachi 3:5)

In the Bible, treating workers unfairly was a grave abomination before God, and the scriptures condemn it repeatedly. By now, none can doubt that the Old Testament prophets were condemning the rich rulers and princes of their day.

Much evidence supports concern that Trump will oppress the poor and those looking to work for a fair wage. It is ironic that so many working class people believe that a rich man who cheated his workers, bought his steel from China rather than from American factories, and ripped off poor people with his Trump University, had their best interests at heart all along and is now their champion.

His first proposed Secretary of Labor is a businessman and political donor who opposes any increase in the minimum wage or expansion of overtime pay. He praises increased automation because businesses won't have to pay machines for vacations, sick leave, overtime, or worker's compensation for job-related injuries.[179] Yet the average blue-collar guy who needs those factory jobs (soon to be automated) believes that Trump and his ilk will make things better for him.

Is it okay to turn a blind eye to Trump's business practices in order to get a few more pro-life judges into the courts? I hope and pray that once Trump has power, he remembers those downtrodden workers he promised to protect. Surely, the pro-life majority can hold him to account for some biblical standard.

Wicked Schemes that Entrap the Poor: A Look at Trump University

It's hard to view Trump University as anything more than a scam. Trump University was not a university at all, although it held itself out as one. It lured people in with promises of gaining Donald Trump's "secrets" in real estate. Trump University claimed that its instructors were handpicked by Trump, when they were not. And Trump came dangerously close to guaranteeing success to applicants by saying, "I can turn anyone into a successful real estate investor, including you." That gives the impression that Trump was intimately involved with the process, although he wasn't. People were asked to pay thousands and tens of thousands of dollars for this fake degree, but in the end they got little—except a picture with a cardboard cutout of Trump.[180]

Trump would have us believe that the class-action lawsuits were just another left-wing campaign conspiracy against him, but these lawsuits were filed before he became a candidate for president. Even conservative media outlets, such as the *National Review*, called Trump out on his deceptive business practices: Trump University sold few, if any, real tips or techniques for real estate but instead sold people a fantasy of being mentored by Trump. Officials claimed that Trump would occasionally stop by the university.[181]

To his credit Mitt Romney spoke out against Trump and his deceptive practices: "His promises are as worthless as a degree from Trump University. He's playing members of the American public for suckers: He gets a free ride to the White House, and all we get is a lousy hat." But Romney was compromised because he had sought Trump's endorsement in 2012[182] and then began sucking up to Trump after he won the election.[183] So far, it looks as if Trump didn't appreciate Romney's newfound conversion to his side.

Regardless of whether you think Romney is a flip-flopper, he was right about Trump University, as were the numerous journalists who covered it. They can't all be wrong and lying about a case that came up long before Trump announced his candidacy. At the least, Trump U was a bait and switch scheme. Some may have little sympathy for gullible people swindled by obvious get-rich-quick schemes. But the law has long expressed the moral principle. "No rogue should enjoy his ill-gotten plunder for the simple reason that his victim is by chance a fool." And biblical justice agrees.

> **For the vile person will speak villany,** and his heart will work iniquity, to practise hypocrisy.... The instruments also of the churl are evil: he deviseth **wicked devices to destroy the poor with lying words,** even when the needy speaketh right. (Isaiah 32:6–7 KJV)

> "Among my people are **the wicked** who lie in wait like men who snare birds and like those who set traps to catch people. Like cages full of birds, their houses are full of deceit; they **have become rich and powerful and have grown fat and sleek.** Their evil deeds have no limit; they do not seek justice. **They do not promote the case of the fatherless; they do not defend the just cause of the poor.** Should I not punish them for this?" declares the Lord. "Should I not avenge myself on such a nation as this? (Jeremiah 5:26–29)

> **In his arrogance the wicked man hunts down the weak, who are caught in the schemes he devises.** He boasts about the cravings of his heart; he blesses the greedy and reviles the Lord. (Psalm 10:2–3)

It's almost as if King David wrote Psalm 10 directly for Trump U, which used lying words to ensnare the poor. The Bible is clear: people who devise get-rich-quick-schemes or other deceptive business practices that cheat the little guy out of his money are wicked.

Some will inevitably cry, "Well, look at the Clinton Foundation; that's no better." It's a false comparison on many levels. Even if you believe the negative assertions that Hillary Clinton, while Secretary of State, pulled strings for or granted access for big Clinton Foundation donors, it doesn't take away from the fact that the Clinton Foundation saves lives,[184] whereas Trump University destroyed livelihoods. The Clinton Foundation took money from the rich and gave it to the poor. So even if she gave big donors favored treatment, she wasn't robbing poor people. Yes, their foundation took donations from some dodgy individuals, but few charities, if any, screen their donors, for all money spends the same.[185]

Regardless, the overall goal and the results of the Clinton Foundation were laudable and effective. Whether it's giving clean water to thirsty villages or lowering the costs of malaria medicines and HIV drugs, the Clintons used their wealth and privilege to make a difference in poor people's lives, and they did so not via big government, but by private philanthropy,[186] which the Republicans purport to adore. My heart rose when James Carville defended the Clinton Foundation by saying, "Somebody is going to Hell over this."[187] Democrats are too squeamish about using religion to make their points, and they need to pick up their Bibles and make a moral case for their policies.

Further, it's totally illogical to compare a profit-making enterprise, Trump University, to a non-profit foundation. The Clinton Foundation didn't target poor people for donations. It courted rich people to give to the poor—what the Bible actually commands. Trump University gained its wealth from lower and middle-income people, who were struggling to get ahead—people who by comparison were poor. Giving Trump the most benefit of the doubt, the best one can say is that he allowed another company to use his name, his brand, for a wicked purpose, and he didn't pay attention to the evil perpetrated in his name.

Even if we use Donald Trump's charitable foundation, as the basis for comparison with the Clinton Foundation, we see that Trump used other people's donations for his own self-aggrandizement and to make donations to politicians. His charity is now being investigated for its violations of nonprofit law.[188] Further, do we see tens of thousands (if not millions) of people benefiting from Trump's philanthropy? Compare that to multitudes being saved by the Clintons' philanthropy, which has partnered with businesses and governments around the world to change health care and make expensive lifesaving drugs affordable to the poor. The Clinton Foundation has a solid A rating by respected charity watch groups, as it spends 88% of its income on program services.[189]

So I'm happy to compare the fruits that Hillary Clinton has produced to the fruits that Donald Trump has produced. But that's not the purpose of this book. Because Donald Trump is the new president, he is held to a higher standard. The point is that the Bible condemns all scams where the rich prey on the poor.

Promoting Hatred of Immigrants Violates God's Law

In researching for this book, we discovered numerous biblical commands to be good to the foreigners who had come to live among the Israelites—the equivalent of our undocumented immigrants of today (See Chapter Four, Jesus Loves Illegal Aliens). We also discussed how Jesus made our conduct toward immigrants one of His key tests for deciding who gets into His kingdom. On this score, where the evidence is overwhelming, Donald Trump has violated God's law. He has given succor to racists and bigots. He's demonized the stranger and used lying words to turn Christians against each other. One could argue that he founded his campaign on racist, divisive rhetoric. Here are Trump's actual words:

> When Mexico sends its people, they're not sending their best. They're not sending you. They're not sending you. They're send-

ing people that have lots of problems, and they're bringing those problems with us. They're bringing drugs. They're bringing crime. They're rapists. And some, I assume, are good people (Donald Trump, June 16, 2015).[190]

How does this compare to God's commands for how we should treat immigrants?

Do not mistreat or oppress a foreigner, for you were foreigners in Egypt. (Exodus 22:21)

The foreigner residing among you must be treated as your native-born. Love them as yourself, for you were foreigners in Egypt. I am the Lord your God. (Leviticus 19:34)

And you are to **love those who are foreigners**, for you yourselves were foreigners in Egypt. (Deuteronomy 10:19)

Do not take advantage of a hired worker who is poor and needy, whether that worker a fellow Israelite **or a foreigner** residing in one of your towns. (Deuteronomy 24:14)

Who among us can say that Donald Trump has demonstrated love for the foreigner when he called them rapists and criminals and when he led the cry to drive 11 million out of our land? Certainly, Latinos felt demonized by his lying words. Trump also fell short of New Testament commandments that admonish Christians not to judge each other based on national origin.

So in Christ Jesus you are all children of God through faith, for all of you who were baptized into Christ have clothed yourselves with Christ. **There is neither Jew nor Gentile**, neither slave nor free, nor is there male and female, for **you are all one in Christ Jesus. If you belong to Christ, then you are Abraham's seed, and heirs according to the promise.** (Galatians 3:26–29)

Consequently, **you are no longer foreigners and strangers, but fellow citizens with God's people and also members of his household**, built on the foundation of the apostles and prophets, with Christ Jesus himself as the chief cornerstone. (Ephesians 2:19–20)

If the "rapists and criminals" comments didn't run afoul of God's commandments, then what about Trump's comments about the Hoosier-born federal judge who was presiding over the Trump

University case. Judge Gonzalo Curiel did have a Mexican heritage, but he was born and reared in Middle America. In May 2016 Trump attacked his Mexican heritage as cause for his disqualification to adjudicate the Trump University case. "He's a Mexican," Trump said to CNN. "We're building a wall between here and Mexico. The answer is, he is giving us very unfair rulings — rulings that people can't even believe." Curiel was a distinguished prosecutor before becoming a judge. In fact, he had prosecuted "fellow Mexicans" by going after the drug cartels in the 1990s. Curiel's "own people" vowed revenge for his prosecution and marked him for death.[191] But Trump didn't like his rulings and immediately chalked it up to his race.

Even Republicans called Trump out for being racist. "Claiming a person can't do their job because of their race is sort of like the textbook definition of a racist comment," House Speaker Paul Ryan said in response to Trump's comments. Ryan disavowed Trump's words as "absolutely unacceptable."[192]

These are just two incidents. We haven't forgotten Trump's slow disavowal of David Duke and the Ku Klux Klan, his Cinco de Mayo Taco Tweet, his renewed vicious attacks on the Central Park Five (wrongly accused black men who were all acquitted by DNA evidence), his approval of beating African American protestors, his attacking the Muslim Gold Star family whose son, U.S. Army Captain Humayun Khan, died serving in Iraq, or his touting of the racist "birther" myth about President Obama—to cite only a few.

One or two comments off the cuff can be a careless mistake, but all this racist rhetoric reveals what's really in Trump's heart—and it ain't Christian love for all mankind. If Christians want to preserve any moral authority on other issues, they must live up to the standards that they profess. You can't say that you want God in the center of your politics but ignore all the racism that directly contradicts God's law. Jesus said how you treat the stranger (that immigrant from another land) has eternal consequences. In this regard Trump seems to be falling far behind. You're free to advocate for

Trump on other grounds, but you can't do it "in the name of Jesus."

The Fruits of Hateful Lying Campaign Words

> There are six things the Lord hates, seven that are detestable to him: haughty eyes, **a lying tongue**, hands that shed innocent blood, a heart that devises wicked schemes, feet that are quick to rush into evil, **a false witness who pours out lies and a person who stirs up conflict in the community.** (Proverbs 6:16–19)

Notice the focus on hostile intentions in the above passage. Lying, slander, and discord rank up there with shedding innocent blood. As Trump's campaign demonstrated, when leaders lie and sow discord, the result often turns violent. In the days following his election, hundreds of hate crimes were committed against immigrants and American citizens who are people of color. Earlier we referenced the 867 cases of harassment and intimidation that the Southern Poverty Law Center documented in the ten days following the November 8 election. Swastikas were spray-painted in many places. One vandal wrote: "Heil Trump." Slogans of "Make America White Again" were often sprayed in conjunction. Another vandal wrote, "Black Lives Don't Matter and neither does your votes." Trump supporters occasionally chanted "White power." Muslims are being assaulted and attacked. Mosques receive death threats and letters calling for their extermination. Latino kids are greeted in school with chants of "Build the Wall."[193] Moreover, open neo-Nazis and other white supremacists are gathering in Washington, and they are celebrating Trump's victory with cries of "Heil Trump" and "Hail Trump," making Nazi-style salutes.[194] Let's look at it this way. If Trump is not a racist, why are these avowed racists ecstatic over his election?

This is not happening in a vacuum. Trump did eventually tell his supporters to stop it, but it took five days for him to do so.[195] And this was after a campaign of whipping up fear and racism. Trump's call for calm was too little too late, and it came only after prompting from the press. Trump presided over a campaign of hatred and division, and his supporters were only reflecting what they saw as acceptable coming from their candidate. So how can Christians look at Trump and the hate his campaign has unleashed and conclude, "Yes, he's following Christ's example"?

Jesus commanded His disciples to judge people by their works, not by their words. So if Trump supporters are committing acts of racism, vandalism, assault, and intimidation to other people, does he not bear some responsibility? If Trump were a humble compassionate Christian who genuinely sowed unity throughout his campaign, why were his supporters acting so terribly?

> Watch out **for false prophets**. They come to you in sheep's clothing, but inwardly they are ferocious wolves. **By their fruit you will recognize them**.... A good tree cannot bear bad fruit, and a bad tree cannot bear good fruit.... **Not everyone who says to me, 'Lord, Lord,' will enter the kingdom of heaven**, but only the one who does the will of my Father who is in heaven. (Matthew 7:15–16, 18, 20–21)

So what are the fruits of Trump's campaign? We have the normalization of racist behavior and hundreds of racist attacks. Trump's supporters will inevitably argue that although some racist incidents occurred, they don't represent Trump or the majority of Trump supporters. Fair enough. An isolated racist comment or one "locker room joke" about women wouldn't be enough. But we've got a pattern here. Trump is seventy years old. He's borne fruit—in business, in his personal life, and in his campaign.

God Loves Leaders Who Embrace Truth, Not Lies

Consider these verses:

> **Mercy and truth preserve the king:** and his throne is upholden by mercy. (Proverbs 20:28 KJV)

King David told his young son Solomon that it was the duty of rulers to seek the truth and to uphold God's law.

Remove from me the way of lying: and grant me thy law graciously. I have chosen the way of truth: thy judgments have I laid before me. (Psalm 119:29–30 KJV)

If lying weren't so tempting for a ruler, King David wouldn't be praying that it be removed. Lying is antithetical to the love of God's law.

I hate and detest falsehood but I love your law. (Psalm 119:163)

As we saw in some earlier scriptures, King Solomon carried on the tradition of extolling the virtues of truth both for those who rule and for everyone else.

The Lord detests lying lips, but he delights in people who are trustworthy. (Proverbs 12:22)

Eloquent lips are unsuited to a godless fool—**how much worse lying lips to a ruler!** (Proverbs 17:7)

Listen, for I have trustworthy things to say; **I open my lips to speak what is right. My mouth speaks what is true, for my lips detest wickedness**. All the words of my mouth are just; none of them is crooked or perverse. (Proverbs 8:6–8)

Lord, who may dwell in your sacred tent? Who may live on your holy mountain? The one whose walk is blameless, who does what is righteous, **who speaks the truth from their heart**; whose tongue utters no slander, **who does no wrong to a neighbor, and casts no slur on others**.... (Psalm 15:1–3)

The Bible is clear: You cannot show forth righteousness unless you speak the truth.

A fool's wrath is presently known: but a prudent man covereth shame. **He that speaketh truth sheweth forth righteousness: but a false witness deceit.** There is that speaketh like the piercings of a sword: but the tongue of the wise is health. (Proverbs 12:16–18 KJV)

While it seems self-evident that God wants honest rulers, most voters expect all politicians to lie. Yet lying comes in multiple forms. There will always be false promises—unrealistic expectations politicians raise to get votes. By now, most voters know that their heroes cannot deliver all that they promise, and it's not always in their power to do so. At law, if you promise something that you did not deliver, but you intended to do so when you promised, it's not considered misrepresentation or lying. Under the law, this kind of false speaking is not considered malicious, even though it disappoints us, for you meant it when you said it and you reasonably believed you would keep your word.

On the other hand, there are fact-based lies, for which our law will hold you accountable. Fact-based lies misrepresent the true facts about present and past reality. Before I went to law school, I thought it redundant to speak of "true facts," for a fact is not a fact unless it is true. But the law separates fact statements from opinion statements. If I say, "Mary was present at the scene of yesterday's accident," that is a fact statement. If it is untrue, i.e., she was not present but home watching TV, then it is a false statement of fact. The law holds us accountable for making false statements of fact, if others rely on those false statements and are injured, or if we lie under oath. Bill Clinton's infamous lie—"I did not have sexual relations with that woman"—was a false statement of fact, and it ended up tainting his entire presidency and legacy, despite his good accomplishments in other areas.

Donald Trump, on the other hand, has taken fact-based lying to a new level. Throughout the presidential campaign, PolitiFact rated both opponents' statements and classified them as true, partly true (conversely partly false), mostly true/false, and then blatantly false ("pants on fire" lies). They called out both sides for their falsehoods. Yet they found that the vast majority of Trump's statements were false, far more so than Hillary's. Of Trump's statements

- 18% were "pants on fire" lies.

- a whopping 33% were just false.

- another 19% were mostly false.

Many conservatives simply dismissed this as "the liberal media being dishonest" or conspiracy against their candidate, but this is not true. Seventy percent of Trump's statements were inaccurate.[196] That's a serious matter, particularly if you want Trump to be the standard-bearer for evangelicals.

The conservative radio talk-show host, Charlie Sykes, now regrets that he did not publicly attack the numerous lies and conspiracy theories spread by the alt-right in the years leading up to and including Trump's campaign. He acknowledges that he and other conservatives downplayed or ignored the valid fact-checking done by such bulwarks as the *Washington Post* and the *New York Times*, for conservatives denigrated their excellent fact-checking as the "liberal media," and so they delegitimized the accurate truth-telling being done. Hence, we have a whole generation of people listening to and believing fake news. It is sad and ironic that Sykes' admissions came on the heels of his retirement. Yet it's exceptional that he had the courage to own the cost of his silence, which in the face of so many lies, helped lead people astray.[197]

Renowned Watergate investigative journalist Carl Bernstein has attacked Trump for being worse than Richard Nixon on lying:

> Trump lives and thrives in a fact-free environment. No president, including Richard Nixon, has been so ignorant of fact and disdains fact in the way this President-elect does. And it has something to do with the growing sense of authoritarianism he and his presidency are projecting. And the danger of it is obvious and he's trying to make the conduct of the press the issue, not his own conduct.[198]

Bernstein encouraged journalists to continue to report facts and pursue the truth as best they could and not to give in to bullying. Not all of the fact-checkers can be disregarded as conspirators out to destroy Donald Trump. At some point, a lie is a lie. When will Republicans stop pretending that every time Trump tells a lie, it's nothing but a media conspiracy? Where are the moral conservatives like John Sherman Cooper, Dwight Eisenhower, Teddy Roosevelt, or William Buckley? If Republicans want to have credibility on other moral issues, they must square how they give Trump a pass on so many false stories when the Bible exhorts everyone, especially leaders, to tell the truth. Explaining away false statements as "alternative facts" leads America straight into the Twilight Zone.

Truth-telling is not just about being moral. It's about being practical. The ancient kings knew that when rulers surround themselves with liars and hucksters, the kingdom suffers. Listening to lies causes real harm. We went to war in Iraq, maimed and lost thousands of our soldiers, killed tens of thousands of innocent Iraqis, whom we termed "collateral damage," and ran up huge deficits—all because President Bush listened to Dick Cheney's lies. Lying perverts justice.

> **No one calls for justice; no one pleads a case with integrity. They rely on empty arguments, they utter lies**; they conceive trouble and give birth to evil.... So justice is driven back, and righteousness stands at a distance; truth has stumbled in the streets, honesty cannot enter. Truth is nowhere to be found, and whoever shuns evil becomes a prey. The Lord looked and was displeased that there was no justice. (Isaiah 59:4,14–15)

Lying rulers are an abomination to the Lord. Trump is now ruling the greatest nation on earth, so people of faith must hold him to a higher standard. Merely claiming, "Well, I don't take him literally" is not good enough. Ignoring his plain words by reinterpreting them to mean something else can only go so far. Trump gets many free passes because his supporters believe he is merely pointing to important issues in a politically incorrect manner.[199] Perhaps they believe he's speaking in hyperbole for dramatic effect, but his lies and distortions are fueling hatred and acts of violence. Words have power. Further, Jesus pointed out that the mouth speaks from the overflow of the heart (Matthew 12:34). Or as Freud would say, there's no such thing as accidental ramblings. We all are responsible for our speaking. Throughout the Bible, lying is wicked and ranks high among the things that God hates.

Rulers Must Listen to Wise Counsel

Many verses in the Bible promote the value of wisdom, knowledge, and understanding.

> Then you will understand what is right and just and fair—every good path. For wisdom will enter your heart, and knowledge will

be pleasant to your soul. **Discretion will protect you, and understanding will guard you.** (Proverbs 2:9–11)

The **prince that wanteth understanding is also a great oppressor**: but he that hateth covetousness shall prolong his days. (Proverbs 28:16 KJV)

This latter verse is a teacher's dream sermon. Ignorant, uninformed people become great oppressors when they gain power. Today, it seems that we glory in ignorance, inexperience, and incompetence. By popular standards today, one would believe that to be a good leader, you must have no experience in government, must not know the law, and need only be good at turning a profit in business. This is a scary form of logic. Nothing in the Bible glorifies ignorance and incompetence.

The first recorded rulers, whom Moses appointed after God led His people out of Egyptian slavery, were wise men.

But how can I bear your problems and your burdens and your disputes all by myself? **Choose some wise, understanding and respected men from each of your tribes, and I will set them over you."** (Deuteronomy 1:12–13)

Like many, I was perplexed when Trump said that he primarily listens to himself on major issues. When asked on MSNBC whom he listens to on foreign policy, he responded, "I'm speaking with myself, number one, because I have a very good brain and I've said a lot of things." When asked to clarify, Trump followed up with, "I know what I'm doing and I listen to a lot of people, I talk to a lot of people and at the appropriate time I'll tell you who the people are, but my primary consultant is myself and I have a good instinct for this stuff."[200] At the time this seemed humorous; now, not so much, particularly as we examine Trump's picks for top positions in his administration. Keep in mind that the Lord wants rulers to have righteous, wise advisers.

He who justifies the wicked, and he who condemns the just, Both of them alike are an abomination to the LORD. (Proverbs 17:15 KJV)

If a ruler listens to lies, all his officials become wicked. (Proverbs 29:12)

Kings take pleasure in honest lips; they value the one who speaks what is right. (Proverbs 16:13)

I don't have a problem with Trump's tapping business experts to come into the government, although I'm concerned if they have been given the post as a reward for prior donations. A conservative businessman might have a unique contribution to make to government reform. But some of Trump's appointments seem immoral. When he was far too cozy with white nationalists during the campaign, I hoped it was all for show. So I was shocked and concerned by the nomination of Alabama Senator Jeff Sessions to be Attorney General, a position where defending the rights of minorities is one of the top responsibilities. In 1986 Senator Jeff Sessions was rejected from the federal bench, even by Republicans, because of his support for black voter intimidation activities, his record of hostility toward enforcement of civil rights laws and rulings, and his vociferous opposition to immigration reform.[201]

Then I was floored when Trump went further in flirting with the racist fringe as he named white nationalist Steve Bannon to be his Chief Strategist.[202] Such appointments suggest that Donald Trump has listened to lies and is justifying wickedness. Steve Bannon was the head of the "alt-right" website Breitbart, which has peddled racist and anti-Semitic propaganda and fake news. The alt-right is nothing more than a smarter, more polished version of the Ku Klux Klan. That's not my interpretation but Breitbart's own conclusion, which states that the key distinction between their recent movement and old school racist movements is their intelligence:

There are many things that separate the alternative right from old-school racist skinheads (to whom they are often idiotically compared), but one thing stands out above all else: intelligence. Skinheads, by and large, are low-information, low-IQ thugs driven by the thrill of violence and tribal hatred. The alternative right are a much smarter group of people.[203] (Breitbart News Website)

That's the key difference between them and the KKK and neo-Nazis: not that they disagree on policies and principles, but just that they are more polished and educated. They will do race prejudice more effectively because they are smarter. NPR reports that the alt-right leaders make fun of conservatives who try to be more open and inclusive by labeling them "cukservative." This is a derogatory term to mean a cuckolded conservative or "race traitor," who has surrendered his masculinity in order to be politically correct.[204]

Breitbart has risen to prominence by trafficking in racist conspiracy theories, anti-Semitic propaganda, and love for the Confederacy.[205] So it's morally untenable for Christians to claim that the racist hate crimes perpetrated in Trump's name don't represent Trump's real feelings, for Trump is giving these racist liars not merely a seat at the table, but a position of high office and influence.

There's nothing in the Bible to justify this amount of hate coming from Trump's supporters and his welcoming racists into his administration, who have made a history of lying about the status of people in America. When will Bible believers speak up?

At times, it was hard to know whether Donald Trump actually believed the outrageous things he said or was merely pandering to the masses to affirm their innate prejudices and get votes. He repeatedly proclaimed that his best advisor was himself—he just knew.

Trump Not Taking His Intelligence Briefings

I was dismayed, though not surprised, when it came to light that Trump wasn't receiving the daily intelligence briefings from the security agencies that do their best to keep this country safe. Trump shrugged the whole thing off as he explained, "You know, I'm, like, a smart person. I don't have to be told the same thing in the same words every single day for the next eight years. Could be eight years—but eight years. I don't need that." Trump went on to say, "I mean, there will be some very fluid situations. I'll be there not every day, but more than that. But I don't need to be told, Chris, the same thing every day, every morning, same words, 'Sir, nothing has changed. Let's go over it again.' I don't need that."[206] Trump apparently takes intelligence briefings once a week.[207]

Of course, that's a 180-degree turnabout from when Trump faulted Obama for not taking daily intelligence briefings. At that point in 2014, Trump decried Obama for not making it a priority. Trump wildly exaggerated his point, but nevertheless, Breitbart and the alt-right picked up the story.[208] But now we see that after he criticized Obama (inaccurately), he does the same thing, even worse. Taking an intelligence briefing at least every two or three days shouldn't be optional. And if he's this casual when it comes to the nation's security, what other policy areas will he neglect? What does this say about his capacity for wisdom and good judgment? I would imagine intelligence briefings bring wisdom and warnings, so it's a good idea to take them more than once a week.

Although the Bible doesn't address intelligence briefings, some verses apply. King David proclaimed, "Therefore, **you kings, be wise; be warned,** you rulers of the earth" (Psalm 2:10).

> When a country is rebellious, it has many rulers, but **a ruler with discernment and knowledge maintains order.** (Proverbs 28:2)
>
> **How much better to get wisdom than gold,** to get insight rather than silver! (Proverbs 16:16)

King Solomon clearly valued intelligence and receiving wisdom. Sadly, given Trump's actions, I fear that Trump will put silver and gold ahead of intelligence and wisdom when it comes to running our country. If Trump continues to ignore his intelligence briefings and other key advisers who present him with good facts, while continuing to enrich his businesses, he may well become a "great oppressor."

Equally as scary is his disdain for the CIA intelligence briefings on the Russian hacking to manipulate our 2016 election. First, he discredited our intelligence community, and then when their evidence was irrefutable, he discounted it. True, the Russians did not hack into our voting machines. They didn't need to. They had already poisoned the minds of the American voters with their fake news and strategic releasing of private emails, which their fake news sites blew out of proportion to defeat the former Secretary of State, who four years earlier had the temerity to point out that Putin had rigged his own election.[209] Given Trump's disbelief of the intelligence reports of Russian hacking, it should not surprise us that he doesn't want his briefings. He doesn't like the information he gets.

God Loves Humble Leaders Who Shun Vainglory

> **Talk no more so exceeding proudly; let not arrogancy come out of your mouth**: for the Lord is a God of knowledge, and by him actions are weighed. (1 Samuel 2:3 KJV)

> **Haughty eyes and a proud heart**—the unplowed field of the wicked—**produce sin.** (Proverbs 21:4)

> They pour out arrogant words; all the **evildoers are full of boasting**. (Psalm 94:4)

> **He [the wicked] boasts about the cravings of his heart**; he blesses the greedy and reviles the Lord. (Psalm 10:3)

Proverbs 16:18 reads: "Pride goes before destruction, a haughty spirit before a fall." It goes on to say, "Better to be lowly in spirit along with the oppressed than to share plunder with the proud" (verse 19). In Trump's case, however, his pride and haughty spirit earned him the presidency of the world's most powerful nation. Whether Trump's been vindicated or whether he's setting America up for a great fall will be left to history. But what worries me is his incessant bragging about his money. It's hard to see this as anything other than pride or a haughty spirit.

> Now listen, you who say, "Today or tomorrow we will go to this or that city, spend a year there, carry on business and make money." Why, you do not even know what will happen tomorrow. What is your life? You are a mist that appears for a little while and then vanishes. Instead, you ought to say, "If it is the Lord's will, we will live and do this or that." As it is, **you boast in your arrogant schemes. All such boasting is evil.** (James 4:13–16)

When I read these biblical admonitions, it's hard not to think of Trump. All politicians fall short of the glory of God. We can use Bible verses against all of us, especially politicians, and find some fault. But Trump is not an ordinary politician. He boasts about his wealth and stature in ways that Mitt Romney never did. His frequent references to his wealth suggest an obsession.

"Part of the beauty of me is that I am very rich," Donald Trump said in 2012 while he was thinking of challenging Obama.[210] And in the 2016 campaign cycle, he's made his wealth and bragging about it the cornerstone of his campaign.

> **And I have assets**—big accounting firm, one of the most highly respected—**$9 billion $240 million**. And I have liabilities of about $500 million. That's long-term debt, very low interest rates. In fact, one of the big banks came to me and said, "Donald, you don't have enough borrowings. Could we loan you $4 billion?" I said, "I don't need it. I don't want it." And I've been there. I don't want it. But in two seconds, they give me whatever I wanted. **So I have a total net worth, and now with the increase, it'll be well over $10 billion**. But here, a total net worth of—net worth, not assets, not— a net worth, after all debt, after all expenses, the greatest assets—Trump Tower, 1290 Avenue of the Americas, Bank of America building in San Francisco, 40 Wall Street, sometimes referred to as the Trump building right opposite the New York—many other places all over the world. So the total is $8,737,540,00. Now I'm not doing that.... **I'm not doing that to brag, because you know what? I don't have to brag. I don't have to, believe it or not.** (Donald Trump, Presidential Announcement Speech, June 2015)[211]

That certainly looks like bragging to me. Is he blessing greed with his boasts?

> I own a big chunk of the Bank of America Building at 1290 Avenue of the Americas, that I got from China in a war. Very valuable. I love China. The biggest bank in the world is from China. You know where their United States headquarters is located? In this building, in Trump Tower. I love China.[212] (Trump, June 2015)

> You know, I may make money running for president. It's very interesting. (Trump in July, 2015)[213]

So then I announced I'm running. Then I wasn't going to file my
FEC original filing because when you do that, you're making a
very big step, and I filed it. And then they had -- oh, but he'll
never put in his financials. Because maybe he's not as rich as people think. **Not that it matters, but I'm much richer and you'll
see that next week.** No, you'll see. I mean, you know, it's like
crazy. So—it is true. You've heard that, right? He'll never file.
These guys, they sit up there. Why, he will never file because he
doesn't want to show that he's not as rich. **And I said to myself,
I want to show that I'm much, much richer than people
say.**[214] (Trump in July 2015)

There were many more similar quotes, but we were concerned
about the length of this book. In the secular realm, a businessman
can and should make his business credentials a selling point. But
Trump didn't talk a lot about what he accomplished in business and
how his business skills will shape his policies and reform the government. Instead, he spent a great deal of time talking about how
great he is and how terrible everyone else is, all the time not pre-
senting the country with concrete policies to consider. Even when
Trump pokes fun at himself, he insists that he's rich.

In 2011 Trump appeared on a Comedy Central Roast and
joked, "What's the difference between a wet raccoon and Donald
Trump's hair? A wet raccoon doesn't have $7 billion." That's kind
of funny—until you learn that the original joke was written to be $2
billion. Trump was annoyed with the writers because he didn't
want people thinking he was less rich than he really was. He demanded that they change the joke to $10 billion. After much nego-
tiation, Trump and the writers settled on $7 billion.[215] If you can't
take the jokes, then why attend the roast in the first place? But this
and other examples demonstrate that Trump is obsessed with people thinking that he's worth billions. Some psychologists have suggested that his behavior fits the textbook profile of a narcissist.[216]
Although such statements are not a fair clinical diagnosis, his brag-
gadocio is extreme. One would expect his boastfulness to give evangelicals pause when they look at Trump's "Me, Me, Me" attitude
and compare it to the Bible's warnings against pride. According to
the Bible, our speech reveals what is in our hearts.

Each tree is recognized by its own fruit. People do not pick figs from thornbushes, or grapes from briers. A good man brings good things out of the good stored up in his heart, and an evil man brings evil things out of the evil stored up in his heart. For the **mouth speaks what the heart is full of**. Why do you call me, "Lord, Lord," and do not do what I say? (Luke 6:44–46)

Trump's speech for decades has proven what his heart is full of, what matters most to him, and it's all about puffing up himself, reminding us of his riches, and touting that everything he does is great.

Is Trump Engaging in Idolatry?

No one can serve two masters. Either you will hate the one and love the other, or you will be devoted to the one and despise the other. **You cannot serve both God and money.** (Matthew 6:24)

For the love of money is the root of all evil: which while some coveted after, they have erred from the faith, and pierced themselves through with many sorrows. (1 Timothy 6:10 KJV)

We know that Trump flagrantly disregards the ninth commandment against lying, but what about the second commandment? Exodus 20:3 states, "Thou shalt have no other gods before me." So my question to faith leaders is this: at what point does Trump's obsession with touting his own wealth and branding his name on land, buildings, products, schools, and resorts around the world turn into a form of idolatry? When do we see that he is mad upon his idols? (See Jeremiah 50:38 KJV "... for it is the land of graven images, and they are mad upon their idols.") An idol is an attachment we elevate above love for God and our fellow man. Whether we are "mad upon our idols" depends not on our words but on our actions that demonstrate our true priorities. As we become obsessed with our own wealth and earthly possessions, we forget about God (the greater Good) and fail to show humble gratitude for our many blessings.

Those who trust in their wealth and boast of their great riches? No one can redeem the life of another or give to God a ransom for them.... (Psalm 49:6–7)

For Bible believers, Trump's words cannot be dismissed as hyperbole, meaningless locker room talk, or strategic campaign hype. Trump's words have been consistent for decades—vainglory, pursuit of riches, and self-aggrandizement.

Trump's bragging brings many other scriptures to mind. The Bible mentions the concept of pride, arrogance, and a haughty spirit more than 100 times. In not one instance is that trait considered a virtue. Even in the days of Moses, the temptation to fall in love with your own wealth and great position was ever present. It seems that the more things change, the more they stay the same. These proud attitudes haven't gone anywhere. And Moses commanded his followers to avoid such presumptuousness and self-glory.

> **Be careful that you do not forget the Lord** your God, failing to observe his commands, his laws and his decrees that I am giving you this day. Otherwise, when you eat and are satisfied, when you build fine houses and settle down, and when your herds and flocks grow large and your silver and gold increase and all you have is multiplied, then **your heart will become proud and you will forget the Lord your God,** who brought you out of Egypt, out of the land of slavery. He led you through the vast and dreadful wilderness, that thirsty and waterless land, with its venomous snakes and scorpions. He brought you water out of hard rock. He gave you manna to eat in the wilderness, something your ancestors had never known, to humble and test you so that in the end it might go well with you. **You may say to yourself, "My power and the strength of my hands have produced this wealth for me."** (Deuteronomy 8:11-17).

> Mark this: There will be terrible times in the last days. **People will be lovers of themselves, lovers of money, boastful, proud, abusive,** disobedient to their parents, ungrateful, unholy, without love, unforgiving, slanderous, without self-control, brutal, not lovers of the good, treacherous, rash, conceited, lovers of pleasure rather than lovers of God—**having a form of godliness but denying its power. Have nothing to do with such people.** (2 Timothy 3:1-5)

> If you harbor bitter envy and **selfish ambition** in your hearts, **do not boast** about it or deny the truth. Such "wisdom" does not come down from heaven but is earthly, unspiritual, demonic. **For**

where you have envy and selfish ambition, there you find disorder and every evil practice. (James 3:14–16)

Arrogant leaders and rich people who boast of their own wealth are not being godly. Have you ever heard Trump say, "To God be all the glory for my wealth and many blessings"? Or without being syrupy religious, has he ever shown a shred of gratitude or humility by saying, "I was fortunate to have received a great start from my father, and many other people who have helped me along the way to achieve extraordinary things"? No. All you hear is "I am great; everything I've done is great; I made myself great...," the very words that the Bible repeatedly condemns.

Trump explains that he started with a million dollar loan from his father. The facts show, however, that he got much more from his dad, who was very rich. Regardless, how many ordinary Americans have a rich dad to "loan" them this kind of money? Did he have anything to do with being born into a wealthy family?[217] You'd think divine providence or a mere accident of birth would get a little credit.

At what stage do we ask our leaders to take on a morsel of humility, given the great power they wield on our behalf? Where is the reverential respect (i.e., "fear of the Lord") for the awesomeness of the privileges he possesses and any sense of gratitude for his great fortune? And since we "anointed" all of this pride, haughtiness, and vanity by blessing it with our votes and the trappings of high office, what does this say about us as a people? Will our own pride be our downfall?

We're listing these scriptures not just to "preach" but because they have value in a purely secular context. Trump's obsession with himself, his brilliance and his wealth (his "self-idolatry") implies that he really feels he does not have to answer to anyone other than himself. If he takes no outside counsel and has only his own internal monolog to guide him, he is far more likely to make monumental mistakes on the global stage. That's one reason the Bible continually warns that pride leads to tragedy, and it extols wisdom and truth: leaders of that day saw continually how arrogance led to ruin.

From Nimrod to Nebuchadnezzar

Two characters from the Bible show some eerie parallels to Trump, which ought to ring a bell of caution in the heart of every God-fearing person. Genesis 11 tells the story of an evil tyrant who defied God in the aftermath of the great flood of Noah's day. This titan of industry built a tower, which was only around 300 feet tall by today's measurements—nothing compared to Trump Tower, but great in his day. The tyrant sought to demonstrate his own greatness and prove that nothing would be out of his reach. But God descended from heaven, divided the people, and gave them all different languages so they could no longer work together to construct the tower. Whether you take Genesis literally or not, the moral remains the same: projects built on self-glory and pride result in confusion and fail to unite people. That tyrant's name was Nimrod, a name synonymous with arrogant stupidity. It's hard not to see parallels with Trump, given his hubris and lack of knowledge of our Constitution.

The story of King Nebuchadnezzar develops the character of a great narcissist even more fully. The entire book of Daniel portrays an amazing story of speaking truth to power and warns rulers against pride and boasting. It's hard to read the story of Nebuchadnezzar without making analogies to Trump. Both were great conquerors—men who occupied large international territories, built wealthy kingdoms, and made their names known.

As princes from Israel who were taken in captivity, Daniel and his three friends had several encounters with this king. Early on, they had refused the king's rich meat and wine in favor of a vegetarian diet (a story that will warm the heart of every vegan). Then after ten days, the strength, glowing health, and wisdom of these four noble youth astounded the king as they outshone all the other princes. Thus Daniel and his friends rose to power.

Later, Daniel twice interpreted the king's dreams and warned him about his arrogance. For the first dream, Daniel told the king that all the great kingdoms of the earth (beginning with his) would fall, as God Almighty would establish a final everlasting reign. This message, in effect, says eternal reign is not in your hands, and there is a power in the universe greater than you. The message was surely intended to help Old Neb recognize his humanity, fallibility, and temporality. The king honored Daniel's great wisdom and promoted him to be governor of the entire province of Babylon.

Still, Nebuchadnezzar missed the point of Daniel's lesson and soon made a huge golden statue of himself, commanding everyone in all his kingdoms to bow down and worship him. How's that for global branding? What is an image? It's a fake replica to make yourself look greater than you truly are and a demand that people pay homage to your hollow glorious self. That's where we find the familiar story of Daniel's three friends—Shadrach, Meshach, and Abednego—who refused to bow down to the king's golden image, were cast into the fiery furnace, yet miraculously survived.

Throughout this drama, Old Neb's message was "I am great, and everything I do is great. Kiss up to me or else." The insistence that all pay obeisance to him is not unlike Trump, who gets furious with anyone who criticizes him. While not throwing his critics into a literal fiery furnace for failing to worship at his self-image, Trump promises to make it hot for those who publish negative stories about him—for they are tarnishing his golden image, and he fires off hostile tweets about any celebrity or reporter who criticizes him or exposes his inaccurate fact statements. He has already suggested retaliation against executives who dared criticize him and lawsuits against women who revealed incidents of his aggressive, lustful behavior.[218]

Like Trump, Nebuchadnezzar was blind to his own self-worship. Even though God created a miracle that defied his decree of death for those who refused to worship him, Old Neb was not in any way transformed by the miracle of the three Hebrews in his fiery furnace. He remained committed to self-glorification.

Throughout this story, we see the spirit of the divine knocking on the hard shell of this proud man's consciousness. So later, God gave Neb another dream, which foretold his downfall and seven years of mental suffering. It was at that point that Daniel warned him that he could make amends for his past iniquities by showing mercy to the poor, a passage we studied earlier (Daniel 4:27). Yet again Nebuchadnezzar disregarded the lessons God was giving him—both in regard to caring for the poor and in perceiving that his pride was wicked.

A year later, we see Old Neb in his palace, still stuck in his self-worship and boasting: "Is not this the great Babylon I have built as the royal residence, by my mighty power and for the glory of my majesty?" (Daniel 4:28–30). His words are hardly different from Trump's: "I am great; I make everyone around me great." At that point Nebuchadnezzar succumbed to insanity, and for seven years he crawled around on all fours, eating grass like oxen, as his hair grew "like eagles' feathers, and his nails like birds' claws" (Daniel 4:33).

Nebuchadnezzar came to his senses only when he acknowledged that he himself was not king of the universe. God didn't die and leave him in charge. Like all inhabitants of the earth, he was just a poor creature subject to greater powers (Daniel 4:34–37). While you can look at the story as using magical thinking to portray God as the one true Supreme Ruler, the moral is clear: preoccupation with our own greatness is borderline insanity—even though we may have achieved extraordinarily great things.

Trump on Seeking Forgiveness from God

> He that covereth his sins shall not prosper: but **whoso confesseth and forsaketh them shall have mercy.** (Proverbs 28:13 KJV)

> **If we confess our sins,** he [Jesus Christ] is faithful and just and **will forgive us our sins** and purify us from all unrighteousness. (1 John 1:9)

Then I acknowledged my sin to you and did not cover up my in-
iquity. I said, "**I will confess my transgressions** to the Lord."
And you forgave the guilt of my sin. (Psalm 32:5)

The Christian religion is based on complete forgiveness: being
able to make a fresh start, for God and His children extend redemption and forgiveness to all, regardless of past mistakes, even crimes.
But first, we must acknowledge our wrongdoing ("confess our sins")
and turn from our former ways ("repent").

I have agnostic friends who are critical of this concept, for they
think that the idea of "sin" fosters low self-esteem and self-
flagellation—being stuck in a guilt trip and groveling in "I'm so terrible that I don't deserve to breathe." But the opposite is true. Moral people on a journey toward self-improvement need the capacity
to recognize their wrongs in order to plan to do better next time.
When I lose my temper with my children, I need to feel a pang of
discomfort to cause me to make it right, to apologize, and learn not
to repeat my mistake. If I'm not mindful that my behavior hurts
others, I have no hope to grow or improve. Christians see the Spirit
of God through Jesus Christ as transformative, as His teachings put
them on a journey of personal growth and mindful living. For true
disciples of Jesus, recognizing and owning our mistakes are key to
achieving forgiveness—and forgiving others who have harmed us.
That is a premise from which we become more like Christ.

In 2015 moderator Frank Luntz asked Trump whether he has
ever asked God for forgiveness for his actions. "People are so
shocked when they find ... out I am Protestant. I am Presbyterian.
And I go to church and I love God and I love my church," Trump
said. "I am not sure I have. I just go on and try to do a better job
from there. I don't think so," he answered. "I think if I do something wrong, I think, I just try and make it right. I don't bring God
into that picture. I don't." Trump said that while he hasn't asked
God for forgiveness, he does participate in Holy Communion. He
went on to say, "When I drink my little wine, which is about the
only wine I drink, and have my little cracker, I guess that is a form
of asking for forgiveness."[219]

Now imagine if Bill Clinton or Barack Obama had referred to the holy sacrament of communion as "my little wine" and "my little cracker." That expression sounds like something Bill Maher or George Carlin, atheistic comedians, would say. In fairness, there was some unease among religious conservatives after this statement, but not enough to cost Trump many votes. Anyone who was truly involved in their Christian church would respond, "All have sinned and fallen short of the glory of God" (Romans 3:23). If you weren't a sinner, you wouldn't need Jesus as your Savior. That is the basic tenet of the Christian faith.

Now, I'm not attacking Trump for not being a true Christian. I'm just exposing the credibility gap here in his proclamations. If Trump wants to play the Christian game and carry the banner for evangelicals, he would do well to read the following scriptures:

If we claim to be without sin, we deceive ourselves and the truth is not in us. (1 John 1:8)

Whoever says, "I know him," but does not do what he commands is a liar, and the truth is not in that person. (1 John 2:4)

For it is by grace you have been saved, through faith—and this is not from yourselves, it is the gift of God—not by works, so that no one can boast. (Ephesians 2:8–9)

And the word *sin* doesn't necessarily mean a heinous crime or that you should go on a big guilt trip. It can include that, of course. But the word itself means *missing the mark*, like an archer who shoots and misses the bull's-eye. The point of the Christian faith is to recognize that all of us humans, regardless of how hard we try and how well intentioned we are, miss the mark. We screw up. We fail. So it is doubly outrageous for any Christian to claim he has done nothing for which he needs to ask God for forgiveness.

I'm not as concerned about whether Trump attends church weekly and doesn't know his Bible. But I do care that his self-introspection mechanisms are so limited that he feels he never did anything that required forgiveness from a higher power. Regardless of whether we believe that an ultimate Supreme Being grants us absolution, as moral human beings, we need the fortitude and humility to say, "I was wrong, please forgive me"—to ourselves and to others. Confession to God is a way of achieving that insight. This only bolsters the previous point that the more Trump seeks only his own counsel, never believing he needs to ask forgiveness, the more likely he is to make bad secular decisions.

But that's not the only indication of Trump's true distance from evangelical Christianity. When he spoke at Liberty University, trying to reach out to evangelicals, he said "Two [sic] Corinthians 3:17, that's the whole ballgame. ... Is that the one you like?"[220] Any preacher's kid would get throttled if they stood in the pulpit and referenced "Two Corinthians" rather than "*Second* Corinthians." I've only known of this happening one other time in my life: at a wedding in a church, when the best man who was atheist for all intents and purposes, read that passage as a blessing to the wedding couple. It's a mistake that only people who rarely go to church would make.

> **The natural person does not accept the things of the Spirit of God, for they are folly to him,** and he is not able to understand them because they are spiritually discerned. (1 Corinthians 2:14 ESV)

This verse in *One* Corinthians seems applicable to Trump; he's simply a man of the world. Of course, this on its own would not be a big deal. But combined with the dismissal of communion as *my little wine* and *my little cracker*, the callous attitude toward women, the racism, the hate speech, the unethical business practices, the lustful comments, the groping, the arrogance, the palpable incomprehension of policy issues and the refusal to learn—these all cause me great concern about our moral future under President Trump. But no man is beyond redemption. Let's hope and pray that he does in fact see the light and amend his ways and that some of his outrageous behavior was Hollywood showmanship—to garner the limelight by being outrageous. Let's pray that the office of presidency transforms him.

We have purposefully omitted a detailed analysis of Trump's lustful behavior toward women. Even Trump admitted that his conduct with women was worse than Bill Clinton's. That horse has been beaten to death, and it made no difference.[221] But something more alarming deserves mention.

Whether he's discussing his Republican female opponent in the presidential primary (giving her a four on his ten point scale and saying she's too ugly to be president), or his beautiful daughter, whom he labels as "hot," Trump's entire adult life has been built on mammon, glamor, and lookism—values that psychologists have shown are detrimental to the development of self-esteem in young girls.[222] Women are rated, even his own daughter, first and foremost on their looks, not on their character or their accomplishments.

> The Lord does not look at the things people look at. **People look at the outward appearance, but the Lord looks at the heart.** (1 Samuel 16:7)

Trump shows the double standard feminists have long opposed in our culture. If a smart beautiful woman like Megyn Kelly dares ask him a fair question in order to do her job, he impugns her menstrual cycle.[223] I don't think many Republicans condoned his behavior and comments, though their silence suggests consent. And Democrats certainly can't throw stones from this glass house. But it bothers me how easily so many evangelicals have dismissed these types of comments.

Setting up women to be valued primarily on their physical beauty is wrong and unbiblical. It shows an inordinate attachment to (and idol worship of) physical appearance. It's demeaning to women who can never compete in such a rigged game: powerful, pudgy old men, whose good looks long ago departed, require women at any age always to compete on their looks. It's a double standard that keeps women oppressed. True Christians, especially holiness evangelicals, shouldn't want this message passed down to their young girls. Nor should they want their young boys emulating such oppressive and shallow thinking.

What Evangelicals Truly Want

Trump's actions on so many fronts are contrary to everything the Bible stands for—whether as Christians we are conservative or progressive—that I'm forced to question whether evangelical Republicans even care whether their leader follows Christian values. In America we are all free to advocate secular humanism, economic greed, and the worship of Mammon, but we need to drop the pretense of doing so from a position of our faith or moral authority. It turns out that by endorsing Trump, evangelicals are more secular than the secularists. Some may argue that they felt the general election gave them two bad choices, so they opted for the lesser of two evils, but Trump won the majority of evangelical voters in the primaries, when they had the opportunity to stop him.

Let's just admit that many Christians wanted a bastard to go into Washington and kick ass and take names, and they don't really care if he is an atheist or a mammon idolater. The good thing about Trump's election victory is that he has acted so egregiously that his conduct has ripped away—let's hope permanently—the mask of piety from many conservatives who gave lip service to wanting a true Christian leader for their party.

In his book, *Don't Think of an Elephant,*[224] George Lakoff, a long-time Republican consultant, demonstrates that people do not vote their self-interests. Rather, they vote their identity and values. So here's your mirror, my evangelical friends. For good or bad, Trump is a true reflection of the values cultivated by Republicans these last three decades. Many who have for years planted seeds of fear, racism, xenophobia, absurdity, and "alternative facts about the world" claim surprise and disdain for his outrageous behavior, his disrespect for career intelligence officers, and his admiration of Putin. But Trump is merely the fruit of the tree that evangelical alliances have planted, fertilized, and watered. The Bible says that we reap what we sow. Someone had better start praying for a crop failure.

Evangelicals have a chance to influence Trump, by insisting that he rein in some of his impulsive, hateful, and cruel thinking. Just remember, how you interact with Trump over the next few years will reveal what you truly believe. If you stay silent and give him a pass, as many have done so far, then you are admitting that Trump represents the values you actually practice, not the ones you profess to hold dear.

8

What Suing a Used Car Salesman Taught Me about Bible-Speak

Permit me to illustrate how I first discovered the power of Bible stories as a tool for persuasion in a secular context. It demonstrates how to apply the techniques I've argued throughout this book. I intuitively stumbled onto this technique—mainly because of my Bible-based upbringing. It illustrates how leaders can work a biblical story into a narrative without coming across as a Bible-thumper or a zealot.

Incorporating the Bible is no great mystery or foreign language. You just have to know the scriptures and key stories. But if you don't know anything about the Bible, you can easily find references at many Bible websites, which have search features that will immediately pull up all scriptures that reference any particular word. Once you have the particular passage, you can quickly do a Google search to find multiple commentaries about that passage—from all points of view. However, since Democratic strategists and activists seldom have time to do this, I did it for you in this book.

Not every instance of using the Bible needs an overt reference. Politicians don't have to use the word *Bible* or quote passages directly. We don't have to say, "Ezekiel says... so we should expand health care." Often politicians can just use the phrase, "There was an ancient story about a shepherd...." Those who know the Bible will hear the ring of familiar truth that will resonate deep within, even if they don't recall that the phrase came from the Bible.

Sometimes, depending on the circumstances, you must hard-peddle biblical citations, especially if you are communicating with evangelicals, for whom this is the only respected authority. Most of the time, however, you don't need to make a big deal out of it. You just subtly work in Bible sayings and metaphors.

My best experience with using a Bible story came to me when I was suing a large used car dealer in town. To protect the guilty, I will refer to it as Best Used Deals (BUD). My clients were a sweet, unsophisticated husband and wife, whom I'll name Carlos and Carrie. They were interested in buying a newer car, but not quite ready to purchase. Late one Saturday evening, the young couple went into Best Used Deals and found a one-year-old Toyota that caught their eye.

Carrie did most of the negotiating. Both were only high school graduates with compliant personalities. Carlos was originally from a Latin American country (relax, he was legal), and he barely read or spoke English. He did odd jobs, mostly cutting grass, while his wife Carrie worked as a babysitter and housekeeper. They had a ten-year-old Ford Escort, which they wanted to replace, but it still had some useful life in it.

BUD's sales staff urged Carrie to "fill out a credit application." Repeatedly, they assured Carrie that she was not signing a binding contract, but was just making an application for credit to see whether she could purchase the car. The binding contract would not occur until after her credit was approved.

The salesman and the finance manager decided to "puppy-dog" the couple. That's the industry's term for sending you home in the newer car. Just as when you bring home a puppy, once you keep it a while, you fall in love with it and can't bear to let it go, so the salesman insisted that she leave her old car at the lot and drive home in the newer car. In fact, Carrie asked to drive home in her own car, but they would not return her keys, insisting that she should drive the newer car and bring it back on Monday. So she acquiesced. Not giving you back your car keys is a long-standing tactic of slick used-car dealers.

The next day Sunday, the BUD car showed problems that made the couple nervous. It was making some funny sounds, and the steering felt "off" during sharp turns. They feared it was a lemon. So on Monday after dropping Carrie off at her work, Carlos took the dealer's car back and asked for his old car to be returned. They gave him the run around and refused. In his limited English, Carlos explained, "The car es in mi name I no sign no paper. Por favor, give me my car." BUD's staff just laughed at him and ignored his pleas—likely assuming he was an illegal alien whom they could bully. So he called someone to come get him and left the newer car at BUD's lot. He didn't know what else to do, and he didn't want to be responsible for a car that was not his.

When Carrie called BUD to ask why they didn't give the car back to her husband, they told her that she had signed a binding contract, could not get her old car back, and must purchase the newer car. Later that week, the finance manager phoned Carrie to explain that her credit wasn't good enough to secure the deal, but he insisted that she get her father to cosign the loan to complete the deal. The finance manager then revealed that Carrie had, in fact, signed a binding contract, a purchase agreement, and the couple was locked in. They were legally bound to buy the new car.

At that point, Carrie phoned me. I knew I could bring a claim against BUD under Kentucky's Consumer Protection Act, which allows punitive damages and legal fees to be awarded to consumers who prevail against a company that has defrauded them. While some people lambast trial lawyers, most people have no idea of the risk that trial lawyers take in advocating for the little guy. Consumer protection laws are the only way that the average person has a chance for justice. No attorney could ever take a case like Carrie's. A 40% contingency over a $500 car is barely worth the lawyer's time to meet with the clients and make a phone call, let alone litigate the case in court.

At first, I thought that upon receiving a strongly worded letter from me, reminding them of the law, BUD would immediately return the couple's raggedy old car. Surely they would not want the bad publicity or the hassle of a lawsuit. But for some reason, the dealership dug in its heels and insisted that Carrie had signed a binding contract to purchase the newer Toyota (at around $12,000—a lot of money in the early '90s). "Just return this lady her car, and she and her husband will go away," I pleaded, but they didn't care. A call from a lawyer didn't concern them at all.

I had told the couple that I would write a letter for them and make a phone call pro bono (free of charge), for often this is enough to get the car dealer to back down. But BUD was adamant and arrogant. My mom raised me to honor my word, and I knew the law provided that I could be reimbursed my hourly fees under the Consumer Protection Act—but only *if* I won the case, and *if* the judge so agreed, for attorney fees are allowed but not required. Yet I dreaded the energy drain and lost time in bringing a lawsuit over a $500 car. I was putting myself at risk of losing thousands of dollars in billable time. Taking on this case meant turning down other paying work, and the couple could not afford to pay me over the interim to take up their fight.

At that point, I had two options. I could tell Carlos and Carrie that they just got a very expensive lesson in not trusting used car salesmen and leave them with no way to pay for the new car or get their old car back. Or I go to war for the side of right, even if it meant that I risked great personal losses for my time and out-of-pocket expenses. This was scary because I was a single mother with bills to pay. And my son could not eat retroactively. But the words of my mother rang in my head: "Do what's right and trust God to take care of the rest." I just couldn't turn my back on them and let Carlos and Carrie be cheated out of everything they had. I rolled up my sleeves and prepared for a fight.

Everyone knocks lawyers, but few know the precarious position most lawyers are in, trying to take up for the little guy against a big wealthy company. For this case, I had to guarantee my own personal earnings to my firm in order to secure the costs of court reporters who charged $30 an hour for depositions and $3.50 per page to type up transcripts, expert witnesses who had to be prepared to testify (usually they charged $200–$500 per hour), and all the other myriad costs of printing, copying, and filing fees. Today, these costs are much higher. Then I put in more than a hundred hours to get the case ready for trial, all the while with no paycheck coming in from the venture. If I lost, then I wouldn't get paid at all. I would lose over $10,000 in expenses and lost billable time. If I won, I'd only recoup my out-of-pocket and hours worked, and a possible contingency bonus if we won punitive damages.[225]

It took a laborious six months to build the case, for in the beginning it looked like it was Carrie's word against the salesmen, who would deny that they told her she was not signing a contract. The papers she signed were titled, "Purchase Agreement." The law holds parties accountable for reading what they sign. So it was not necessarily an easy case. I had to take several depositions and subpoena records from the bank. I had to do extensive legal research. Trying to coordinate schedules with opposing counsel and witnesses caused even more delay. Finally I deposed the bank officer, who testified that the bank had rejected Carrie's credit application three days after she signed the purchase agreement. At that point, I had solid proof that the contract, under anyone's interpretation, was void, for it was conditional on her credit's approval. Within the first week, BUD should have automatically released the couple from the deal.

At that point, BUD offered to return to the couple their $500 car. I said:

> Fine, but you owe my clients for six months' deprivation of their car, and you owe me for six months' worth of legal fees and expenses. You knew all along that the deal was dead, and you had no right to keep their car, yet you strung us along and forced me to take the bank officer's deposition to prove what you knew all along.

Yet BUD was adamant: they wouldn't pay a dime. I explained their duties under the law, how it was unfair for us to incur thousands of dollars because of their contempt for the law and their callous disregard of my clients. But they didn't care. I had no choice but to go to trial. The trial was scheduled to take place more than six months later, so my clients ended up being without a car for over a year, and I had even more work to do.

At trial, I subpoenaed the finance manager, who had helped to puppy-dog the couple and along with BUD's owner had refused to return their original car. By that time, however, he had left the employ of BUD (a stroke of divine intervention) and was working at another company, so he could testify freely without fear of retaliation. And who knows, BUD may have mistreated him in some way. This finance manager honestly and freely stated, "Yes, I knew I had no right to keep their car because I knew the credit application was turned down, but I was trying to keep the customers at bay so I could make the deal go through." He admitted that he thought he could still complete the sale by forcing her to get her dad to cosign on her loan. He also admitted that he indeed had assured her that she was not signing a binding contract but was only making a credit application when she signed those initial documents that fateful Saturday night. Few of us read what we sign, let alone the fine print, and car salesmen, like all seducers, will tell us what we want to hear so they can get what they want.

We gave evidence of the hardships the couple faced in being without their only car for over a year. The husband had an old truck he used for his grass-cutting jobs. During this time the wife became pregnant and had to make extra trips to the doctor. He had to take off work to drive her. One of the children she babysat was chronically ill, and she worried that she couldn't get that child to the hospital if something went wrong and that her employer would replace her with another sitter who had more reliable transportation. They were humiliated to be begging and borrowing rides from friends and family, not to mention all the embarrassing explanations of how they came to lose their only car. They were the butt of jokes in front of their friends, who teased, "What kind of idiot do you have to be to go to a car lot to buy a new car and you end up giving them your car?"

Then, after all the evidence was in, after we established how the couple had asked BUD "pretty please" several times to return their car, how I had written asking them merely to return the car, and after flaky arguments that Carrie had signed a binding contract (which were refuted by the plain wording of the documents and by the finance manager who corroborated Carrie's testimony), BUD'S guidance to the jury was this:

> If you find for the plaintiffs, then the only thing you should do is award them $500, the value of their old car, for that is all they have lost.

On behalf of my clients, who had suffered a tremendous amount of hardship due to BUD's unethical and illegal behavior, I asked, however, for the $500 car back *and* for punitive damages, because the company's behavior had been willfully fraudulent and abusive to this young couple and had for more than a year intentionally imposed a serious hardship on them.

For my closing argument, I went to the ancient wisdom found in the Bible. Although lawyers are not allowed to reference the Bible explicitly when making closing arguments, they are allowed to tell stories from any source of literature that they may feel are relevant to the case at hand. So my argument went something like this:

> This situation today reminds me of an old story I heard when I was a child. There was a rich man, and he had a thousand sheep, and his wealth was beyond all compare. But he looked around one day and saw his neighbor, a poor man, who had only one sheep. So the rich man decided to take his neighbor's one sheep. The rich man didn't need the sheep. He was already rich. But he took it because he was greedy, and he could. Since he was so powerful, he knew he could get away with it. What could the poor man do?

> And when the king heard the story, he was furious and wanted to punish the rich man severely. But other people asked the king,

"Why should the rich man be punished severely? He only took one sheep. Just let the rich man pay back the one sheep he took."

But the wise king said, "Oh no. Paying back one sheep is nothing to the rich man who had so much, for when the rich man stole his neighbor's one sheep, he took *everything* that his poor neighbor had. He must be punished severely so he feels the sting of what it was like for his neighbor to lose it all."

And here today, when Best Used Deals took this young couple's one old car, it was nothing to this car dealer. They all thought it was a big joke. And you heard how BUD sells two or three hundred cars every month. But to this young couple, this was the only car they had.

They suffered a whole year without adequate transportation. They were humiliated in front of their friends and lived in fear of what they would do if while the wife was at work, she needed to get to the hospital for herself, her unborn child, or one of the children in her care. So is it justice to make Best Used Deals give back the one car? For someone who sells 200 cars per month, giving back one car would be a huge joke to them.

The question is how much should Best Used Deals pay to feel the sting of what they did to their neighbor? Please look into your hearts and return a number for punitive damages that will help BUD feel the sting of what they did to this young couple and also teach this company never to do that again.

The jury returned a verdict of compensatory damages in the amount of $500 and punitive damages in the amount of $50,000.

The next week when we lawyers met to file our post trial motions (that's where lawyers ask the judge to set aside the jury verdict and tie up other loose ends), the defense counsel asked the judge to throw out the verdict on the grounds that I had used a Bible story, which they acknowledged I had told brilliantly. The judge denied their motion and also awarded us additional attorney fees, as provided under the consumer protection statute.

Nothing in the rules of professional responsibility prohibits lawyers from using material from the Bible. The only thing we cannot do is appeal directly to religion or divine authority. So I could not have said, "Punish Best Used Deals because the Bible says so," or "Punish them because God wants you to." But using literature from the Bible as a metaphor to help the jury feel compassion for my clients was ethical and appropriate.

This Bible story presented the best analogy I could find, even when I scoured famous literature for comparable examples. (I was an English teacher before I became a lawyer.) The logic and metaphor were a great fit. A rich man or wealthy company can freely oppress little people, who are totally screwed unless a system of justice holds such oppressors accountable. I also knew that in Kentucky, many people on the jury were likely Bible believers, and the story would ring a familiar chord, even if the jurors didn't remember the original Bible story. The story is powerful, even for those with no Bible connection. This analogy could prove useful when leaders are attacking the deceptive practices of large US banks and financial institutions. I give my blessings to lawyers and activists to use it freely.

The story of the rich man and the thousand sheep was taken from the story of King David's adultery with Bathsheba, found in 2 Samuel 11 and 12. King David saw Bathsheba bathing one day and developed a serious case of lust for her. Being the king, he called her in and seduced her. Remember, women were property back then, and refusing a king could bring certain death, and who knows, the attraction may have been mutual, or she may have been flattered by the king's attention.

Bathsheba's husband was fighting on the front lines at war for his country and his king. When Bathsheba turned up pregnant, the king tried to cover his misdeed by bringing her husband Uriah home and letting him spend time with his wife so that later he would think the baby was his. But Uriah was a man of integrity and refused to enjoy the comforts of his wife while his men, deprived of their wives, were fighting at the battlefront. So King David sent Bathsheba's husband back to the war and ordered his men to retreat at a strategic point and leave him to be killed.

When the prophet Nathan heard of Uriah's murder (you can't keep that level of conspiracy hidden for long), he went to King David and told him the story of the man with a thousand sheep. King David wanted to put the rich man to death, for he saw that in taking the poor man's sheep, the rich man had taken all that the poor man had. Then Nathan said, "You, O King, are that rich man." King David already had many wives and concubines, and Bathsheba was Uriah's only wife. That revelation pierced the hard shell of King David's heart. Overcome with guilt, he fell on his face, weeping in remorse for his crimes. Obviously, King David knew the law of Moses, which made oppressing the poor a capital offense.

Of course, Old Testament justice had a few strange twists. Polygamy was the status quo, and it was okay for the king to have a stable of concubines who didn't get the full status of being wives. Nor were there legal checks and balances to make David pay for murdering Uriah; however, in the story, God punished David by causing the first child born with Bathsheba to die before age two. Yet King Solomon and his magnificent reign of splendor came from this union that began in adultery and murder. And we are left to presume that Bathsheba became David's favorite wife.

This story gives a brilliant lesson in how to confront people about their wrongs, especially those in authority. Had Nathan directly accosted the king for his wickedness, the king likely would have rejected his counsel and had him killed. People in power don't welcome criticism. Just ask Dick Wilson and Valerie Plame, who contradicted the faulty intelligence supporting the Iraq war only to see their careers in the CIA destroyed as a result and the law violated in order to out Valerie as a CIA spy. But by using a story first, the prophet Nathan got the king to drop his defenses and open his conscience to assess the situation objectively. Only after the king pronounced judgment on the rich man's wicked conduct did the prophet Nathan disclose the identity of the real culprit. We all can learn a thing or two from Nathan. Sometimes, the best way into a heart is by analogy.

In my lawsuit, I didn't bring up King David. I softened King David's punishment from "that man should be killed" to "that man should be punished severely." A punishment of death would have made me look vindictive and have been over the top. And, of course, I left out the plot of adultery and the fact that the king himself was the rich man guilty of stealing his neighbor's sheep. Those parts were irrelevant to the sound principle I was advocating.

The story itself demonstrates two principles of justice: proportionality so you feel what it's like to stand in someone else's shoes and the wickedness of harming someone else when you have no need to do so. Stealing a loaf of bread because you are hungry is not the same as stealing your neighbor's only bread because you are greedy, arrogant, and vindictive. This is just one example of how we can use the Bible to champion a just cause—holding Goliath corporations accountable for the way they treat defenseless little guys. This shows how we can speak up for those who have no voice, as the Bible commands in Proverbs 31:8.

During the 2007 Kentucky gubernatorial race, the Democrat Steve Beshear masterfully used biblical references. As a Democrat, he didn't make grandiose references to Scripture. He made his quotes subtly. Proverbs and Ecclesiastes are wonderful sources for powerful, zippy sayings. Politicians are missing it by not using phrases that undergird the heritage of most Americans.

One of Beshear's ads went something like this: "There is a proverb that says a person who answers before he listens is a fool. I have been traveling our state for over two years listening to what Kentuckians have to say, and that's why I'm now running to be your governor...." The point was "I am now speaking because I have listened." When I heard the ad, I cheered, for at last a Democrat was getting it.[226] Beshear was using Proverbs 18:13: "To answer before listening—that is folly and shame."

Beshear's would-be Democratic successor, Jack Conway, did not approach Bible-speak at all. I'm not saying that would have swayed the election since Republicans were more energized than the Democrats. But it certainly couldn't have hurt. While the old proverb is just a proverb, it has a strong ring of truth to Bible believers because they instinctively recognize it as "the Word of God." By subtly incorporating the Bible into his message, Beshear won the election—not merely because of this quote, but partly because his Bible references and his emphasis that he came from a family of Christian ministers prevented his Republican opponent from casting him in an anti-Christian light—even though Beshear himself came out in favor of casino gambling.

Bible stories acknowledge the common moral, religious, and spiritual heritage that underlies our social fabric and that speaks to many in our population. We are calling forth genuine, honest biblical principles that support our point of view. And as shown in the case of the used car dealer, a Bible story may be the best metaphor to capture the morality of the situation. There's a lot of wisdom in the Bible ready to enlighten our thinking. Using Bible stories is more authentic than merely playing a word game. It frames moral principles in language people can relate to and gives us fresh insight into our relationships and moral standards.

Conclusion

In the book *Words That Work*,[227] Frank Luntz talks about using words that reframe a situation in order to shift one's perspective. For instance, today casinos refer to their industry as the gaming industry, not as gambling, for going somewhere to play some games seems a lot more wholesome than going somewhere to gamble, an activity long stigmatized as a vice. Republicans have been more masterful at labeling and framing issues than Democrats. For instance, they renamed estate taxes as "death taxes." Who wants to owe taxes just because they die? It automatically sounds unfair, even though our estate tax system has been our country's only means of preventing the super wealthy from snowballing their wealth and power from generation to generation.

Similarly, being pro-life is more appealing than being pro-abortion; even pro-choice is a weaker term. Sister Joan Chittister, a prominent Roman Catholic nun, has aptly used reframing, by pointing out that being pro-birth is not the same as pro-life, especially when we insist that children be born, but refuse to provide them with food, clothing, education, and health care once they are here.[228]

Republicans have effectively relabeled laws designed to curb workers' pay and benefits as "right to work" laws. Wake up. These are union busting laws, or "right to low pay" laws. And if you've ever been privy to hear CEO's talk about these matters, as I have, being an attorney, you know they are "right to oppress workers" laws. But it sounds wholesome, and our entire culture has bought into their terminology.

The power to name is the power to define—and then to control. Sometimes, dear moderate Republican friends ask me, "Why do Democrats give Republicans all the power to frame the issues?" Throughout this book I've argued that progressives are missing the boat by not using the abundance of Bible authority that corroborates their social and legal policies. What can be better than framing debates for evangelicals by using their most sacred authority—an authority they have unwittingly abandoned?

That's why my son came up with the phrase, "Jesus Loves Obamacare." Let conservatives argue that our collective efforts to obey the words of Jesus are wrong or immoral. Even in a secular context, one can refer to our national common faith heritage without sounding like a zealot or wanting to install a theocracy. Knowing the scriptures comes in handy when debating our conservative friends or a crazy right-wing uncle at Thanksgiving. We need to speak up and remind conservative Christians that Jesus Christ clarified that the *only* way to align with God's kingdom was to feed the hungry, clothe the naked, give drink to the thirsty, take in the immigrant, care for those in prison, and care for the sick, as laid out in Matthew 25. In fact, Jesus Christ said that when we fail to care for the least of the people in any of these categories, we fail to care for Him, and He will reject us as being part of His fold. This is one of the strongest moral imperatives in the New Testament, and it's one that deserves serious consideration, even by those who don't take the entire Bible literally.

Jewish people or Muslims can modify the statements in this book to be in integrity with their faith, for the Old Testament law charged the nation's rulers with taking care of the sick, the poor, and the immigrant, as well as enacting proper justice for prisoners. In the New Testament Jesus was merely upholding Old Testament law. And these other two faith traditions don't even debate these well-established principles. They understand that societies have collective responsibilities to care for the poor and the sick. Even an agnostic could simply change the beginning and state, "I'm not a person of faith, but I think Jesus had the right idea when He said...." Everyone can and should call Christians to account for refusing to follow the religion they purport to uphold.

When conservative Christians inevitably play the small government card, be sure to mention that the Old Testament had legal mandates of taxation that took care of the poor and the immigrant. These weren't optional acts of charity. Be sure also to refer to the Old Testament prophets, who discuss how rulers and leaders have a moral duty to use their power to help the poor, the immigrant, and the sick—not just by individual charity but by making just laws. If they try to dismiss that as "Old Testament" or no longer relevant, be sure to bring up Acts chapters 4 and 5, which describe how Christians banded together as a community to solve the problem of poverty and to take care of each other; remind them how the early Christians practiced massive wealth redistribution. They will really squirm if you discuss the story of Ananias' dying for not giving over all of his money to the church. I have a feeling that suddenly your conservative friend will get a lot less literal very quickly.

You might also try asking them to quote a scripture that specifically forbids people from asking the government to take care of those in need. You might also ask them to find verses that lay out where giving massive tax cuts to the rich is moral and righteous. There's nothing about "Blessed are the job creators" in Christ's Beatitudes. There are no verses extolling the virtues of social Darwinism. Hopefully, you will stump your cantankerous uncle or loud-mouthed mall biddies if you know the scriptures we have set out previously in this book.

In addition, we need to use biblical references to reframe dissent. Somehow, in our country conservative evangelicals have come to see critics of our government or its leaders as being unpatriotic and traitors to their church communities. I have been repeatedly shocked at the hostility from my own Christian culture toward anyone who spoke up against the Vietnam War in the 1960s or the Iraq War in 2003. Yet history has proven both sets of critics, decades apart, to be morally and legally on the better side.

I stand with my country, right or wrong, because it is my country, but I don't have to pretend that my government is always right or makes wise choices, nor am I compelled to help leaders perpetrate lies. Most of us loving parents stand by our children, right or wrong, but we certainly reserve the right to tell them when they may venture down a dangerous or ill-advised path. Growing up, I heard many sermons that parents who love their children chasten (correct) them. Those who care about their children will suffer the inconvenience and disapproval of their children to teach them good behaviors and moral principles that will help them succeed. And wise people admit that true friends tell us the truth about something, even when it's not what we want to hear. It is a challenge to speak the truth in love, and it comes with great personal risk. I always say, "The truth will set you free, but first it will offend you."

Some of my progressive friends might suggest that it's silly to inject the Bible into politics. But in my personal life, I don't see a hard line between the sacred and the secular. It's all God's world; it's all God's money, and if I go to church on Sunday, I must practice Bible values Monday through Saturday. Our values and principles must pervade all areas of our lives, if we have any integrity with our doctrines. I can and must advocate government policies that are consistent with my personal Christian values, even though legally, I do not impose my faith on others, and I believe in a strong division between church and state under the law. Many of our laws are based on moral principles that share origins with the Bible. The key is having a rational basis that can be enforced across the board without reference to or favoritism of any one religion.

For my dear evangelical friends and associates who may be offended at my audacity in writing this book, I remind you of the following scriptures from the KJV:

Am I therefore become your enemy, because I tell you the truth? (Galatians 4:16)

He that refuseth instruction despiseth his own soul: but **he that heareth reproof getteth understanding.** (Proverbs 15:32)

It is better to hear the rebuke of the wise than the song of fools. (Ecclesiastes 7:5)

Reprove not a scorner, lest he hate thee: **rebuke a wise man, and he will love thee.** Give instruction to a wise man, and he will be yet wiser: teach a just man, and he will increase in learning. (Proverbs 9:8–9)

These are my answers to those who assume that we progressives are always protesting, criticizing, and tearing down America. Those who love their country will rebuke their country. Yet somehow in fundamentalist culture this Bible logic is seldom applied. Many unwittingly adopted the mentality that "the king can do no wrong" (well, that is their stance so long as the king is a Republican). Those who rebuke our leaders are labeled as unpatriotic liars. It's always risky to criticize anyone in authority. But the Bible says, "**Faithful are the wounds of a friend...**" (Proverbs 27:6 KJV). Hence, if we love our friends, we will speak the truth to them, even if we have to risk their ire.

In this book I have gone to great lengths to remind all of us of our biblical heritage. I put my law practice on hold and invested considerable resources in getting this message out into both our progressive and conservative cultures. I have no illusions about its success or that I would even recoup my costs. I only pray it makes a difference. The urgency of the message required me to self-publish in order to get it to market quickly. Given the movement to abolish health care benefits and other compassionate social policies sweeping our nation by a now controlling minority of Americans, I had to go on the record to hold the mirror of the Bible up to popular thinking. I also believe it is political malpractice for Democrats and conservatives with a conscience, like John Kasich or Mitt Romney, not to use the authority of the Bible when defending efforts to bring affordable health care to all Americans.

Using Bible stories is a way of acknowledging our common moral, religious, and spiritual heritage that underlies our social fabric and that speaks to many in our population. We are calling forth genuine, honest biblical principles that support our point of view. And as shown in the case of the used car dealer, a Bible story may be the best metaphor to capture the morality of the situation. There's a lot of wisdom in the Bible ready to enlighten our thinking.

For too long many of us have let one wing of the faith community frame issues as if they are the only ones who love God and their country. Liberals, progressives, moderates, Democrats, and moderate wise-thinking Republicans have failed to stand up for their moral convictions that have a strong basis in the Bible. Right-wingers can still refuse to apply it, but they will have to admit that their beliefs and conduct often oppose their own Bible, and they lose the giant club of "moral values" with which they've been bashing Democrats for decades. You can advocate the policies of Ayn Rand, but no longer will you get away with doing it in the name of Jesus.

Perhaps, this book will encourage those who've long felt like a voice crying in the wilderness. I hope it's been informative, or at the very least thought provoking. While I would appreciate a nice review on Amazon, it's more important that we call our congressional representatives and senators. Let them know that saving the Affordable Care Act is important to us and that we will be voting in 2018. Call them and your governors to show that Obamacare should be reformed (and potentially expanded) not repealed. Even if we don't have a preexisting condition, we can take a stand for those that do. We can speak up for the least of these in society.

My son jokes, "Bernie Sanders shouldn't be afraid of quoting the Bible; he was there when it was written." If national Democrats can spend hundreds of millions on consultants and spin doctors, they can take a few hours and learn some Bible verses to help them connect with evangelical Republican voters. The coastal elites in our party have been far too squeamish about using the Bible as moral authority for their policies, despite the fact that so much of it reads like a Bernie Sanders campaign speech. In fact, we found so many scriptures on economic reform that we had to omit them here and plan a second book so that we could focus on health care and other welfare policies that appear at immediate risk with the new Trump administration.

We need to use all the resources at our disposal in order to change hearts and minds, and that includes quoting the Bible. We may not be able to convince all Bible believers to embrace the more than 200 scriptures we've quoted in this book, scriptures that reinforce Jesus' words in Matthew 25, but if we can convince just 2% of conservative evangelicals in swing states to embrace Jesus' words to care for the sick and the poor and to stop demonizing immigrants, then that's more than enough to win the next election and begin building a national consensus for a fair, compassionate society that promotes the common welfare.

Take back your power, liberals! The ability to reframe and argue the issues is right there in front of you in the Good Book. As Obama said, "Let's get fired up and ready to go."

Index to Scripture References

Genesis 12

Genesis 26

Genesis 42

Leviticus 19:34

Deuteronomy 14:28–29

Deuteronomy 26:8–13

Leviticus 19:9–10

Leviticus 23:22

Leviticus 19:34

Deuteronomy 24:19–21

Exodus 22:21

Exodus 22:21

Exodus 23:9

Exodus 23:9

Deuteronomy 24:14

Deuteronomy 10:17–19

Leviticus 19:33–34

Exodus 12:43–48

Isaiah 14:1

Isaiah 56:1–8

Ezekiel 47:22, 23

Exodus 12:49–51

Leviticus 24:22

Numbers 9:14

Numbers 35:15

Leviticus 25:6

Leviticus 16:29–30

Leviticus 18:26–27

Leviticus 24:16

Isaiah 1:7

Deuteronomy 17:14–20

Psalm 146:9

Luke 17:12–19

Luke 10:22

Luke 10:30–37

John 8:48

Acts 22:21–24

Acts 11:18

Acts 15:7–9

Galatians 3:26–29

Colossians 3:9–12

Ephesians 2:12–20

Hebrews 13:1–2

2 Timothy 1:7

Proverbs 25:29

Chapter Five:

Zechariah 7:10

Isaiah 32:7–8

Ezekiel 22:1–8

Zechariah 7:9–11

Zechariah 11:15–17

Malachi 3:5–6

Psalm 10:2–12

Psalm 109:16

Psalm 9:17–18

Psalm 37:14

Psalm 94:3–8

Proverbs 14:31

Proverbs 21:13

Proverbs 28:27

Proverbs 29:7

Isaiah 58:6–11

Jeremiah 5:26–28

Jeremiah 7:3–7

1 Timothy 5:8

Exodus 22:22–24

2 Samuel 12:1–7

Leviticus 25:17

Deuteronomy 15:6–11

Deuteronomy 23:24–25

Isaiah 32:7

2 Timothy 3:16

1 Timothy 5:8

Matthew 19:21–22

Mark 10:20–22

Luke 18:18–23

Luke 12:33

Matthew 19:24

Mark 10:25

Luke 18:25

Luke 14:12–14

Deuteronomy 14:22–27

James 1:26–27

James 2:15–17, 26

James 2:5–7

Philippians 2:4

Luke 6:38

Galatians 6:2

I John 3:17

1 Timothy 6:17–19

Proverbs 3:27

2 Thessalonians 3:10

Psalm 41:1–3

Psalm 12:5

Psalm 35:9–10

Psalm 113:7–8

Psalm 140:12

Proverbs 14:21

Proverbs 19:17

Proverbs 22:9

Psalm 82:1–5

Chapter Six:

Matthew 25:43

Mark 2:17

Luke 14:16–19

Hebrews 13:3

Psalm 69:33–34

Psalm 102:19–20

Psalm 146:6–8

Job 3:17–19

Isaiah 42:6–8

Psalm 66:10–12

Ephesians 4:28

Lamentations 3:31–36

Proverbs 30:7–9

Genesis 1:29

Genesis 9:3

Ezekiel 47:12

II Kings 2:19–22

Chapter Seven:

Endnotes

1   See Mary Pipher, *Reviving Ophelia: Saving the Selves of Adolescent Girls* (Riverhead, 2005).

2   Norman Vincent Peale, "Mr. Positive Thinking" himself, opposed Kennedy on these grounds. https://www2.gwu.edu/ ~ erpapers/mep/displaydoc.cfm?docid = erps-acism.

3   https://en.wikipedia.org/wiki/Bloody_Monday. See also, Gustavus Myers, *History of Bigotry in the United States* (Capricorn, 1960).

4   The summary in the link below corroborates my personal memory of this history. https://thinkprogress.org/the-ferocious-fight-against-the-mlk-national-holiday-cc5debdbb86a#.s5w0egz6r.

5   https://partners.nytimes.com/library/national/race/060400sack-church-side.html.

6   See Scott C. Billingsly, *It's a New Day: Race and Gender in the Modern Charismatic Movement* (U of Alabama Press, 2008).

7   John R. Rice, 1941. This book is still available on Amazon.

8   For a hilarious time the whole family can enjoy, see https://smile.amazon.com/Bill-Engvall-Heres-Your-Sign/dp/B0002EJ7X0/ref = sr_1_2?ie = UTF8&qid = 1483887409&sr = 8-2&keywords = bill + engvall + here%27s + your + sign.

9   http://www.pewhispanic.org/2015/11/19/more-mexicans-leaving-than-coming-to-the-u-s/.

10 I am indebted to a sermon by Rob Bell for the insight to connect Nineveh with the Assyrians and the horrendous evils they had inflicted on the Israelites.

11 See Matthew 23:25–28.

12 See Matthew 12:43–45.

13 The doctrine of *sola scriptura* ("only scripture") is a fundamental build-
    ing block of Protestantism, ever since the Reformation. See, for in-
    stance, http://www.sbts.edu/wp-
    content/uploads/sites/5/2016/05/Sola-Scriptura-in-the-Strange-Land-
    of-Evangelicalism.pdf.

14 The scholarship it took to create this reference tool in the nineteenth
    century without computers is mind-boggling.
    https://en.wikipedia.org/wiki/Strong's_Concordance.

15 There is a free version of Touch Bible, but if you are a Bible student,
    pay the $5 and buy the better version, so that with a mere tap on each
    word, you see the pop-up definition from *Strong's Concordance*.

16 "Male and female created he them; and blessed them, and called their
    name Adam…" (Genesis 5:2; see also, Genesis 1:27).

17 I remember when many Republicans were conservative fiscally, but in
    favor of civil rights, a time when they reached across the aisle to pass
    voting rights, end segregation, and support educational opportunity.
    My own state's Senator John Sherman Cooper was an excellent exam-
    ple of wise Republican leadership. But this was before Reagan brought
    the Dixiecrats into the Republican Party.

18 Courtesy Strong's Exhaustive Concordance of the Bible.

19 http://www.biblestudytools.com/dictionaries/bakers-evangelical-
    dictionary/psalms-theology-of.html.

20 We will address this more fully in Chapter Five.

21 http://www.consumerfinance.gov/about-us/newsroom/consumer-
    financial-protection-bureau-fines-wells-fargo-100-million-widespread-
    illegal-practice-secretly-opening-unauthorized-accounts/;
    http://fortune.com/2016/11/23/american-bank-regulators-sanctions-
    wells-fargo/.

22 https://www.ministrymagazine.org/archive/1958/09/the-three-tithes-
    of-the-old-testament. It's noteworthy that this 1958 evangelical pastor
    was advocating collective efforts to give welfare to the poor. Evidently,
    the trend for evangelicals to oppose collective efforts is a more recent
    phenomenon. This pastor notes: "The Jewish historian, Flavius Jose-
    phus, mentions the custom of paying three tithes: 'In addition to the

two tithes which I have already directed you to pay each year, the one for the Levites and the other for the banquets, ye should devote a third every third year to the distribution of such things as are lacking to widowed women and orphan *children.'—Antiquities* IV. 240; Loeb ed."

23 https://bible.org/seriespage/lesson-4-why-you-should-not-tithe-selected-scriptures, quoting Charles Ryrie, *Balancing the Christian Life* (Moody Press 1969), 86.

24 http://www.jewishencyclopedia.com/articles/14408-tithe.

25 https://www.theguardian.com/us-news/2015/may/11/presidential-hopeful-ben-carson-bases-10-tax-plan-on-biblical-tithing. Four years earlier, Herman Cain echoed similar sentiments with his 9-9-9 plan, which may have come from a video game. http://www.huffingtonpost.com/2011/10/20/herman-cain-defends-999-plan_n_1020992.html; http://www.dailymail.co.uk/news/article-2048969/Did-Herman-Cain-999-tax-plan-SimCity-video-game.html.

26 The following site lists quotations of the Old Testament by the New: http://www.kalvesmaki.com/LXX/NTChart.htm.

27 History shows that Romans citizens had the right to vote, could stand for public office, and had rights of appeal. For a detailed review of Roman legal history and analysis of Paul's use of the legal system of his day to seek justice, see Boyd Reece, "The Apostle Paul's Exercise of his Rights as a Roman Citizen...." https://biblicalstudies.org.uk/pdf/eq/1975-3_138.pdf/.

28 See https://www.christiancourier.com/articles/1552-when-was-the-book-of-revelation-written; see also, http://www.jewishvirtuallibrary.org/jsource/Judaism/revolt.html.

29 Interpretations of the Beast (of Revelation): https://en.wikipedia.org/wiki/The_Beast_ (Revelation)#Interpretations; see also, Symbolism of the Whore of Babylon: https://en.wikipedia.org/wiki/Whore_of_Babylon#Symbolism.

30 Elaine Pagels, *Revelations: Visions, Prophecy, and Politics in the Book of Revelation* (Viking, 2012).

31 Piecing together a historical view of Domitian requires much research, not the purpose here, but an interesting review and bibliography is found at http://www.biblearchaeology.org/post/2010/01/18/The-King-and-I-The-Apostle-John-and-Emperor-Domitian-Part-1.aspx.

[32] His own statements about his name and Ayn Rand are on YouTube
      and also repeated here: http://www.motherjones.com/blue-
      marble/2010/05/aynt-true-rand-paul-not-named-after-novelist. See also,
      http://www.politico.com/story/2012/04/7-pols-who-praised-ayn-rand-
      075667; see also https://thinkprogress.org/rand-pauls-favorite-
      philosophers-think-poor-people-are-parasites-
      e464616f8512#.10mc682h8.

[33] https://pjmedia.com/news-and-politics/2015/11/28/rand-paul-if-you-
      want-to-help-people-give-of-your-own-money/ (This is a conservative
      news blog, not a liberal reporter ragging on Rand.)

[34] https://www.thenation.com/article/rand-paul-americas-hungry-
      seniors-let-them-eat-private-charity/.

[35] https://en.wikipedia.org/wiki/Sichuan_schools_corruption_scandal;
      see also, http://erm-academy.org/publication/risk-management-
      article/bangladesh-and-reasons-buildings-collapse.

[36] https://en.wikipedia.org/wiki/Beverly_Hills_Supper_Club_fire.

[37] "Bevin Invites Tragedy By Cutting State Oversight of Building Codes."
      http://www.kentucky.com/opinion/op-ed/article125072754.html.

[38] https://www.nytimes.com/2016/01/30/us/lead-poisoning.html.

[39] http://www.cnn.com/2016/01/11/health/toxic-tap-water-flint-
      michigan/; http://www.cnn.com/2016/03/04/us/flint-water-crisis-fast-
      facts/.

[40] https://www.washingtonpost.com/news/powerpost/wp
      /2016/09/28/house-leaders-reach-deal-on-flint-aid-potentially-averting-
      shutdown/?utm_term=.665852f4c7d9.

[41] See http://www.politifact.com/truth-o-
      meter/statements/2009/oct/02/michael-moore/michael-moores-film-
      capitalism-claims-richest-paid/ and
      https://www.bloomberg.com/view/articles/2013-01-02/1950s-tax-
      fantasy-is-a-republican-nightmare.

[42] This was the June 19, 2007 edition of The View. The quoted conversa-
      tion occurs about two minutes into the clip, as Star Parker kept ram-
      bling before she could formulate her question to Moore.
      https://www.youtube.com/watch?v=b7UTm0UpX5g.

43 Michael Moore appeared before the Judiciary Committee in Washington, D.C. on June 20, 2007. https://youtu.be/pIL6be7WwvM.

44 https://www.youtube.com/watch?v=bgQQ7_BAUaE.

45 http://www.factcheck.org/2009/10/37th-in-health-performance/.

46 http://www.usnews.com/opinion/articles/2014/05/30/no-the-us-doesnt-have-the-best-health-care-system-in-the-world. See also, http://www.commonwealthfund.org/publications/issue-briefs/2015/oct/us-health-care-from-a-global-perspective, which gives many more statistics as to birth, deaths, life expectancy, and chronic conditions.

47 For example, see Deuteronomy 28:58–61.

48 As noted earlier, https://youtu.be/pIL6be7WwvM.

49 http://ldi.upenn.edu/news/overview-israels-universal-health-care-system.

50 http://www.nytimes.com/1997/03/14/us/hatch-joins-kennedy-to-back-a-health-program.html.

51 http://www.politifact.com/colorado/statements/2016/feb/17/hillary-clinton/hillary-clinton-wrong-sanders-claim/.

52 For a general overview, see https://en.wikipedia.org/wiki/Special_education_in_the_United_States.

53 https://www.washingtonpost.com/news/fact-checker/wp/2016/09/19/fact-checking-clintons-story-of-meeting-disabled-children-in-new-bedford-in-1973/?utm_term=.5aef5a1e17b5.

54 Elizabeth Warren and Amelia Warren Tyagi, *The Two Income Trap: Why Middle Class Parents Are Going Broke* (Basic Books, 2004). Elizabeth Warren discusses her book in the following legal interview, which can be seen here: https://youtu.be/8GHg3GAeQ1Y.

55 http://www.nytimes.com/1990/07/26/us/house-backs-bush-veto-of-family-leave-bill.html.

56 http://acasignups.net/15/12/01/aca-may-have-saved-87000-lives-and-im-not-even-talking-about-through-medicaid-expansion. See also, http://www.dailykos.com/story/2015/4/2/1375090/-Fact-check-Has-Obamacare-helped-save-50-000-lives-Why-yes-it-nbsp-has.

57 http://www.nytimes.com/2015/12/10/us/politics/marco-rubio-
    obamacare-affordable-care-act.html?_r=0;
    http://america.aljazeera.com/opinions/2015/12/how-marco-rubio-
    sabotaged-obamacare.html.

58 https://www.bloomberg.com/news/articles/2016-10-24/obamacare-
    benchmark-premiums-to-rise-25-in-sharpest-jump-yet;
    http://fortune.com/2016/10/25/obamacare-insurance-premiums-2017-
    health care/.

59 https://www.ncbi.nlm.nih.gov/pmc/articles/PMC2690175/.

60 http://www.aging.senate.gov/imo/media/doc/
    02_Hoadley_5_22_13.pdf.

61 http://www.huffingtonpost.com/d-brad-wright/did-the-heritage-
    foundati_b_551804.html;
    http://krugman.blogs.nytimes.com/2011/07/27/conservative-origins-
    of-obamacare/?_r=0.

62 http://www.bostonglobe.com/lifestyle/health-
    wellness/2004/11/24/plan-for-massachusetts-health-insurance-
    reform/d1I1xFpnfLcQ8Ipz4nCdpJ/story.html; see also,
    http://www.motherjones.com/mojo/2015/10/mitt-romney-
    obamacare-romneycare.

63 See Reform Coalitions in Massachusetts Health care Reform:
    https://en.wikipedia.org/wiki/Massachusetts_health_care_reform#Ref
    orm_coalitions.

64 https://www.healthreformvotes.org/congress/300025.

65 https://www.healthreformvotes.org/congress/300091.

66 http://www.usatoday.com/story/theoval/2013/04/24/obama-
    olympia-snowe-health-care-joan-of-arc/2109765/.

67 Why Senator Chuck Grassley Turned On Health Care Reform:
    http://content.time.com/time/magazine/article/0,9171,1920306,00.ht
    ml. See also, Grassley's Big Blunder on Health Care Law:
    http://www.desmoinesregister.com/story/opinion/columnists/iowa-
    view/2016/07/22/grassleys-big-blunder-health-care-law/87411958/; and
    David Axelrod, *Believer: My Forty Years in Politics.* (Penguin, 2015).

68 https://www.mentalhealth.gov/get-help/health-insurance/.

69 http://www.nytimes.com/2015/11/03/health/death-rates-rising-for-middle-aged-white-americans-study-finds.html; http://www.theatlantic.com/health/archive/2016/01/middle-aged-white-americans-left-behind-and-dying-early/433863/.

70 http://kff.org/health-costs/report/2016-employer-health-benefits-survey/.

71 http://robertreich.org/post/123327070510. See also http://www.fiercehealth care.com/payer/health-insurance-stocks-hit-all-time-highs.

72 http://www.salon.com/2016/10/28/making-a-killing-under-obamacare-the-aca-gets-the-blame-for-rising-premiums-while-insurance-companies-are-reaping-massive-profits/.

73 https://www.theguardian.com/business/2016/aug/24/epipen-ceo-hiked-prices-heather-bresch-mylan.

74 https://www.whitehouse.gov/blog/2013/07/18/refund-your-health-insurance-company-thank-affordable-care-act; http://abcnews.go.com/Politics/obamacare-health-insurance-rebates-check/story?id=19701785.

75 http://money.cnn.com/2014/07/24/pf/insurance/health-insurance-refund/.

76 http://www.nytimes.com/2015/03/16/opinion/medicaid-expansion-in-red-states.html?_r=0.

77 http://www.washingtonpost.com/sf/national/2016/01/05/deciderskasich/.

78 http://www.dispatch.com/content/stories/local/2013/06/18/kasich-will-never-give-up-fight-to-expand-medicaid.html.

79 http://talkingpointsmemo.com/livewire/jan-brewer-to-gop-expand-medicaid-or-i-ll-veto-all-bills; http://www.politico.com/story/2013/06/arizona-medicaid-expansion-jan-brewer-092723.

80 http://www.slate.com/articles/news_and_politics/politics/2016/11/can_tennessee_s_trey_hollingsworth_buy_a_congressional_seat_in_indiana.html.

81 https://www.hhs.gov/health care/facts-and-features/fact-
    sheets/preventive-services-covered-under-
    aca/#CoveredPreventiveServicesforChildren.

82 *Ibid.*

83 http://obamacarefacts.com/obamacare-womens-health-services/.

84 At the time of this writing, the information was at
    https://www.whitehouse.gov/sites/default/files/docs/the_aca_helps_
    women.pdf; however, the new administration has removed this infor-
    mation from the White House. See the next footnote for the same in-
    formation.

85 http://www.babycenter.com/0_how-the-affordable-care-act-aca-affects-
    pregnant-women-and-f_10371090.bc.

86 http://www.commonwealthfund.org/~/media/Files/Publica
    tions/Issue%20Brief/2009/May/Women%20at%20Risk/PDF_1262_R
    ustgi_women_at_risk_issue_brief_Final.pdf.

87 https://www.hhs.gov/health care/facts-and-features/fact-
    sheets/preventive-services-covered-under-aca/.

88 https://www.cdc.gov/cancer/dcpc/data/men.htm.

89 http://kff.org/health-reform/poll-finding/kaiser-health-tracking-poll-
    march-2014/.

90 http://www.americamagazine.org/content/all-things/pope-calls-
    guaranteed-health-care.

91 https://www.catholicculture.org/news/headlines/index.cfm?
    storyid=28266.

92 The cover story in the August 2009 Jewish Journal addressed "Why We
    Must Support Universal health Care."
    (http://www.jewishjournal.com/articles/print/why_we_must_suppor
    t_universal_health_care_20090826) This link stopped working, but
    similar arguments are found at
    http://www.chabad.org/library/article_cdo/aid/1914545/jewish/Wha
    t-Does-the-Torah-Say-About-Obamacare.htm.

93 The following sites are a good place to begin to see America's history
    of intolerance: http://www.pri.org/stories/2015-11-26/brief-history-
    america-s-hostility-previous-generation-mediterranean-migrants;

https://en.wikipedia.org/wiki/Anti-Irish_sentiment;
https://en.wikipedia.org/wiki/Anti-Polish_sentiment;
https://en.wikipedia.org/wiki/History_of_antisemitism_in_the_Unite
d_States; Gustavus Myers' *History of Bigotry in the United States*, is still
a classic (Random House, 1943). Used copies are available on Amazon.

94 https://en.wikipedia.org/wiki/Ku_Klux_Klan.

95 The statistics on modern genocide are sobering. And more mass murders were performed by supposed "Christian" regimes than even by Muslims. See http://www.juancole.com/2013/04/terrorism-other-religions.html. Yet the facts show that religion is often just a subterfuge and that wars are waged for conquest. http://www.huffingtonpost.com/rabbi-alan-lurie/is-religion-the-cause-of-_b_1400766.html.

96 The NIV is equally as cogent: "The **foreigner residing among you must be treated as your native-born. Love them as yourself,** for you were foreigners in Egypt. I am the Lord your God" (Leviticus 19:34).

97 https://www.theguardian.com/society/2016/nov/29/trump-related-hate-crimes-report-southern-poverty-law-center.

98 There are several links to this vicious event on Facebook. http://themountainvoice.com/2016/12/23/woman-verbally-attacks-hispanic-woman-j-c-penny-video/.

99 Although it was seen as controversial and "bleeding hearted," the US Supreme Court (stacked with Republican appointees) declared in 2006 in *Hamdan v. Rumsfeld*, 548 U.S. 557 (2006), that George W. Bush could not unilaterally set up special courts to try suspected terrorists apprehended in Afghanistan after 9/11. In the *Hamdan* case, the Supreme Court found that the Bush Administration violated the Geneva Conventions. The Geneva Conventions and other international agreements were set up to prevent the victors in war from executing the losers. Even in war, there are universal truths that show mercy to our harshest enemies. And this universal truth is evidenced here in the Bible.

100 See http://www.catholic.com/quickquestions/who-were-the-samaritans-and-why-were-they-important.

101 A whopping 77%—comprised mostly of Catholics and evangelicals. http://www.pewforum.org/religious-landscape-study/racial-and-ethnic-composition/latino/.

[102] http://money.cnn.com/2014/11/20/news/economy/immigration-myths/. See also https://www.fns.usda.gov/sites/default/files/Non-Citizen_Guidance_063011.pdf.

[103] See, for instance, http://www.cnn.com/2015/07/08/politics/immigrants-crime/.

[104] See http://www.bbc.com/news/magazine-27373131. See also http://www.jewishvirtuallibrary.org/jsource/Holocaust/stlouis.html.

[105] http://www.bbc.com/news/world-us-canada-34849891.

[106] The 1951 Refugee Convention, a multi-national treaty, states: "No Contracting State shall expel or return ('refouler') a refugee in any manner whatsoever to the frontiers of territories where his life or freedom would be threatened on account of his race, religion, nationality, membership of a particular social group or political opinion" (Article 33(1)). https://en.wikipedia.org/wiki/Non-refoulement; https://en.wikipedia.org/wiki/Convention_Relating_to_the_Status_of_Refugees. See also http://crfimmigrationed.org/index.php/lessons-for-teachers/145-hl6.

[107] http://www.politifact.com/truth-o-meter/article/2015/dec/29/what-citizenship-status-terrorists-united-states/.

[108] A Google search will enable you to pull up copies of Sartre's essay.

[109] See "Welfare Cadillac" by Guy Drake, https://www.youtube.com/watch?v=hq-hx73or30.

[110] http://mentalfloss.com/article/30142/when-johnny-cash-met-richard-nixon.

[111] https://www.youtube.com/watch?v=HNU9nNY-v0g.

[112] For more examples of "lying words" that create a false impression about the cushy life of the poor, see the following, which fact-checks common myths. http://www.politifact.com/rhode-island/statements/2015/feb/01/rhode-island-center-freedom-and-prosperity/do-common-welfare-programs-pay-equivalent-2083-hou/.

[113] http://thehill.com/blogs/blog-briefing-room/news/222003-catholic-bishops-criticize-ryan-budget-cuts-to-food-stamps.

[114] http://www.msnbc.com/rachel-maddow-show/paul-ryans-faith-based-troubles-continu.

[115] https://sojo.net/articles/hole-y-bible-gets-digital-makeover.

[116] Lest anyone misinterpret, I'm not in favor of adultery. From my own broken marriage and experience as a lawyer, I'm a witness to the devastation that a cheating spouse brings.

[117] Dietrich Bonhoeffer, *Letters and Papers from Prison* (Minneapolis: Fortress Press, 2015), see pp. 9–11.

[118] Please notice in the above passage that while requiring aid to the poor, God commanded Israel to give foreign aid to other countries. Being able to lend to other nations was a testimony of prosperity and superiority.

[119] http://www.rollcall.com/news/policy/gop-budget-plan-cut-23-billion-food-stamps.

[120] https://thinkprogress.org/26-lawmakers-live-off-food-stamps-to-protest-republican-cuts-a42da27ec4af#.o0c6c5swq.

[121] https://thinkprogress.org/aide-to-republican-congressman-fails-to-live-on-food-stamps-for-a-week-795118a84013#.bh3mp16qp.

[122] http://www.msnbc.com/msnbc/cutting-food-stamps-angry-nun-gives-the.

[123] http://www.msnbc.com/msnbc/congress-passes-farm-bill-food-stamp-cuts#50092.

[124] http://www.salon.com/2016/12/30/fox-news-apologizes-for-getting-a-report-on-food-stamp-fraud-so-very-very-wrong/.

[125] http://www.motherjones.com/kevin-drum/2016/12/fox-news-and-food-stamp-fraud-plot-thickens.

[126] See above Salon story at footnote 124.

[127] For an array of interpretations, see http://www.biblicalhebrew.com/nt/camelneedle.htm. Likely, it was intended as a hyperbole.

[128] A number that is way too high, for one in six or seven Americans has food insecurity. See http://www.feedingamerica.org/hunger-in-america/impact-of-hunger/hunger-and-poverty/hunger-and-poverty-fact-sheet.html.

[129] See *Perfectly Legal: The Covert Campaign to Rig our Tax System to Benefit the Super Rich—and Cheat Everybody Else* (New York: Penguin, 2003). Johnston updated these figures in 2012 in his blog: http://blogs.reuters.com/david-cay-johnston/2012/04/12/taxed-by-the-boss/.

[130] See Chapter Two, Debunking the Myth....

[131] http://www.forbes.com/sites/theapothecary/2016/05/19/new-report-proves-maines-welfare-reforms-are-working/#eab0afda4c75; http://dailysignal.com/2016/04/08/why-more-states-are-requiring-work-requirements-for-food-stamps/.

[132] http://www.nytimes.com/2016/08/30/us/controversial-gov-paul-lepage-maine-list.html; http://www.msnbc.com/rachel-maddow-show/maines-lepage-comes-unglued-after-racial-controversy.

[133] http://www.forbes.com/sites/theapothecary/2016/05/19/new-report-proves-maines-welfare-reforms-are-working/#eab0afda4c75.

[134] See Barbara H. Young, "Higher Education for Welfare Mothers," *Social Work*, Vol. 22.2, pp. 114-118 (1977).

[135] See, e.g., Kate Pickett and Richard Wilkinson, *The Spirit Level: Why More Equal Societies Almost Always Do Better* (Penguin, 2010), which outlines the "pernicious effects that inequality has on societies: eroding trust, increasing anxiety and illness, (and) encouraging excessive consumption." Available on Amazon.

[136] https://en.wikipedia.org/wiki/Helen_Prejean.

[137] https://en.wikipedia.org/wiki/Amazing_Grace.

[138] https://www.thenation.com/article/prison-education-reduces-recidivism-by-over-40-percent-why-arent-we-funding-more-of-it/.

[139] In 1995 in *Nicholas v. Riley*, the U.S. District Court for the District of Columbia held that denying Pell funding to state and federal prisoners did not violate equal protection, due process, or the Administrative Procedures Act (874 F. Supp. 10 (D.D.C. 1995)). In 1996 in *Tremblay v. Riley*, a federal district court rejected claims that the ban violated the ex post facto clause and the Eighth Amendment's prohibition on cruel and unusual punishment (917 F. Supp. 195 (1996)).

140 https://en.wikipedia.org/wiki/Violent_Crime_Control_and
_Law_Enforcement_Act.

141 SpearIt, "The Return of Pell Grants for Prisoners?" *Criminal Justice*,
Summer 2016;
http://www.americanbar.org/content/dam/aba/publications/criminal
_justice_magazine/v31/SpearIt.authcheckdam.pdf.

142 The average community college costs $3,500 a year, about one-tenth of
the $30,000 a year cost of incarceration, and several states spend $50-
60,000 per year per prisoner. http://www.topuniversities.com/student-
info/student-finance/how-much-does-it-cost-study-us. See also,
https://bigfuture.collegeboard.org/pay-for-college/college-
costs/college-costs-faqs. The following site gives a more detailed state-
by-state analysis. https://smartasset.com/insights/the-economics-of-
the-american-prison-system.

143 One moving personal story of the value of such evidence is *Picking
Cotton: Our Memoir of Injustice and Redemption* (St. Martin's Griffin,
2010) by Jennifer Thompson-Cannino, Ronald Cotton, and Erin Tor-
neo. Their journey through hell and then to forgiveness and reconcilia-
tion was heart-breaking and inspiring. This woman, a rape victim, had
picked Cotton out of a line-up, and she was absolutely and honestly
sure that he was the man who had raped her. He was convicted, despite
his solid alibi only because he resembled her attacker. Later, DNA evidence exonerated him, and she had to come to terms with the harm she
had done by robbing an innocent young man of eleven years of his life.
We lawyers know that eyewitness identification can be seriously
flawed.

144 http://www.rand.org/pubs/research_reports/RR564.html shows a
research report, "How Effective Is Correctional Education, and Where
Do We Go from Here?"

145 *Ibid*.

146 http://www.npr.org/sections/ed/2015/07/31/427741914/measuring-
the-power-of-a-prison-education.

147 https://msu.edu/~webbsuza/115/underclassarticlegalleys.pdf.

148 Christian Henrichson and Ruth Delaney, "The Price of Prisons: What
Incarceration Costs Taxpayers," *Center on Sentencing and Corrections*,
2012.

[149] http://www.nytimes.com/2016/02/16/opinion/a-college-education-for-prisoners.html.

[150] http://money.cnn.com/infographic/economy/education-vs-prison-costs/.

[151] JaPaula Kemp, & Marcia Johnson, "The Effect of Educating Prisoners," *University of Pennsylvania Journal of Law and Social Change*, Vol. 7.1 (2003). Available at: http://scholarship.law.upenn.edu/jlasc/vol7/iss1/2.

[152] "Schools v. Prisons: Education's the way to cut prison population," https://ed.stanford.edu/in-the-media/schools-v-prisons-educations-way-cut-prison-population-op-ed-deborah-stipek.

[153] See, e.g. https://ca.news.yahoo.com/blogs/dailybrew/dog-grooming-prison-farms-and-other-animal-150458718.html ; http://krex.k-state.edu/dspace/bitstream/handle/2097/1028/NikkiCurrie2008.pdf ; http://www.academia.edu/2181681/A_history_of_prison_inmate-animal_interaction_programs ; http://www.npr.org/sections/thesalt/2014/01/12/261397333/prison-gardens-help-inmates-grow-their-own-food-and-skills ; https://www.washingtonpost.com/local/can-gardening-transform-convicted-killers-and-carjackers-prison-officials-get-behind-the-bloom/2015/06/07/bf5c4cf0-0afb-11e5-a7ad-b430fc1d3f5c_story.html?utm_term=.074cbe55781f.

[154] http://rightoncrime.com/the-conservative-case-for-reform/. See also, "How Conservatives Learned to Love Prison Reform," by Shane Bauer, *Mother Jones*, March/April 2014, available at: http://www.motherjones.com/politics/2014/02/conservatives-prison-reform-right-on-crime.

[155] http://thefederalist.com/2015/02/24/seven-reasons-conservatives-are-leading-criminal-justice-reform/.

[156] https://www.aclu.org/gallery/marijuana-arrests-numbers.

[157] http://www.nj.com/politics/index.ssf/2015/03/booker_and_paul_re-introduce_legislation_to_overha.html.

[158] http://europe.newsweek.com/would-president-rand-paul-legalize-all-drugs-418651?rm=eu.

159 http://edition.cnn.com/2013/08/07/health/charlotte-child-medical-
marijuana/; see also updates at:
http://www.cbsnews.com/news/charlottes-web-marijuana-a-hope-for-
kids-with-seizures-despite-unproven-medical-benefits/; and
http://www.nbcnews.com/health/health-news/parents-demand-
medical-marijuana-epileptic-kids-n411186.

160 https://www.theguardian.com/world/2013/apr/02/americans-obama-
anti-christ-conspiracy-theories.

161 Jefferson's history is most meticulously documented and told by An-
nette Gorden Reed, a professor of law at New York Law School and a
professor of history at Rutgers University in *The Hemmingses of Monti-
cello* (Norton 2009). A quick summary is on Wikipedia:
https://en.wikipedia.org/wiki/Thomas_Jefferson_and_slavery.

162 http://www.detroitnews.com/story/news/politics/2016/09/03/
trump-tax-mexican-built-cars-seeks-retribution/89851280/. The irony
of this proposal is that tariffs only raise the price of goods for consumers.

163 See Reuters, "Here's How Much of His Own Money Donald Trump
Spent on His Campaign." *Fortune* online, December 9, 2016,
http://fortune.com/2016/12/09/donald-trump-campaign-spending/.
Two different numbers are found at
https://www.washingtonpost.com/graphics/politics/2016-
election/campaign-finance/ and
https://www.bloomberg.com/politics/graphics/2016-presidential-
campaign-fundraising/.

164 https://www.washingtonpost.com/news/post-
politics/wp/2016/12/09/the-six-donors-trump-appointed-to-his-
administration-gave-almost-12-million-with-their-families-to-his-
campaign-and-the-party/?utm_term=.f2240e22cd1f.

165 http://www.commondreams.org/news/2016/12/27/trump-who-cant-
be-bought-rewards-big-donors-cabinet-roles.

166 http://www.nytimes.com/2016/11/21/us/politics/donald-trump-
conflict-of-interest.html?_r=1.

167 http://www.vox.com/policy-and-
politics/2016/11/23/13715150/donald-trump-emoluments-clause-
constitution.

168 https://www.washingtonpost.com/business/capitalbusiness/
2016/11/18/9da9c572-ad18-11e6-977a-
1030f822fc35_story.html?utm_term=.d31e4784e56a.

169 http://www.vox.com/policy-and-
politics/2016/11/23/13715150/donald-trump-emoluments-clause-
constitution.

170 http://www.newsweek.com/2016/12/23/donald-trump-foreign-
business-deals-jeopardize-us-531140.html.

171 *Ibid.*

172 http://www.npr.org/2016/05/09/477350889/donald-trumps-messy-
ideas-for-handling-the-national-debt-explained.

173 http://www.usatoday.com/story/news/politics/elections/2016/
06/09/donald-trump-unpaid-bills-republican-president-
laswuits/85297274/.

174 *Ibid.*

175 *Ibid.*

176 http://www.wsj.com/articles/donald-trumps-business-plan-left-a-trail-
of-unpaid-bills-1465504454.

177 http://edition.cnn.com/2016/09/13/politics/trump-small-business-
owners/.

178 http://www.usatoday.com/story/news/politics/elections/2016
/06/09/donald-trump-unpaid-bills-republican-president-
laswuits/85297274/.

179 https://www.nytimes.com/2016/12/08/us/politics/andrew-puzder-
labor-secretary-trump.html.

180 http://www.newyorker.com/news/john-cassidy/trump-university-its-
worse-than-you-think.

181 http://www.nationalreview.com/corner/432010/trump-university-
was-massive-scam.

182 http://edition.cnn.com/2016/03/03/politics/mitt-romney-presidential-
race-speech/.

[183] http://edition.cnn.com/videos/politics/2016/11/30/donald-trump-mitt-romney-jean-georges-dinner-impressed-sot-ctn.cnn.

[184] http://www.vox.com/policy-and-politics/2016/9/22/12893444/clinton-foundation-effectiveness.

[185] http://www.slate.com/blogs/outward/2016/08/25/Clinton_foundation_scandal_aids_relief_work_is_a_success.html.

[186] http://www.vox.com/policy-and-politics/2016/9/22/12893444/clinton-foundation-effectiveness.

[187] http://thehill.com/blogs/blog-briefing-room/news/292319-carville-somebody-is-going-to-hell-over-clinton-foundation.

[188] https://www.theguardian.com/us-news/2016/oct/05/donald-trump-foundation-allegations-charity-new-york; see also http://www.bbc.co.uk/news/election-us-2016-37369515.

[189] See two charity organization's ratings: https://www.charitywatch.org/ratings-and-metrics/bill-hillary-chelsea-clinton-foundation/478; https://www.charitynavigator.org/index.cfm?bay=search.summary&orgid=16680; see also http://fortune.com/2016/08/27/clinton-foundation-health-work/.

[190] https://www.washingtonpost.com/news/post-politics/wp/2015/06/16/full-text-donald-trump-announces-a-presidential-bid/?utm_term=.658c318578ab.

[191] http://www.huffingtonpost.com/entry/donald-trump-racist-examples_us_56d47177e4b03260bf777e83.

[192] http://www.cnn.com/2016/06/07/politics/paul-ryan-donald-trump-racist-comment/.

[193] http://www.cnn.com/2016/11/10/us/post-election-hate-crimes-and-fears-trnd/.

[194] http://www.theatlantic.com/politics/archive/2016/11/richard-spencer-speech-npi/508379/.

[195] http://www.huffingtonpost.com/entry/donald-trump-hate-crimes_us_5828f3f6e4b02d21bbc952be.

[196] Politifact Profile on Trump:
http://www.politifact.com/personalities/donald-trump/.

[197] A transcript of his NPR interview on December 18, 2016 is at
http://www.npr.org/2016/12/18/506076747/radio-host-charlie-sykes-
on-being-a-contrarian-conservative-in-the-age-of-trump.

[198] Carl Bernstein on CNN:
http://edition.cnn.com/2016/12/11/us/bernstein-on-trumps-disdain-
cnntv/.

[199] http://www.theatlantic.com/politics/archive/2016/09/trump-makes-
his-case-in-pittsburgh/501335/.

[200] http://www.politico.com/blogs/2016-gop-primary-live-updates-and-
results/2016/03/trump-foreign-policy-adviser-220853.

[201] See http://fortune.com/2016/11/19/jeff-sessions-race-civil-rights/ and
http://www.nytimes.com/2016/11/21/opinion/jeff-sessions-other-
civil-rights-problem.html?_r=0. See also
https://www.washingtonpost.com/news/the-fix/wp/2016/11/18/10-
things-to-know-about-sen-jeff-sessions-donald-trumps-pick-for-attorney-
general/?utm_term=.3ba4f2fad268.

[202] http://www.motherjones.com/politics/2016/11/donald-trumps-white-
nationalist-bannon-sessions-alt-right.

[203] http://www.breitbart.com/tech/2016/03/29/an-establishment-
conservatives-guide-to-the-alt-right/.

[204] http://www.npr.org/2016/08/26/491452721/the-history-of-the-alt-
right.

[205] http://www.motherjones.com/kevin-drum/2016/11/steve-bannon-
racist-lets-find-out.

[206] http://www.politico.com/story/2016/12/trump-briefings-232479.

[207] http://www.cnbc.com/2016/12/12/trump-claims-he-doesnt-need-
daily-intelligence-briefings-because-hes-a-smart-person.html.

[208] http://www.huffingtonpost.com/entry/trump-obama-intelligence-
briefings_us_584dd82fe4b04c8e2bb053b3.

[209] http://www.cnn.com/2017/01/06/politics/trump-russia-intelligence-
briefing/; see also http://www.ibtimes.co.uk/former-us-ambassador-
russia-says-putin-wanted-revenge-clinton-1595970.

210 http://blogs.wsj.com/washwire/2011/03/17/trump-on-2012-part-of-beauty-of-me-is-im-very-rich/.

211 http://time.com/3923128/donald-trump-announcement-speech/.

212 https://www.washingtonpost.com/news/post-politics/wp/2015/06/16/full-text-donald-trump-announces-a-presidential-bid/?utm_term=.29b6ea0c9cba.

213 http://www.whatthefolly.com/2015/08/05/transcript-donald-trumps-speech-in-phoenix-arizona-on-july-11-2015-part-2/.

214 http://edition.cnn.com/TRANSCRIPTS/1507/11/cnr.06.html.

215 http://www.dailymail.co.uk/news/article-3833033/The-inside-story-Trump-s-Comedy-Central-roast-Donald-edited-jokes-make-richer-banned-discussion-bankruptcies-sensitive-hair.html.

216 http://www.theatlantic.com/magazine/archive/2016/06/the-mind-of-donald-trump/480771/; https://www.washingtonpost.com/news/the-fix/wp/2016/07/22/is-donald-trump-a-textbook-narcissist/?utm_term=.76113c5c1be7; http://edition.cnn.com/2016/10/28/opinions/trump-campaign-narcissism-lipman/.

217 https://www.washingtonpost.com/news/fact-checker/wp/2016/03/03/trumps-false-claim-he-built-his-empire-with-a-small-loan-from-his-father/?utm_term=.57cd940246a0.

218 https://www.washingtonpost.com/news/the-fix/wp/2016/12/06/did-donald-trump-tank-boeings-stock-because-he-was-mad-about-a-news-article/?utm_term=.1cfd1030c548; http://www.cbsnews.com/news/donald-trump-threatens-to-sue-sexual-assault-accusers-after-election/; https://www.washingtonpost.com/news/post-politics/wp/2016/10/22/trump-threatening-nearly-one-dozen-sexual-assault-accusers-vows-to-sue/?utm_term=.6bdd84d5ca60.

219 http://edition.cnn.com/2015/07/18/politics/trump-has-never-sought-forgiveness/.

220 http://www.npr.org/2016/01/18/463528847/citing-two-corinthians-trump-struggles-to-make-the-sale-to-evangelicals.

221 http://www.independent.co.uk/news/world/americas/us-elections/donald-trump-sexist-quotes-comments-tweets-grab-them-by-the-pussy-when-star-you-can-do-anything-a7353006.html.

222 See Mary Pipher, *Reviving Ophelia: Saving the Selves of Adolescent Girls* (Riverhead, 2005).

223 Remember, "You could see there was blood coming out of her eyes, blood coming out of her wherever." More of Trump's comments can be seen at: https://www.buzzfeed.com/andrewkaczynski/donald-trump-said-a-lot-of-gross-things-about-women-on-howar?utm_term=.dudY0qVB1#.jjG1Owpdz; and http://www.independent.co.uk/news/world/americas/us-elections/donald-trump-sexist-quotes-comments-tweets-grab-them-by-the-pussy-when-star-you-can-do-anything-a7353006.html.

224 Chelsea Green Publishing, 2004.

225 When a lawyer is successful, often he merely recoups his normal hourly rate and has waited at least one or two years to collect his paycheck. Occasionally, an attorney may hit "the big one," but the vast majority of plaintiffs' cases do not return large judgments, for juries often lowball the value of damages, and compensation for damages must be reasonable.

226 Incidentally, Beshear was the last Democratic governor in the south in recent years.

227 Hyperlon, 2007.

About the Authors

 Barbara Young holds bachelor's and master's degrees in English and a Juris Doctorate (J.D.) from the University of Louisville Brandeis School of Law, where she graduated first in her class, summa cum laude. She also holds a doctorate in higher education administration (Ed.D.) from Indiana University Bloomington. For more than two decades, she was a community college administrator over federally funded institutional development programs, and she taught English at the remedial, freshman, and sophomore levels. She has been licensed to practice law in Kentucky and Indiana since 1989. She is currently winding down her law practice in order to devote more time to writing and conducting leadership, communication, and legal seminars.

Stuart Young graduated summa cum laude with a B.A. in religion from Emory University. He holds an M.S. from the London School of Economics in information systems, and a J.D. from Harvard Law School. He has worked in international finance, in television news at the BBC, and in policy research and international  affairs in the British Parliament. He has also advised U.S. Congressional candidates. He has published numerous op-ed pieces in major newspapers on international politics.

Both Barbara and Stuart have drawn from their extensive formal and informal training in the study of religion, extensive Bible study, their family background in the Pentecostal "old time" religion, and their literary and legal scholarship. To contact the authors, write barbara@jesuslovesobamacare.com.